An Unfortunate Coincidence

AN UNFORTUNATE COINCIDENCE:

Jews, Jewishness, and English Law

Didi Herman

OXFORD
UNIVERSITY PRESS

Great Clarendon Street, Oxford OX2 6DP

Oxford University Press is a department of the University of Oxford.

It furthers the University's objective of excellence in research, scholarship,
and education by publishing worldwide in

Oxford New York

Auckland Cape Town Dar es Salaam Hong Kong Karachi
Kuala Lumpur Madrid Melbourne Mexico City Nairobi
New Delhi Shanghai Taipei Toronto

With offices in

Argentina Austria Brazil Chile Czech Republic France Greece
Guatemala Hungary Italy Japan Poland Portugal Singapore
South Korea Switzerland Thailand Turkey Ukraine Vietnam

Oxford is a registered trade mark of Oxford University Press
in the UK and in certain other countries

Published in the United States
by Oxford University Press Inc., New York

© D. Herman 2011

The moral rights of the author have been asserted
Database right Oxford University Press (maker)

First published 2011

British Library Cataloguing in Publication Data

Data available

Library of Congress Cataloging in Publication Data

Data available

Typeset by SPI Publisher Services, Pondicherry, India
Printed in Great Britain
on acid-free paper by
CPI Antony Rowe

ISBN 978–0–19–922976–5

1 3 5 7 9 10 8 6 4 2

For Davina

ACKNOWLEDGMENTS

Some of the material in this book has appeared elsewhere. Portions of Chapter 2 appeared in D. Herman, ' "An Unfortunate Coincidence": Jews and Jewishness in 20th century English Judicial Discourse' (2006) 33 *J. of Law and Society* 277–301. Chapter 4 is a revised version of S. Jivraj and D. Herman, ' "It is Difficult for a White Judge to Understand": Orientalism, Racialisation, and Christianity in English Child Welfare Cases' (2009) 21(3) *CFLQ* 283. Chapter 5 is a revised version of D. Herman, ' "I Do Not Attach Great Significance To It": Taking Note of "the Holocaust" in English Law' (2008) 17 *Social & Legal Studies* 427–52.

Throughout the five years or so that I have worked on this project, I have been fortunate to have had many friends and colleagues who have either read earlier versions of what became chapters in this book, and/or passed on to me helpful material. I thank: Nicola Barker, Brenna Bhandar, Doris Buss, David Cesarani, Ray Cocks, Alison Diduck, David Fraser, Jonathan Boyarin, Sander Gilman, Jon Goldberg-Hiller, Ruth Fletcher, Marie Fox, Michael Freeman, Lisa Herman, Rosemary Hunter, Suhraiya Jivraj, Reina Lewis, Les Moran, Qudsia Mirza, Stewart Motha, Helen Reece, Sally Sheldon, Noel Whitty.

There are three people whom I bombarded with drafts and who have been exceptionally generous in this regard and I would like to particularly thank Maleiha Malik, Daniel Monk, and David Seymour. All responsibility for content, errors, comedy, etc. is of course my own.

I could not have completed this project without the financial assistance of Kent Law School and the AHRC Research Centre for Law, Gender and Sexuality, and the three research assistants I employed over the years, each of whom is now an established academic in their own right. I thank Brenna Bhandar, Sarah Lamble, and Suhraiya Jivraj.

I would also like to thank my editors at Oxford University Press, Natasha Knight, Alex Flach, and Fiona Stables.

Finally, this project would not have gone anywhere without Davina Cooper: she is a wonder.

CONTENTS

TABLE OF CASES

Chapter 1

AN INTRODUCTION

In the mid 1920s, a fire led Sapsy Glicksman, a tailor in London's East End, to make a claim on his insurance policy. Unfortunately, he failed to disclose on his application that he had been refused insurance in the past, and so the claim of this 'wretched little ladies' tailor', this 'little Polish Jew', as a judge in the House of Lords referred to Mr Glicksman, was unsuccessful.[1] Fifteen years or so later, Barnett Samuel's will was challenged in court by several of his children who had married Christians, contrary to the terms of the will's inheritance provisions. The children won their action, the judges finding that they had no idea what the phrases contained in the will—'Jewish parentage' and 'Jewish faith'—meant.[2] A few years after that, in 1947, Sabine Greenburg, on behalf of herself and five others, claimed she was being unlawfully detained in a ship at sea. Ms Greenberg, a Jewish European refugee, had been travelling from France to Palestine along with 1,500 others when the ship was apprehended by the British navy. According to the judge, these passengers were 'illegal immigrants', and his decision authorized their transport to detention camps in Germany where they were incarcerated.[3]

In the early 1950s, Napoleon Ryder sought to recover money he claimed was his sister's, a woman who, as the judge put it, had 'failed to emerge from the ghetto of Krakow'.[4] In putting a legal end to his claim, the judge was clearly unimpressed with Mr Ryder,

---

[1] *Glicksman (Pauper)* v *Lancashire & General Assurance Co Ltd* [1927] AC 139.
[2] *Clayton* v *Ramsden* [1943] 1 All ER 16.
[3] *R* v *Sec of State, ex parte Greenberg* [1947] 2 All ER 550.
[4] *Loudon* v *Ryder (No 2)* [1953] Ch. 423.

describing him as 'foreign ... impulsive and emotional'.[5] In the late 1970s, Mr Seide complained that he had suffered discrimination in his workplace. The judges disagreed, finding, instead, that Mr Seide had brought his troubles on himself.[6] And, in the late 2000s, a Jewish father claimed a Jewish school was discriminating against his son by imposing a 'matrilineal descent' test for the purposes of admission to the school. In this case, the only reported action ever won by a Jewish claimant under the UK's Race Relations Act 1976, the UK Supreme Court found the matrilineal test to be a 'racial' one, and thus contrary to English equality law.[7]

At first glance, the reported judicial decisions arising from all these legal actions might appear to have little in common. They occur over a nearly 100-year period, and involve a diverse range of judges and legal areas: contract law; trust law; criminal law; race relations law. In the book as a whole, I also consider legal decisions in the areas of family law, tax law, and child welfare law. All the litigants share at least one thing: they either identified, or were identified in the legal decisions, as Jewish. Their Jewishness was rarely the main subject of the legal action; there are very few reported cases of people complaining of 'antisemitism' (and where they have, they almost invariably, like Mr Seide, lose their cases: see Chapter 6). Nonetheless, all the judges in these diverse areas of law noted the litigants' Jewishness in one way or another, some very extensively.

In this book, I examine a wide range of cases in order to begin mapping the terrain of English judicial representations of Jews and Jewishness.[8] In contrast to a popular narrative of England becoming more secular, multicultural, and tolerant over time, I will argue that the relationship between Englishness and Jewishness in English law is far more complex and uneven than this story suggests. As I will show, there are both continuities and discontinuities in this relationship that no simple narrative of 'progress' can properly capture.

---

[5] *Loudon* v *Ryder (No 2)* [1953] Ch. 423.   [6] *Seide* v *Gillette Industries Ltd* [1980] IRLR 427.
[7] *R(E)* v *Governing Body of JFS* [2010] IRLR 136.
[8] This book is thus *not* about Jewish-related legislation, nor is it about how Jewish people themselves understand Jewishness (there is a voluminous literature on the latter, and some historical literature on the former). Given my subjects are English judges, neither is this book about working-class racial thinking.

Unfortunately, there is virtually no existing scholarship on this topic. While there is a small literature on how Jewish and Islamic law have influenced the development of English law (a literature largely ignored in my own discipline of legal studies), no other work exists in the field.[9] When Davina Cooper and I wrote a piece over a decade ago on 'the Jew' of twentieth-century English trust law, we were inspired by Jonathan Bush's work about the deployment of Jewish concepts in early modern English legal developments;[10] unfortunately, since the publication of our piece in 1999, to the best of my knowledge, only one further, related, piece has been published in the area by other scholars.[11]

The absence, in the UK, of legal studies scholarship on Jews and Jewishness is not surprising given the paucity of work on law and racial representation more generally. While numerous socio-legal scholars have written about the content and impact of race relations legislation, very few can be said to work in the more humanities-inflected field of 'critical race legal studies'. While an impressive body of critical race scholarship has existed in North America for some time,[12] albeit with little taking account of Jews and Jewishness,[13] Qudsia Mirza, amongst others, has noted the extraordinary underdevelopment of this field in the UK.[14] In searching

[9] On the influence of Jewish law, see J. Bush, ' "You're gonna miss me when I'm gone": Early Modern Common Law Discourse and the Case of the Jews' (1993) 5 *Wisconsin Law Journal* 1225–85; J.A. Shapiro, 'The Shetar's Effect on English Law—A Law of the Jews Becomes the Law of the Land' (1983) 71 *The Georgetown Law Journal* 1179–200. On the influence of Islamic law, see A. Avini, 'The origins of the modern English trust revisited' (1995–1996) 70 *Tulane L. Rev* 1139–63; G. Makdisi, 'The Guilds of Law in Medieval Legal History: An Inquiry into the Origins of the Inns of Court' (1985–1986) 34 *Cleveland St. L. Rev* 3–18; J. Makdisi, 'Islamic Origins of the Common Law' (1999) 77 (5) *North Carolina L. Rev* 1635–1739. Legal scholars tend to be far more interested in Roman influences than Islamic and Jewish ones.

[10] D. Cooper and D. Herman, 'Jews and Other Uncertainties: Race, Faith and English Law' (1999) 19(3) *Legal Studies* 339–66. Bush, ibid.

[11] See G. Godfrey, 'The Judges and the Jews' (2003) *Ecclesiastical Law Journal* 50–61, although this short piece is not a scholarly critique. David Fraser's important contribution, *The Jews of the Channel Islands and the Rule of Law, 1940–1945* (Brighton: Sussex Academic Press, 2000), is not about judicial discourse, but about the role of law and legal professionals in the Holocaust. Anthony Julius's recent book on English antisemitism does not address the subject of legal discourse: see A. Julius, *Trials of the Diaspora: A History of Anti-Semitism in England* (Oxford: Oxford University Press, 2010).

[12] See, for example, R. Delgado, J. Stefanic, A. Harris (eds), *Critical Race Theory* (New York: New York University Press, 2001); K. Crenshaw, N. Gotanda, G. Peller, K. Thomas (eds), *Critical Race Theory: The Key Writings That Formed the Movement* (New York: New York University Press,1996); A. Wing, R. Delgado, D. Bell (eds), *Critical Race Feminism: A Reader* (New York: New York University Press, 2003).

[13] But see J.W.St.G. Walker, *'Race', Rights and the Law in the Supreme Court of Canada* (Waterloo: Wilfrid Laurier University Press, 1997), ch. 4 in particular.

[14] Q. Mirza, 'Critical Race Feminism: The Anglo-American Experience', Paper presented at the Annual Meeting of the Law & Society Association, Chicago, May, 2004. Although see D. Fraser,

the legal literature for studies of racial knowledge and representation in English law very little presents itself, and so a legal literature on Jews and Jewishness cannot be expected.

Sociologists have provided the bulk of the work on UK race and racism over the past few decades. This is a significant and influential field, and my reference to its limitations is not in any way meant to diminish its value. My intention here is not to undermine or dismiss this work, but, rather, to observe its partiality. For example, the singular focus on the white vs Black/Asian frame is illustrated in a series of iconic and other texts that contain virtually no references to any other dynamics or histories of racialized encounters.[15] Perceived skin colour tends to be treated as 'fixed', with little recognition that 'whiteness' (like non-whiteness) is historically, culturally, and politically contingent.[16]

Historical work on English racialization processes emphasizes overseas colonial encounters to the virtual exclusion of others,[17]

'To Belong or not to Belong: the Roma, State Violence and the New Europe in the House of Lords' (2001) 21(4) *Legal Studies* 569–93.; P. Fitzpatrick, 'Racism and the Innocence of Law' (1987) 14 *J. of Law and Society* 119–32 and *The Mythology of Modern Law* (London: Routledge, 1992); R. Sandland, 'The Real, the Simulacrum, and the Construction of "Gypsy" in Law' (1996) 23(3) *J. of Law and Society* 383–405; P. Tuitt, *Race, Law and Resistance* (London: Glasshouse, 2004); P. Goodrich and L. Mills, 'The Law of White Spaces: Race, Culture, and Legal Education' (2001) 51(1) *J. of Legal Education* 15–38. I return to this literature below.

[15] M. Banton, *Racial Theories* (Cambridge: Cambridge University Press, 1998); J. Solomos and L. Back, *Race, Politics and Social Change* (London: Routledge, 1995); J. Solomos, *Race and Racism in Britain* (Basingstoke: Palgrave Macmillan, 3rd edn, 2003); Centre for Contemporary Cultural Studies, *The Empire Strikes Back: Race and Racism in 70s Britain* (London: Routledge, 1982); T. Blackstone, B. Parekh, and P. Sanders (eds), *Race Relations in Britain: A Developing Agenda* (London: Routledge, 1998); M. Anwar, P. Roach, and R. Sondhi (eds), *From Legislation to Integration: Race Relations in Britain* (Basingstoke: Palgrave Macmillan, 2000). See also Tony Kushner's critique of some of this literature, T. Kushner, 'Remembering to Forget: Racism and Anti-racism in Postwar Britain' in B. Cheyette and L. Marcus (eds), *Modernity, Culture and 'the Jew'* (Stanford: Stanford University Press, 1998) 226–41. For a different account of British racism, one that gives reasonable attention to the history of Jews and Jewishness in England, see P. Panayi, *Immigration, Ethnicity and Racism in Britain, 1815–1945* (Manchester: Manchester University Press, 1994). A similar critique has been made by Mary Hickman in relation to the absence of 'the Irish' in scholarship on race and ethnicity: 'Reconstructing Deconstructing "race": British Political Discourses about the Irish in Britain' (1998) 21(2) *Ethnic and Racial Studies* 288–307. See also M. Mac An Ghaill 'The Irish in Britain' (2000) 26(1) *J. of Ethnic & Migration Studies* 137–64 and 'British Critical Theorists: The Production of the Conceptual Invisibility of the Irish Diaspora' (2001) 7(2) *Social Identities* 179–201.

[16] But see Eric Goldstein, *The Price of Whiteness: Jews, Race, and American Identity* (Princeton: Princeton University Press, 2006) for a different approach. See also D. Roediger, *The Wages of Whiteness: Race and the Making of the American Working Class* (London: Verso, 1999, orig. pub. 1991).

[17] For example, the otherwise excellent: C. Hall, K. McCelland and J. Rendall, *Defining the Victorian Nation: Class, Race, Gender, and the Reform Act of 1867* (Cambridge: Cambridge University Press, 2000). Robert Young's work is one obvious example of the failure to understand this history, indeed, his *Colonial Desire: Hybridity in Theory, Culture and Race* (New York: Routledge, 1995) arguably rewrites the English history of racialization to entirely erase Jews (except as an example of English 'acceptance' of those racially classified as 'Caucasian', see pp 84–5). While Ann McClintock's *Imperial Leather* is a far more nuanced account than Young's, and she refers to the racialization of Jews several

Paul Gilroy's discussion of Jews and Jewishness in *The Black Atlantic* being a notable exception here.[18] This partiality is also true for early modern studies of race; for example, Kim Hall's fascinating account of race and gender marginalizes the racial and religious role of 'the Jew' in shaping the categories she explores.[19] Work in a variety of disciplines on the making of English national identity exhibits a similar constricted lens.[20]

The absence of Jews appears also largely true of work in diaspora studies in the UK. Despite nods towards 'the Jews' as the classic or paradigmatic example of the diasporic phenomenon, the literature is overwhelmingly concerned with modern processes of colonialization and globalization.[21] I am not suggesting that all these scholars ought to have centred Jewishness in their analysis, only that their theoretical claims need to be assessed with the history of Jews and Jewishness in mind, and that there is clearly a large gap in the literature.

Within my own discipline, conventional and socio-legal texts on 'discrimination' also tend to tell a story that begins and ends with mid-twentieth century notions of perceived skin colour,[22] with some references to 'Jews' and 'Gypsies' found in texts on 'ethnic minorities and the law'.[23] Pieces by David Fraser and Ralph Sandland on judicial representations of Roma peoples are exceptions to

times, her 'imperial' framework prevents 'the Jew' from making more than a cursory appearance, *Imperial Leather: Race, Gender and Sexuality in the Colonial Contest* (London: Routledge, 1995). See also Robert Miles's critique of an approach to race focusing solely on processes of colonialization, *Racism after 'Race Relations'* (London: Routledge, 1993), ch. 3. For work on race (but not Jewishness) in the 'metropole', see A. Burton, *At the Heart of the Empire: Indians and the Colonial Encounter in Late-Victorian Britain* (Berkeley: University of California Press, 1998); R. Wheeler, *The Complexion of Race: Categories of Difference in Eighteenth-Century British Culture* (Philadelphia: University of Pennsylvania Press, 2000).

[18] *The Black Atlantic: Modernity and Double Consciousness* (London: Verso, 1993), ch. 6.

[19] K.F. Hall *Things of Darkness: Economies of Race and Gender in Early Modern England* (Ithaca: Cornell University Press, 1995).

[20] L. Colley, *Britons: Forging the Nation 1707–1837* (New Haven: Yale University Press, 1992); K. Kumar, *The Making of English National Identity* (Cambridge: Cambridge University Press, 2003); P. Mandler, *The English National Character: The History of an Idea from Edmund Burke to Tony Blair* (New Haven: Yale University Press, 2006); K. Wilson, *The Island Race: Englishness, Empire and Gender in the Eighteenth Century* (London: Routledge, 2003).

[21] See, for example, Anthias's otherwise useful analysis of this field, 'Evaluating "Diaspora": Beyond Ethnicity' (1998) 32(3) *Sociology* 557–80.

[22] For example, M. Connolly, *Townshend-Smith on Discrimination Law: Text, Cases and Materials* (London: Cavendish, 2004), also suggesting Jews arrived in Britain at the end of the nineteenth century, p. 4; A. McColgan, *Discrimination Law* (Oxford: Hart, 2005).

[23] R. Jones and W. Gnanapala, *Ethnic Minorities in English Law* (Stoke-on-Trent: Trentham Books, 2000); S. Poulter, *English Law and Minority Customs* (London: Butterworths, 1986) and *Ethnicity, Law and Human Rights* (Oxford: Oxford University Press, 1999).

the rule here.[24] While Sandra Fredman's *Discrimination Law* briefly notes some Jewish history in England,[25] Nicholas Bamforth, Maleiha Malik and Colm O'Cinneide's antidiscrimination law text stands out for the attention paid to the complexity and histories of racialization processes in the UK.[26]

Critical legal studies on race and racialization tend to suffer from similar limitations. Peter Fitzpatrick's impressive body of work, for example, is relatively silent on racialization processes that are not easily captured by analytical frames of colour, imperium, and post-coloniality.[27] Peter Goodrich and Linda Miles's piece on 'white spaces', while very welcome, is again dependent on assumptions about skin colour,[28] while Patricia Tuitt's significant monograph *Race, Law, and Resistance* does not refer to the racialization of Jews, Irish, and Roma.[29] Again, my comments here are not intended to undermine the value of the important work undertaken by these scholars, but, rather, to draw attention to the lacunae within the field.

One might expect more attention to judicial representations of Jewishness in the field of 'law and religion'; however this is not the case. This work tends to follow one of three paths. One trajectory focuses on the rights of minority religious groups to practise their faith, not usually highlighting how and in relation to what norms 'minorities' are understood, nor considering racial and religious knowledge formation amongst the judiciary.[30] The second path

[24] D. Fraser, 'To Belong or not to Belong: the Roma, State Violence and the New Europe in the House of Lords' (2001) 21(4) *Legal Studies* 569–93;. R. Sandland, 'The Real, the Simulacrum, and the Construction of "Gypsy" in Law' (1996) 23(3) *J. of Law and Society* 383–405.

[25] Oxford University Press, 2007, p, 37.

[26] N. Bamforth, M. Malik and C. O'Cinneide, *Discrimination Law, Theory and Context* (London: Sweet & Maxwell, 2008), ch. 12.

[27] For example, 'Racism and the Innocence of Law', and *The Mythology of Modern Law*.

[28] P. Goodrich and L. Mills, 'The Law of White Spaces: Race, Culture, and Legal Education' (2001) 51(1) *J. of Legal Education* 15–38.

[29] P. Tuitt, *Race, Law and Resistance* (London: Glasshouse, 2004). Very new work, unfortunately not yet available when I was completing this book, promises to redress this imbalance. See, for example, S. Auerbach, *Race, Law, and 'The Chinese Puzzle' in Imperial Britain* (New York: Palgrave Macmillan, 2009); E. Darian-Smith, *Religion, Race, Rights: Landmarks in the History of Modern Anglo-American Law* (Oxford: Hart, 2010).

[30] R. Ahdar and I. Leigh (eds), *Religious Freedom in the Liberal State* (Oxford: Oxford University Press, 2005); A. Bradney, *Religions, Rights and Laws* (Leicester: Leicester University Press, 2003) and *Law and Faith in a Sceptical Age* (London: Routledge, 2009); C. Hamilton, *Family, Law, Religion* (London: Sweet & Maxwell, 1995); S. Knights, *Freedom of Religion, Minorities and the Law* (Oxford: Oxford University Press, 2007); R. O'Dair and A. Lewis (eds), *Law and Religion* (Oxford: Oxford University Press, 2001); P. Oliver, S. Douglas-Scott, V. Tadros (eds) *Faith in Law: Essays in Legal Theory* (Oxford: Hart, 2000); St. J.A. Robillard, *Religion and the Law* (Manchester: Manchester University Press, 1984); S. Poulter, *English Law and Ethnic Minority Customs* (London: Butterworths,1986) and *Ethnicity, Law*

considers the development of internal religious norms and practices, and the third the relationship between religious self-governance mechanisms and English law.[31] Again, while important and welcome, this work rarely considers how *judicial* norms and practices understand and produce minority subjects, nor how religious minorities are racialized, nor does this work take account of scholarship problematizing the concept of 'religion' itself.[32] Suhraiya Jivraj's study on religion, race and law is one notable exception.[33]

And yet, if we turn to the humanities, work on racial representation has been highly attentive to Jews and Jewishness for some time. Bryan Cheyette, for example, has written a ground-breaking book on images of 'the Jew' in English literature, arguing for the centring of 'a dominant racialised discourse at the heart of what constitutes the received definitions of literary "culture"'.[34] Michael Ragussis's *Figures of Conversion* is a similarly significant work, as is James Shapiro's *Shakespeare and the Jews*; Nadia Valman's more recent account of representations of Jewish women in English literature is a welcome contribution to this scholarship.[35] At the

---

and Human Rights (Oxford: Oxford University Press, 1999). For a view more critical of the accommodation of religion, one assuming England is a secular and not a Christian nation (an assumption with which I disagree, see later in this chapter), see A. McColgan 'Class Wars? Religion and (In)Equality in the Workplace' (2009) 38(1) *ILJ* 1–29.

[31] For example, M. Freeman, 'Is the Jewish *Get* any Business of the State?', in R. O'Dair and A. Lewis, (eds), *Law and Religion*;. See also sources on Islamic and Jewish influences on English law, n. 9. But see also B. Jackson, 'Brother Daniel: The Construction of Jewish Identity in the Israel Supreme Court', 17 *Intl J. for the Semiotics of Law* 115–46 for a different approach.

[32] Scholarship that includes: T. Asad, *Formations of the Secular: Christianity, Islam, Modernity* (Palo Alto: Stanford University Press, 2003); H. De Vries and L. Sullivan (eds), *Political Theologies* (Fordham University Press, 2006); H. De Vries, *Religion, Beyond a Concept* (Fordham University Press, 2008); T. Fitzgerald (ed.), *Religion and the Secular: Historical and Colonial Formations* (London: Equinox, 2007); T. Fitzgerald, *Discourses on Civility and Barbarity* (Oxford: Oxford University Press, 2007); T. Masuzawa, *The Invention of World Religions* (Chicago: University of Chicago Press, 2005).

[33] S. Jivraj, *Interrogating 'Religion' and 'Race' in Child Welfare and Education Law* (PhD thesis, forthcoming, University of Kent).

[34] B. Cheyette, *Constructions of 'The Jew' in English Literature and Society* (Cambridge: Cambridge University Press, 1993) 4, also (ed), *Between 'Race' and Culture: Representations of 'the Jew' in English and American Literature* (Stanford: Stanford University Press, 1996).

[35] M. Ragussis, *Figures of Conversion: 'The Jewish Question' and English National Identity* (Durham: Duke University Press, 1995); J. Shapiro, *Shakespeare and the Jews* (New York: Columbia University Press, 1996); N. Valman, *The Jewess in Nineteenth-Century British Literary Culture* (Cambridge: Cambridge University Press, 2007). See also, A. Bale, *The Jew in the Medieval Book: English Anti-semitism, 1350–1500* (Cambridge: Cambridge University Press, 2006); M. Metzger, ' "Now by my hood, a Gentle and no Jew": Jessica, The Merchant of Venice, and the Discourse of Early Modern Identity' (1998) 113(1) *PMLA* 52–63; D. Boyarin and J. Boyarin, *Jews and Other Differences: The New Jewish Cultural Studies* (Minneapolis: University of Minnesota Press,1997); B. Cheyette and L. Marcus, *Modernity, Culture and 'the Jew'* (Stanford: Stanford University Press, 1998); D Cohen and D. Heller,

same time, British historians have also made an impressive contribution to our understanding of the relationship between dominant
English culture and Jews, Judaism, and Jewishness.[36] Sander
Gilman's huge body of work, much of which pertains to England,
constitutes perhaps a discipline in itself.[37]

Taken as a whole, this humanities scholarship represents a significant consideration of the role of Jewishness and 'the Jew' in
English culture, a role left largely unexcavated when it comes to
legal studies and the social sciences. As literary, cultural studies, and
history scholars repeatedly remind us, understanding the role of
'the Jew' is as important for what it reveals about 'the English' and
Englishness as for what it tells us about Jews and Jewishness.[38]
Jews, for centuries, have been 'at the centre of European metropol-
itan society'.[39] Legal discourse, I will argue, is one of the key sites
throwing this encounter 'of the interior' into relief.[40]

In mapping the terrain of Jews and Jewishness in English legal
judgments, I will draw extensively on the cultural studies and
historical work above; however, whilst judicial discourse on Jews
and Jewishness is heavily indebted to the texts of English literature, most explicitly Dickens and Shakespeare, they are not
equivalents. Legal judgments, especially those that function as
'precedent', are authoritative statements of official state discourse.
Judicial pronouncements have immediate and often long-lasting

---

Jewish Presences in English Literature (Montreal: McGill-Queen's University Press, 1990); J. Steyn, *The Jew: Assumptions of Identity* (London: Cassells, 1999).

[36] See, G. Alderman, *Modern British Jewry* (Oxford: Oxford University Press, 1992); D. Cesarani (ed.), *The Making of Modern Anglo-Jewry* (Oxford: Blackwell, 1990); T. Endelman, *The Jews of Britain, 1656 to 2000* (Berkeley: University of California Press, 2002); D. Feldman, *Englishmen and Jews: Social Relations and Political Culture 1840–1914* (New Haven: Yale University Press, 1994); C. Holmes, *Anti-Semitism in British Society 1876–1939* (New York: Holmes & Meir, 1979); David S. Katz, *The Jews in the History of England 1485–1850* (Oxford: Clarendon Press, 1994); T. Kushner, *The Persistence of Prejudice: Antisemtism in British Society During the Second World War* (Manchester: Manchester University Press, 1989); T. Kushner (ed.), *The Jewish Heritage in British History: Englishness and Jewishness* (London: Frank Cass, 1992). This is obviously a very small selection of the historical scholarship, but see also sources noted below in the 'Jewish legal history' part of this chapter.

[37] For the purposes of this book, the main texts of Gilman's I have found helpful are, *The Jew's Body* (New York: Routledge, 1991); *Difference and Pathology: Stereotypes of Sexuality, Race, and Madness* (Ithaca: Cornell University Press, 1985); *Freud, Race, and Gender* (Princeton: Princeton University Press, 1993).

[38] I am not suggesting that the concept of 'the Jew' is unique in this respect, only that its role is underappreciated in legal studies.

[39] Cheyette, *Constructions of 'the Jew'* 12.

[40] On the concept of the 'interior', and the need to study racializations there, see R. Miles, *Racism After 'Race Relations'*, ch. 3 and A. Burton, *At the Heart of the Empire.*

material consequences. When the UK Supreme Court finds a Jewish school guilty of racial discrimination against Jews, the effects are far-reaching. More specifically in relation to the themes of this book, judges are active creators of official *racial knowledge*. How they go about coming to their decisions in cases implicating Jews and Jewishness involves a process, sometimes simple, sometimes complex, of determining character and characteristics. Thus, judges are also *nation-builders*, defining what it means to be—and not to be—English. While some legal scholars might argue that judges are little more than prisoners of precedent and legal formalism, my contention in this book is that, while judges certainly operate under constraining conditions, they are at the same time active agents, making deliberate choices (I expand on this later in the chapter).[41]

A SHORT HISTORY OF 'JEWS AND THE LAW' IN ENGLAND

As I worked on this project, I was struck by how few people seemed aware of the lengthy history of Jewish (and Muslim) presence in England.[42] While Judaism has a much longer presence in England than does Anglicanism, the idea that the relationship between Christian England and Jews and Jewishness should be explored as fundamental to any understanding of Englishness itself is unknown outside the small scholarly world of 'Jewish Studies'. While the historical summary I present here is very partial to say the least, I do believe that some longer view is necessary in order to understand the contemporary legal discourses. Readers already familiar with the historical scholarship may wish to move on to the next section as I do no more than attempt to distil some selected literature here.

Prior to the twelfth century, Jewish history in Britain is not well known. Henry Henriques, for example, who, in 1908, published

---

[41] For an excellent example of work showing such choices, see R. Hunter, C. McGlynn and E. Rackley (eds), *Feminist Judgments: From Theory to Practice* (Oxford: Hart Publishing, 2010).

[42] On Muslim history in England, see, for example, A. Ansari, *'The Infidel Within': Muslims in Britain Since 1800* (London: C. Hurst & Co., 2004) which, despite its title, contains some history on sixteenth- and seventeenth-century Muslim populations; also, N. Matar, *Islam in Britain 1558–1685* (Cambridge: Cambridge University Press, 1998), which is not a history of Muslim communities in England, but of Christian converts to Islam in Ottoman territories, and English Christian representations of Islam in popular culture of the period as a result of anxieties surrounding these conversions.

what still remains the definitive study of Jews and English legal
history, suggests that as there is evidence of laws forbidding various sorts of relations between Christians and Jews from the mid
seventh century, Jews must have come originally to the British
Isles with the Romans.[43] Others dispute drawing any conclusions
from this.[44] It seems likely that there were some individual Jews
in England after the Roman invasion but no identifiable Jewish
communities.

Following the Norman Conquest, a more substantial social and
legal record exists.[45] Jews during this period had the status of the
King's chattel. They were assigned a monopoly over money-lending
(usury being forbidden to Christians), and the Crown's revenues
from this economy led Richard I to establish an 'Exchequer of the
Jews'.[46] By the mid/late thirteenth century, a set of laws, some of
which were to remain on the books for nearly 600 years, had been
put in place: Jewish land ownership was restricted; usury was
forbidden to Jews; Jews could not employ Christian servants;
Jews must not pray so loudly that Christians could hear them;
Jews must wear a yellow badge and pay special taxes.[47] Some of
these measures were religiously motivated, while others were applied at the instigation of Christian landowners who owed Jewish
money-lenders great sums they preferred not to pay. Many were
preceded by outbreaks of anti-Jewish violence, accompanied by
'blood libel' accusations.[48] By the 1270s and 80s, Jewish communities
in England were largely impoverished, undergoing coerced conversion, subject to violence, or in exile.[49]

---

[43] H. Henriques, *The Jews and English Law* (Clifton: Augustus M. Kelley, 1974, orig. pub. 1908) 52–3.
[44] R.B. Dobson, *The Jews of Medieval York and the Massacre of March 1190* (York: University of York, Bothwick Paper No. 45, 1974) 1.
[45] Much of this is usefully collected in J.A. Romain, *The Jews of England: A Portrait of Anglo-Jewry Through Original Sources and Illustrations* (London: Michael Goulston Educational Foundation and Jewish Chronicle Press, 1988).
[46] Ibid., 49–57. See also Henriques, *The Jews and English Law* 54. For a comprehensive discussion of the legal position of Jewish people in medieval England, see S. Herman, 'Legacy and Legend: The Continuity of Roman and English Regulation of the Jews' (1991–1992) 66 *Tulane Law Review* 1781–1851, 1801–3, 1808. More generally, see R. Mundill, *England's Jewish Solution: Experiment and Expulsion, 1262–1290* (Cambridge: Cambridge University Press, 1998).
[47] See Romain, *The Jews of England*, 49–50. See also C. Roth, *A History of the Jews in England* (Oxford: Oxford University Press, 1941) for a history of the 'badge'.
[48] E.g., Dobson, *The Jews of Medieval York*. See also Romain, *The Jews of England*, 37–40, regarding anti-Jewish riots and blood libel, 27–31. See also Mundill, *England's Jewish Solution*, and Julius, *Trials of the Diaspora*, chs 2 and 3.
[49] Shapiro, *Shakespeare and the Jews* 55.

In late 1290, the combination of landowners' pressure, the loss of revenue from the Crown's Jewish chattel, popular anti-Jewish sentiment (often violently fuelled by the departure of Crusaders), and a constitutional crisis, led to King Edward I's decree of property confiscation and expulsion.[50] Official documents guaranteed the safe passage of England's Jews out of the Cinque Ports.[51] For the next 300 years or so, there were almost no Jewish persons living openly as Jews in England. There were some Jews of Spanish and Portuguese origin, who, escaping the Inquisition there, came to England and lived as public Christians, but private Jews.[52] But, as might be expected, little evidence of their Jewish lives is available. Nevertheless, as Anthony Bale has comprehensively demonstrated, medieval England remained fascinated, repelled, and otherwise obsessed with Jews and Jewishness throughout this 'Jew-free' period.[53]

By the mid 1600s, Jewish communities again began to grow in England. There is some debate as to the role played by Oliver Cromwell in the return of Jews (living as Jews) to England. Henriques assesses the evidence as showing Cromwell did little or nothing,[54] while others suggest otherwise.[55] Nevertheless, it is clear from the historical record that by the 1650s a small Jewish community could be identified in England, and that a synagogue had been established in London.[56] David Katz assesses the historical evidence as demonstrating that conversion was the key factor leading to readmission: Christian millenarianism was very powerful at the time and 'the conversion of the Jews' was viewed as an essential precursor to the Second Coming (as it still is in contemporary

---

[50] Reproduced in Romain, *The Jews of England* 58.   [51] Ibid., 59.

[52] See Katz, *The Jews in the History of England*, ch. 2. See also Friedman, 'Jewish Conversion, the Spanish Pure Blood Laws and Reformation: A Revisionist View of Racial And Religious Antisemitism'(1987)18(1)*Sixteenth Century Journal* 3–30, on 'New Christians' coming to England; and Spanish Inquisition testimony reproduced in Romain, 63–6.

[53] Bale, *The Jew in the Medieval Book*. Shapiro has also shown how Elizabethan society was 'obsessed' with Jews and Jewishness (including their perceived 'stench', the so-called *'foetor judaicus'*) and argued that what is particularly interesting is how there is such an investment in this formative period of English identity-building being 'Jew free', see Shapiro, *Shakespeare and the Jews*, 62–3. But this is not something I can pursue further here. See also J.P. Rosenblatt, *Renaissance England's Chief Rabbi: John Seldon* (Oxford: Oxford University Press, 2006) for a discussion of the major influence of rabbinical scholarship on this early-sixteenth century political philosopher.

[54] Henriques, *The Jews in English Law* 94–114.

[55] P. Johnson, *A History of the Jews* (London: Weidenfeld & Nicholson, 1987) 277–8 and Katz, *The Jews*, ch. 3.

[56] Henriques, *The Jews in English Law*, 121–2.

millenarian thinking).[57] James Shapiro argues that the very notion of 'Readmission' is both a misnomer and a myth—that Jews had been trickling into England for some time and continued to do so. The issue for Cromwell, Shapiro suggests, was what *status* they should have there.[58]

In any event, following the restoration of Charles II in 1660, although laws against Jews in particular remained in place and others applying to non-Anglicans in general were revived, it seems that Jews in England openly defied the prohibition on their religious worship with the King's tacit approval. Gradually, English courts began to deal with the rights of Jewish persons (for example, as witnesses or litigants).[59] Charles II provided various dispensations from certain legal disabilities as did James II after him. However, new restrictions continued to be initiated—for example, legislation was passed in 1702 requiring Jewish and Catholic parents to financially support their Anglican convert children.[60] Nevertheless, by the late eighteenth century, the Jewish community was expanding, as were its institutionalized self-governance mechanisms.[61]

However, for the next 150 years or so, Jewish people were prevented from entering many professions, from becoming naturalized, and from holding political office. While certain exclusions, for example from the teaching profession, applied to all non-conformists, others were the result of a requirement that entrants swear a Christian oath. In terms of naturalization, the only route

---

[57] Katz, *The Jews in the History of England*, ch. 3. On contemporary millenarian thinking vis a vis 'the Jews', see D. Herman, *The Antigay Agenda: Orthodox Vision and the Christian Right* (Chicago: University of Chicago Press, 1997), ch. 2.

[58] Shapiro, *Shakespeare and the Jews*, ch. 2.   [59] Henriques, *The Jews in English Law*, 126–52.

[60] Katz, *The Jews*, 195–6. Anti-Catholic measures were also rife throughout this period, see J.A. Bush, '"Include Me Out": Some Lessons of Religious Toleration in Britain' (1991) 12 *Cardozo Law Review* 881–923.

[61] The Board of Deputies, uniting the Sephardic and Ashkanazi communities, was established in 1760, adopting a formal constitution in 1836, see documents in Romain, *The Jews of England*, 92–3. By the late eighteenth century, the phrase 'Chief Rabbi' came to designate the overall Jewish religious authority, including the English Sephardim, see also M. Persoff, *Faith Against Reason: Religious Reform and the British Chief Rabbinate, 1840–1990* (Edgeware: Valentine Mitchell, 2008). Records from the Bet Din, the Jewish religious court, exist from the early nineteenth century, although it is clear the Bet Din was operating before then. By the provisions of the Marriage Act 1753, Jewish marriage, and thus divorce, had been entirely a matter for the Bet Din. For some history of the English Bet Din, see J.I. Pfeffer, *'From One End of Earth to the Other': The London Bet Din, 1805–1855, and the Jewish Convicts Transported to Australia* (Brighton: Sussex Academic Press, 2010). The United Synagogues Act 1870 brought the 'orthodox' Ashkenazi synagogues together under the auspices of the Chief Rabbi.

for foreign-born Jews was to convert. The attempt to remove some of these disabilities in the 1750s—known as the 'Jew Bill'—resulted in an outpouring of anti-Jewish sentiment and ended in failure.[62] Some of these obstacles to full citizenship were not removed until the 1870s.[63] The period covered by this book, then, begins a short while after what has been called 'full emancipation'.[64]

In terms of twentieth-century history, I have attempted to give some historical texture to each chapter where relevant to its subject. In brief here, the relationship between Jews, Jewishness, and English judges during the twentieth century was shaped by several factors. In the first half of the century, some of these included: the initial waves of Jewish immigration from eastern Europe at the turn of the century; the gradual settlement and, to some extent, uneven embourgeoisement of these communities; Jewish refugees arriving in the 1930s, largely from western Europe; world war two (including the internment and deportation of Jewish refugees in England); the British colonial administration in Palestine and the founding of Israel; and the persistence of Christian anti-Jewish practice and thinking in England throughout these periods.[65] In the second half of the century, as I hope to show in subsequent chapters, the gradual acknowledgment of the Holocaust, and the particular forms this acknowledgment took, shaped judicial discourse on Jews and Jewishness to a large degree, as did the emergence of 'race relations' culture and legislation.

KEY CONCEPTS AND ARGUMENTS

Limitations of Existing Scholarship

Drawing upon the insights contained in the diverse literatures I noted earlier, I read the cases in order to make five main arguments. First, as I noted above, there is a serious lacuna in existing scholarship

---

[62] Jewish Naturalization Act, 1753. See Shapiro, *Shakespeare and the* Jews, ch. 7; Katz, *The Jews in the History of England*; Endleman, *The Jews of Britain*. In 1771, the government explicitly restricted Jewish entry into England, see *Halsbury's*, v. 10, p. 396.

[63] See Henriques, *The Jews in English Law*, for a detailed history of these developments, chs VII–X.

[64] However, as Jonathan Bush has documented, there remain on the books several anti-Catholic and anti-Jewish provisions (in addition to the provisions 'establishing' the Church of England), see 'Include Me Out' 900–11.

[65] See individual chapters for sources.

on race, ethnicity, religion and law. Most of this literature fails to consider judicial knowledge of Jews and Jewishness on any level. As a result, we currently have a very partial picture of racialization processes in England, and there is an erasure of peoples who do not conform to phenotypical or twentieth-century postcolonial paradigms. However, integrating the legal history of Jews and Jewishness into existing theoretical frameworks is not easily achieved; attempting to do so in fact troubles these approaches as I go on to demonstrate in subsequent chapters. In addition, some of this work, in socio-legal studies in particular, is influential at a policy and law-making level. I argue that some scholars' failure to consider the complexity of a concept such as Jewishness can lead to harmful forms of law reform advocacy (for example, in relation to circumcision: see Chapter 4). In this sense, I suggest that academic scholarship in this area can itself be studied as a form of orientalizing and racializing discourse (see below). Finally, a more muted point in the book that follows from this literature critique is that current attempts to analyse Islamophobia in England would greatly benefit from some historical knowledge of how Jews and Jewishness have been understood.

Orientalizing and Racializing Processes

Moving on to my case studies, my second argument is that judges draw on and contribute to orientalizing and racializing processes to find their way around and through Jews and Jewishness. Although my approach here is indebted to Edward Said's development of the concept of orientalism,[66] I am not using 'orientalism' as a term of art and do not wish to contribute to debates about its limitations and possibilities. For me, orientalism provides a useful shorthand to signify a range of judicial practices towards Jews and Jewishness.[67] These include particular ways of characterizing people and practices that have come from 'the east', along with recurring restatements of what is 'English'. An orientalist approach, as I use that phrase, is also about comparing civilizations—most

---

[66] *Orientalism* (New York: Vintage, 1979).
[67] See also, R. Lewis, *Gendering Orientalism: Race, Femininity and Representation* (London: Routledge, 1996), particularly ch. 5 on the orientalization of Jews.

specifically a Christian one with others. In 1663, Samuel Pepys attended a Simchat Torah service that led him to write:

But, Lord! To see the disorder, laughing, sporting, and no attention, but confusion in all their service, more like brutes than people knowing the true God, would make a man forswear ever seeing them more; and indeed I never did see so much, or could have imagined there had been any religion in the whole world so absurdly performed as this. Away thence with my mind strongly disturbed with them, by coach and set down my wife in Westminster Hall.[68]

This, I would argue, is both racialized and orientalist (and patri-archal) thinking and I intend to demonstrate that many (not all) of the legal cases I discuss in this book, including the *JFS* decision of 2009,[69] can be read similarly in terms of their understanding of non-Christian culture. While there is discontinuity in terms of how the forms and emphases of this orientalizing gaze change over time (modern judges would never describe Jews as 'brutes'), there is a continuity in terms of how Jewishness is understood as inferior to Christianity (Jewish practices, circumcision or the matrilineal test, for example, remain 'barbaric' or 'primitive'). Thus, there is, in my view, a *theological* component to orientalism, one that places Chris-tianity at the civilizational apex of 'world religions' (see further below). As Gil Andijar has argued, orientalism is, at its heart, *Christian imperialism*.[70] Or, as Tomoko Masuzawa has put it: 'it has become exigent that the discourse on religion(s) be viewed as an essential component, that is, a vital operating system within the colonial discourse of Orientalism'.[71]

I also draw on the concept of racialization,[72] and see this as intertwined with orientalism, particularly when it comes to Jews

---

[68] *Diary of Samuel Pepys* (1663), reproduced in Romain, 85.

[69] *R (E) v Governing Body of JFS* [2010] IRLR 136.

[70] G. Anidjar, *Semites: Race, Religion, Literature* (Stanford: Stanford University Press. 2008) 52.

[71] T. Masuzawa, *The Invention of World Religions* 21.

[72] R. Miles and M. Brown, *Racism* (London: Routledge, 2nd edn, 2003), define racialization as 'a representational process whereby social significance is attached to certain biological (usually pheno-typical) human features, on the basis of which the people possessing those characteristics are designated as a distinct collectivity', 100. Also, see M. Omni and H. Winant, *Racial Formations in the United States: From the 1960s to the 1990s* (London: Routledge, 1994); D. Goldberg, *The Racial State* (Malden, MA: Blackwell, 2001). For a child welfare analysis using the concept of 'racial ideologies', see M. Kline, 'The "Colour" of Law: Ideological Representations of First Nations in Legal Discourse' (1994) 3 *Social & Legal Studies* 451–76. For a thorough recounting of sources on the concept of 'race', see D. Cohen, 'Who Was Who?: Race and Jews in Turn-of-the-century Britain' (2002) 41(4) *J. of*

and Jewishness. Again, I do not use the words 'racialization' and 'racialized' as terms of art (and this book is not a contribution to theories of 'race' per se), but to signify a particular form of under-standing and way-finding—often (although not always) through phenotypical signifiers or characteristics—when encountering per-sons perceived as alien to the 'home' environment. Racialization, as I shall use that concept here, refers to the process whereby the judiciary—quite literally if not 'scientifically'—analyses the blood of individuals or peoples they define as 'races', invariably leaving white, English, Christian blood unremarked upon. I argue that racialization overlaps with, yet is distinct from, orientalizing pro-cesses as, while there is a 'civilizational mission' that can be per-formed on 'orientals', their blood will always tell the truth of their 'race'. I suggest that this orientalist, racialized, and Christian (see further on this last one below) thinking leads to particular forms of characterizations and decision-making with significant implications for the litigants, and for how judges envision English law. I argue that when judges elucidate the character of English law they are involved in a racializing process.

Secularism, Christianity and Conversion

Third, I argue that a Christian normativity underlies these orien-talizing and racializing processes, and that 'secularism' becomes a term that facilitates judicial Christian thinking. For many judges, Jews and Jewishness represent the particular, and Christianity, often referred to as 'the secular' in my cases, represents the uni-versal. This claim, that the courts are not secular but Christian, seems to be controversial, particularly in light of some recent case law refusing to protect discriminatory acts based on Christian belief, and judges' constant reiteration of their secularity.[73] But my argument about Christianity is not that it receives special legal protection (although it has and does and this forms a significant

---

British Studies 460–83, 460 (n. 1). For a set of interesting pieces on 'race', some of which engage critically with the US literature on racialization above, see the special issue of Social Analysis (2005) 49(2).

[73] See, for example: LB Islington v Ladele [2009] IRLR 154, affirmed by Court of Appeal [2010] IRLR 211; McFarlane v Relate Avon [2010] IRLR 196. See also, Eweida v British Airways [2009] IRLR 78. For a good and typical statement of judicial secularity, see Munby J's comments in X v X [2002] 1 FLR 508, paras 111–113: 'although historically this country is part of the Christian west, and although it has an established church which is Christian, I sit as a secular judge serving a multi-cultural community', para. 112.

backdrop for my study),[74] but that judicial understandings of Jews and Jewishness cannot be adequately analysed without recognizing that the impositions that take place on the bodies, culture, and aspirations of Jewish litigants are often Christian ones. I also make the argument that English law itself becomes, for many judges, the embodiment of good, Christian values, and Jewish behaviour, including in relation to English law, its opposite. My analysis here draws on scholarship exploring the concepts of 'religion', 'secularism', and 'Christianity' from a critical perspective,[75] although, again, very little of this literature considers Jews and Jewishness.

Drawing on many of the insights in these writings, I go on to suggest that, in relation to Jews, Jewishness and English law, the imposition of Christian norms can result in the courts sanctioning de facto 'conversions'. There is a de-Judification taking place as ties to Judaism and Jewish communities are broken, that could, if the rhetoric is permitted, be seen as a form of symbolic ethnic cleansing. I accept this is strong language; however, I hope to show that a reading of the cases sustains the argument, or, at least, makes it plausible. And it is not as if processes of conversion have not been imposed on Jews by Christians for centuries in England so my claim to see them at work in contemporary judicial discourse is not outlandish.[76] The 'conversion of the Jews' has been an integral aspect of English Christianity since at least the thirteenth century—I am simply arguing that these conversionary processes

---

[74] The official privileges of Christianity in England are many and include the reigning monarch being the Head of the Church of the England and taking an oath to uphold Protestanism, the right of Anglican and Catholic bishops to sit as legislators in the House of Lords, and compulsory Christian education in English schools. On the latter, see D. Cooper, 'Defiance and Non-Compliance: Religious Education and the Implementation Problem' (1995) 48 *Current Legal Problems* 253–79.

[75] G. Anidjar, *Semites: Race, Religion, Literature* (Stanford: Stanford University Press, 2008); T. Asad, *Formations of the Secular: Christianity, Islam, Modernity* (Palo Alto: Stanford University Press, 2003); H. De Vries and L. Sullivan (eds), *Political Theologies* (New York: Fordham University Press, 2006); H. De Vries, *Religion, Beyond a Concept* (New York: Fordham University Press, 2008); T. Fitzgerald, *Discourses on Civility and Barbarity* (Oxford: Oxford University Press, 2007); T. Fitzgerald (ed.), *Religion and the Secular: Historical and Colonial Formations* (London: Equinox, 2007); J.R. Jakobsen and A. Pellegrini (eds), *Secularisms* (Durham: Duke University Press, 2007); T. Masuzawa, *The Invention of World Religions* (Chicago: University of Chicago Press, 2005).

[76] See generally, Katz, *The Jews in the History of England*. On conversion in English legal history, see Bush, 'You're Gonna Miss Me'; in Elizabethan England, see Shapiro, *Shakespeare and the Jews*; see also Metzger, '"By my hood"' on the politics of conversion in *The Merchant of Venice*; on the eighteenth century, see Ragussis, *Figures of Conversion*.

remain at work today, albeit more subtly, and we can see them at work in the courts.

My deployment of the term 'Christian' is not intended to homogenize Christianity or ignore the very significant history of Protestant and Catholic conflict in England. Nor is my intent to marginalize the fact that Christianity is riven by historical and contemporary dissent and fissures, that English Christianity takes a particular form in its establishment (the Church of England), and that English religious and legal history is replete with violence and discrimination against Catholics, non-conforming Protestants, and others.[77] Nonetheless, it is my contention, and I would ground that contention in a wide-ranging and interdisciplinary scholarship,[78] that Christianity, despite the different forms it takes, can nonetheless be analysed as a set of organizing principles or constellation of elements.[79] These would include not only clearly theological principles—for example, a belief in the divinity of Jesus and his eventual return—but also ways of knowing and being that are articulated, in legal as well as in political and popular culture, as non-religious or secular, and, in mainstream forms, associated with reason, civility, and progress. As a number of scholars have argued, despite the enunciation of these values as 'secular' and 'universal', they are, rather, deeply embedded in Christianity, more particularly, in England, in Anglicanism.[80]

Perhaps most importantly for my purposes here, it must be possible to name the asymmetric power Christianity in various forms has in the world today and has had ever since its early form fused with imperial state power in the Roman and Byzantine empires. This is a power that has had material effects through, amongst other things: a long European history of anti-Jewish and anti-Islamic thinking and practice; in past colonial projects of

---

[77] See Bush, 'Include Me Out'.

[78] Much of this scholarship is referenced in and engaged with by the contributions to Jakobsen and Pellegrini (eds), *Secularisms*.

[79] H. De Vries, *Religion, Beyond a Concept* (New York: Fordham University Press, 2008).

[80] For a comprehensive study of how Enlightenment thinkers deployed 'reason' to disparage Jews and Judaism (one written long before it became fashionable to talk about 'civilizational discourse'), see J. Katz, *From Prejudice to Destruction*. Of course, some forms of Christianity may also be characterized as exhibiting 'unreason', see, for example, *Re R* [1993] 2 FLR 163 on the Christian Brethren. Historically, Catholicism also was often viewed as lacking reason, see, for example, *Gilmour v Coats* [1949] AC 426.

domination, and in current ones that justify the post 9/11 'war on terror' on the grounds that Christian civilization (and democracy)—associated with the Western values of North America and Europe—are under threat.[81] It is possible, then, to recognize the heterogeneity of Christianity, while at the same time highlighting its dominating, imperial, cross-cultural, and trans-national dimensions, and also recognizing that, as many others have argued and is hardly a controversial claim, a central narra-tive of all forms of Christianity has been that it is the 'true' faith that superseded Judaism (as Islam, for some religious Muslims, is the 'true' faith superseding Christianity, and Judaism, for that matter, was seen to supersede Middle Eastern polytheism). This narrative of Christian supersession—of Christian 'progress'—is important to my project, as hopefully will become clear in subsequent chapters.[82]

'The Jew' and Myth-Making

My fourth argument is that the concept of 'the Jew' has, over many centuries in English legal discourse, achieved a kind of disembod-ied agency. In other words, judges draw on their conception of 'the Jew' which, in many instances, has nothing whatsoever to do with actual Jews or Jewish issues of any sort: 'the Jew is rarely given a subjective space in which to operate, but is dependent and contin-gent on the greater narrative in which he (or less frequently she) is placed'.[83] As Jonathan Bush has comprehensively demonstrated, the figure of 'the Jew' became an exemplar deployed by judges in many legal cases in the seventeenth century, despite very few actual Jews living openly as Jews in England at the time.[84] While Bush explores a considerably older period of legal history than I do

---

[81] See, for example, G. Anidjar, *Semites*; T. Asad, *Formations of the Secular*; B. Bhandar, 'The Ties That Bind: Multiculturalism and Secularism Reconsidered' (2009) 36(3) *J. of Law & Society* 301–26; W. Brown, *Regulating Aversion: Tolerance in the Age of Identity and Empire* (Princeton: Princeton University Press, 2006); J. Butler 'Sexual Politics, Torture, and Secular Time' (2008) 59 *The British J. of Sociology* 1–23; M. Malik, *Feminism and Minority Women* (Cambridge: Cambridge University Press, 2010); S. Motha, 'Veiled Women and the *Affect* of Religion in Democracy' (2007) 34 *J. of Law and Society* 139–62 and 'Liberal Cults, Suicide Bombers, and other Theological Dilemmas' (2008) 5 *J. of Law, Culture and the Humanities* 228–46. S. Razack, 'Imperilled Muslim Women, Dangerous Muslim Men and Civilised Europeans: Legal and Social Responses to Forced Marriages' (2004) 12 *Feminist Legal Studies* 129–74.

[82] See also Mandler, *The English National Character*, ch.4, for a discussion of how English character was deeply embedded with civilizational beliefs.

[83] Bale, *The Jew in the Medieval Book* 5.   [84] Bush, 'You're Gonna Miss Me'.

here, I argue that 'the Jew' retains to this day a kind of conceptual agency, divorced from its association with 'real' Jewish people. As Hannah Arendt wrote over 70 years ago:

> ... Jews are turned into little more than an example, almost a mere pretext... they are seen by their 'friends' in particular as nothing but a principle within a process, and never once in the sad course of history over the last 150 years have they been regarded by others as living human beings.[85]

In modern judicial discourse, 'the Jew' remains deployed as exemplar and symbol—often now as the paradigmatic victim. In certain cases, judicial discourse on the Holocaust for example, a complicated iconography emerges where, through a set of juxtapositions and 'stock footage' clips, Jewish suffering is both revered and orientalized.[86] In this and in other contexts, a process of myth-making is taking place that involves a significant amount of historical revisionism, as I explore further in Chapter 5. Bush argues that, in seventeenth-century England, Jews 'were part of the intellectual landscape of Christian jurists',[87] and I argue that this remains the case today.

Judicial Agency

Another argument that touches on issues of agency is to do with the role of judges. While some legal scholars suggest that judges have little autonomy, that they are virtual prisoners of the forms of law they adjudicate, my study suggests otherwise. I argue that judges are active agents in the production of orientalist, racialized, and Christian discourse and that legal formalism only goes so far in terms of explaining judicial rhetoric and case outcomes. Orientalism, for example, as Said wrote, is 'willed human work'.[88] Judges articulate, reflect, and, importantly, re-present ubiquitous understandings.

[85] H. Arendt, *The Jewish Writings*, J. Kohn and R.H. Feldman (eds) (New York: Shocken Books, 2007) 64 (orig. pub. 1938–9). Arendt points to the abstraction of 'the Jew' as being a defining difference between medieval and modern antisemitism, but my argument is not dependent on this distinction; Bale's work would also seem to challenge this line of thinking.

[86] These judicial renderings parallel the deployment of 'the Jew' in certain leftist writings, as provocatively analysed by David Seymour in his *Law, Antisemitism and the Holocaust* (London: Routledge/Cavendish, 2007). See also J. Boyarin, *Thinking in Jewish* (Chicago: University of Chicago Press, 1996) and M. Silverman, 'Refiguring "the Jew" in France', in B. Cheyette and L. Marcus (eds), *Modernity, Culture and 'the Jew'* (Stanford: Stanford University Press, 1998).

[87] Bush, 'You're Gonna Miss Me' 1276. [88] Said, *Orientalism* 15.

These cases about Jews and Jewishness show that judges have choices—choices about what aspects of a wider cultural discourse they incorporate, choices about what parts of a narrative they leave in or out, choices about what sort of rhetorical stance to adopt, and choices about what kinds of juxtapositions they make to advance their reasoning. While choices about outcome may often (although by no means always) be greatly constrained, my concern in this book is not solely or even predominantly with outcomes, but with judicial knowledge production about Jews and Jewishness.

The cases I analyse here represent a range of substantive legal areas. While there are obviously considerable formal and substantive differences between the cases, for example those with which I opened this book, my contention is that there is a genealogical trajectory of Jews and Jewishness that can usefully be traced over several decades, apart from considerations of the character of particular forms of law at particular times. An analysis of such a trajectory can tell us something about the continuities and discontinuities in these terms' meaning, the work they do at particular moments; 'Jew' and 'Jewish' are not terms constituted afresh in the context of each usage but have an inevitable relationship to wider understandings of race and religion in a Christian society.

In presenting some of this work prior to its completion, I was often asked the question: which of your judges are Jewish? Do Jewish judges come to different decisions? I have not undertaken serious investigative work into the background of the judges, except where I found myself curious about an unusual judgment. So, for example, I occasionally encountered a thoughtful and sympathetic decision and would then seek to discover something about its author. I sometimes found that Catholic judges showed a more nuanced understanding of Jewishness than Protestant judges, but I would not wish to make any general claim following from this observation. My concern is not with the background, politics, prejudice, or ethnicity of any individual judge, although a cursory perusal of the *Dictionary of National Biography* will show any reader just how homogenous this group was, certainly in the earlier part of the twentieth century. But my argument is about pervasive approaches in judicial discourse about Jews and Jewishness, and it does not matter to me whether a judge is Christian or Jewish.

Jewish judges who believe themselves to be adjudicating in a secular court system are also capable of engaging in orientalizing, racializing, and normative Christian impositions. Having said that, with a very few exceptions, the judges appearing in these pages come from Christian, in the main Anglican, backgrounds—not because I have specially selected them this way, but because very few Jewish judges participated in cases where Jews and Jewishness were discussed, particularly earlier in the twentieth century.

A WORD ABOUT METHODOLOGY

I have read several hundred twentieth- and twenty-first century legal cases for this project. I make no claim that the coverage is complete (my database consisted, with a few exceptions, of electronically reported cases only); although I do think it is comprehensive. I restricted my collection to English cases, and thus make no claims in this book about Scottish or Northern Irish courts. I also found that almost none of my cases had a Welsh context, and so I am excluding any discussion of 'Welshness'. When I use the words English and Englishness, that is what I mean. With the exception of Chapter 5, I chose the cases I analyse by whether they explicitly discuss Jews or Jewishness in some way. Thus, with the exception of Chapter 5, cases involving Jewish litigants where the words 'Jew' or 'Jewish' do not appear are necessarily outside the ambit of a project concerned with judicial articulations of Jews and Jewishness.[89] Of the several hundred cases I read, I focus on 50 or so with richer discussions of Jews and Jewishness, although I note about 100 others in passing. There are also many more cases where the words 'Jew' or 'Jewish' appear that are not cited in these pages as there is no further discussion of these concepts.

In Chapter 5, my selection of cases was premised on the presence of a different term—'holocaust'. I also searched within my 'Jews and Jewishness' cases for related terms, for example, 'extermination'. This is because, as the project proceeded, it became apparent to me that judicial mention of 'the Holocaust' was also, often, about

---

[89] Note that there are some cases where one report mentions the Jewishness of a litigant, and another one does not—this has also complicated things. For example, see the two reports in *Vyner* v *Waldenberg Bros* [1946] KB 50, [1945] 2 All ER 547.

understandings of Jews and Jewishness even if those latter words never appeared in the case report. Aside from conducting textual analysis here, appreciating how and when judges took note of 'the Holocaust' also impacts on their approach in other cases involving Jews and Jewishness more explicitly, as I go on to argue.

I should note that there are two groups of judgments to which I do not give much attention in this book. First, there are the cases to do with how English courts review decisions of the Bet Din—the orthodox Jewish courts. These cases largely concern judicial reviews of marriage and divorce decisions,[90] but occasionally something else, such as the review of a rabbi's appointment, or the licensing of shochetim, or the issuing of a Kashrut certificate, for example.[91] Judicial review of the Bet Din is one area of law that has received a certain amount of attention, for example by Michael Freeman, Susan Maidment, and Stephen Poulter, amongst others.[92] Technically, these decisions are often lengthy disquisitions on conflict of laws principles, and they do not lend themselves to the analysis I pursue in this project. Where they do, I have referred to them in relevant chapters.

Second, criminal law cases do not feature in the book. This is because in some ways these cases were too easy a target—in other words, as one of the judges himself says (see Chapter 2), references to Shylock and Fagin abound in the criminal courts. I am far more interested in other areas of law, less obviously amenable to popular stereotypes. At the same time, criminal law cases are largely settled

[90] On nineteenth-century cases, see Pfeffer, 'From One End of Earth to the Other'. Some twentieth-century ones include: *Har-Shefi* v *Har-Shefi* [1953] 2 All ER 373; *Joseph* v *Joseph* [1953] 2 All ER 710; *Corbett* v *Corbett* [1957] 1 All ER 621; *Brett* v *Brett* [1969] 1 All ER 1007; *Berkovits* v *Grinberg* [1995] 2 All ER 681; *N* v *N* [1999] 2 FCR 583; *X* v *X* [2002] 1 FLR 508. Some of these cases concern the *get*, the Jewish divorce, and are concerned with the position of women whose husbands refuse to give them a *get*; note that the Divorce (Religious Marriages) Act 2002 made it impossible to get a civil divorce without first taking steps to dissolve the marriage in the Bet Din.

[91] On a rabbi's appointment, see *R* v *Chief Rabbi of the United Hebrew Congregations, ex parte Wachmann* [1993] 2 All ER 249; on the licensing of shochetim, see *R* v *Rabbinical Comm. For the Licensing of Shochetim, ex parte Cohen* (14 December 1987); on Kashrut, see *R* v *London Beth Din, ex parte Bloom* (18 November 1997). See also *Soleimany* v *Solemainy* [1999] 3 All ER 847, finding that English courts will not enforce a Bet Din award when a contract is illegal under English law, and *R* v *London Committee of Deputies of British Jews, ex parte Helmcourt Ltd.* (14 July 1981), finding that the Board of Deputies was best placed to issue 'Sunday opening' certificates. I do not discuss any of these, better known, cases in this book.

[92] M. Freeman, 'Is the *Get* Any Business of the State?' in R. O'Dair and A. Lewis (eds), *Law and Religion* (Oxford: Oxford University Press); S. Poulter, *Ethnicity, Law and Human Rights* (Oxford: Oxford University Press, 1999); S. Maidment, 'The Legal Effect of Religious Divorces' (1974) 37 *Modern Law Review* 611–26. See also J. Pfeffer, 'From One End of Earth to the Other'.

at first instance, by jury, and without lengthy judgments issued by judges. Thus, judicial discourse, the subject of this book, is minimal. Finally, there is already a large literature on discourses of Jewish criminality.[93]

This project would undoubtedly have benefited from incorporating two further dimensions: a much longer historical lens, as well as a comparative one. In other words, while I can and do make some arguments about time, change, and socio-political context in the over 100 years of my study, much more could be said if I had been able to consider the nineteenth- and eighteenth-century legal cases as well. On the other hand, as I explained earlier, the twentieth century was (with some caveats) the first to contain no explicit anti-Jewish discriminatory measure, and so I am quite consciously interested in this 'post-emancipation' context. Comparing judicial discourse on Jews and Jewishness with understandings of Irishness, Muslimness, and other persons and concepts would no doubt make also for a richer text. Unfortunately, resources did not permit me to pursue all these avenues and this work remains to be done.

In terms of my approach to reading the cases I have chosen, I draw from humanities scholarship (see discussion above), including Edward Said's methodological approach in *Orientalism* where he argued for work that highlighted processes of *representation*.[94] I also rely methodologically on a rich history of feminist scholarship that has studied legal discourse to explore how judges understand, produce, and deploy gender.[95] Like these scholars, who are less interested in documenting 'sexism' as they are in analysing gendered discourse, I am less interested in identifying 'antisemitism',[96] and more interested in exploring racialized understandings. With the exception of some of the cases I discuss in Chapter 6,

---

[93] Much of Sander Gilman's work addresses this aspect, see, in particular, *The Jew's Body*, chs 4 and 9. See also, Shapiro, *Shakespeare and the Jews*, ch. 3, for a discussion of 'Jewish crime' in early modern England; P. Knepper, 'British Jews and the racialisation of crime in the age of empire' (2007) 47(1) *British J. of Criminology* 61–79 for early twentieth century. See also, M. Berkowitz, *The Crime of My Very Existence: Nazism and the Myth of Jewish Criminality* (Berkeley: University of California Press, 2007).

[94] Said, *Orientalism* 23 and 273.

[95] E.g., C. Smart, 'The woman of legal discourse' (1992) 1 *Social & Legal Studies* 29; R. Graycar and J. Morgan, *The Hidden Gender of Law* (Annandale: Federation Press, 2002, rev'd edn). Note that few of the cases I encountered involve representations of 'the Jewish woman'; however, I do highlight depictions of Jewish masculinity where relevant. For a discussion of 'the Jewess' in English literature, see N. Valman, *The Jewess in Nineteenth-Century British Literary Culture* (Cambridge: Cambridge University Press, 2007).

[96] But see Julius, *Trials of the Diaspora*, for one recent attempt to do this.

none of the legal decisions in this book are about Jewish people complaining of discrimination. Perhaps contrary to some popular (mis)perceptions, English law is not replete with such examples. In fact, the number of legal actions motivated by claims of anti-Jewish discrimination is minute, and, where they have occurred, under race relations legislation, they are almost invariably unsuccessful (as I show in Chapter 6).

Furthermore, for reasons well explored by many critical Jewish studies scholars, I do not find the term 'antisemitism' helpful, and I rarely use it in this book other than to identify a general trend. Antisemitism is a shorthand for processes that require greater depth of analysis. As David Feldman has written, 'antisemitism' has a 'tendency to reduce the historical question to one of whether an individual was for or against the Jews'.[97] I am not interested in labelling judges 'antisemites'—I do not think this advances knowledge about racialization processes in England. Anthony Julius, in his recent text, defines antisemitism as involving 'hatred', 'malice'—and as an 'idée fixé'.[98] Although I do not think the concept of antisemitism needs to be defined this way, I avoid its use in this book precisely because I am not accusing individual judges of 'hatred' and 'malice' towards Jews and Jewishness. What I have found in the cases is not 'hatred', but *distaste*, not 'malice', but *unease and confusion*. Thus, my analysis is more in keeping with critical Jewish studies scholars who describe the relationship between Jews, Jewishness and English culture as one of 'ambivalence'.[99]

In taking this approach, I am also indebted to the critical race approaches noted earlier in this chapter that seek to analyse racial discourse, rather than to catalogue instances of 'racism'. While, as I explained earlier, virtually none of this work considers Jews and Jewishness in English law, I adopt its methodologies in terms of being attentive to what is less on the surface, reading cases not

---

[97] Feldman, *Englishmen and Jews* 77. I find the term 'philosemitism' also problematic as its use implies that it is 'antisemitism's' opposite. However, as Reisenover has shown, philosemitism can go hand in hand with anti-Jewishness, see 'Anti-Jewish Philosemitism: British and Hebrew Affinity and Nineteenth Century British Antisemitism' (2008) I (1) *British Scholar* 79–104. See also Bale, *The Jew in the Medieval Book*, who makes a similar point 20.

[98] Julius, *Trials of the Diaspora* xxxiii.

[99] 'Ambivalence' in relation to Jews and Jewishness in England has been most comprehensively developed by Bryan Cheyette, *Constructions of 'the Jew'*. Cheyette has recently re-stated his argument about 'ambivalence' in (forthcoming), 'English Anti-Semitism: A Counter Narrative', *Textual Practice*.

simply for doctrinal reasoning, but for socio-political exercises in categorization and the making of a 'common-sense'. Much legal analysis focuses on the decision or doctrinal argument of a case; my primary focus in this book is on how judges compile the 'facts' in a written decision, what elements are recorded and juxtaposed, what information is rendered irrelevant, and on the thinking behind this compilation. The 'facts' of the case become part of a historical record and it is the making of this record, or, this documentary montage, that interests me. How can we analyse the juxtapositions in which 'the Jew' is enmeshed? How do Jews and Jewishness work in conjunction with other terms in legal discourse? Jonathan Bush, in his discussion of how early modern jurists envisioned Jews and Jewishness, wrote:

To focus on the rules reached by these late-medieval and early modern lawyers, and not their intellectual vocabulary and approach is to miss the essence of their endeavour, and frequently to misjudge their results.[100]

My approach in this book is similar—while rules and outcome are by no means irrelevant, my focus is elsewhere.

CHAPTER OUTLINE

The next two chapters consider cases from the start of the twentieth century and into the twenty-first. In Chapter 2, I explore decisions covering a range of legal areas to focus particularly on the relationship between race, character, nation, class, and English law over time. I argue that in the earlier part of the century, judicial assessments of 'character' were often dependent on notions of race and nationality. In the latter part of the century, a concern with nationality disappeared. However, Jewish people continued to be considered un-English based on an assessment of their behaviour. At the same time, there was a significantly racialized aspect to the ways in which the judiciary extolled the virtues of English law.

Chapter 3 takes one legal area—the law of trusts—and traces the courts' approach to understandings of Jews and Jewishness, again, over the course of the last century. While judges at the turn of the twentieth century had no trouble finding valid clauses in

---

[100] Bush, 'You're Gonna Miss Me' 1283.

wills requiring progeny to 'marry in' in order to inherit, by the early 1940s this had all changed. In the middle of the century, judges developed an understanding of Jews and Jewishness that relied on theological/racial assumptions, while, at the same time, they claimed total ignorance about anything Jewish. As they struck down clauses in the wills of Jewish testators, they upheld those of Christians through a form of Christian universalist discourse. While the judges did not engage in overt orientalizations of Jewish persons, as in the cases in Chapter 2, they did orientalize Judaism.

Chapter 4 explores how judges consider the cultural futures of children in parental dispute and adoption cases. I argue that objections to minority persons and practices as harmful to children can involve not just racializing and orientalizing processes, but conversionary ones as well. In other words, under the veil of 'secularism', judges authorize the conversions of non-Christian children to Christianity. At the same time, there is evidence in some cases of a more nuanced, sophisticated understanding of children's cultural identities.

Chapter 5 takes a somewhat different trajectory by exploring judicial references to 'the Holocaust'. I first trace the evolution of the term in English case law, demonstrating that, with just two exceptions, English judges did not take account of 'the Holocaust' until the 1990s. Once the phrase did enter the judicial repertoire, I argue that it was deployed by many judges in ways that were abstract, mythologizing, and routinized. I also suggest that 'the Holocaust' can be seen to facilitate judicial presentations of the un-English behaviours I discuss in Chapter 2.

In Chapter 6, I review the history of race relations law in England, and consider the various appearances of Jews and Jewishness in race relations law. I explore how parliamentarians made use of the abstracted Jewish victim in both sides of the debates on race relations legislation, and then consider the cases—both those with Jewish parties and those without. I argue that despite the 'abstracted Jew' facilitating the development of antidiscrimination law in relation to other groups, no 'real' Jew had ever, until 2009, won a reported Race Relations Act 1976 case. This chapter ends with a discussion of the first two decisions in the *JFS* case.

In the final chapter, I restate the book's main arguments, and then show how the Supreme Court's final decision in the *JFS* case reinforces them. I argue that the judicial discourse in this judgment is highly racialized, orientalist, and conversionary, and that there is a continuity with older discourses to which we should attend. Finally, I suggest some additional avenues for further research.

Chapter 2

'AN UNFORTUNATE COINCIDENCE':[1] RACE, NATION, AND CHARACTER

This chapter looks back at the whole of the twentieth century, and into the twenty-first, covering a wide variety of legal areas, in order to trace a set of ideas that I continue to examine in subsequent chapters. In considering judicial knowledge of Jews and Jewishness over the course of the last 100 years or so, I ask: first, how do English judges comprehend and represent Jews and Jewishness over time?; second, are contemporary judicial understandings of Jewishness different in substance to earlier ones? I have chosen for the purposes of this first substantive chapter to extract from selected cases how judges articulate the relationship between race, nation, and character.

The articulation of race to 'nation', and the role these concepts play in shaping how fundamental aspects of personhood and character are understood, has a long history in England.[2] Kim Hall's work has been particularly influential in explaining these relations in early modern England, and other scholars have considered different periods of English history.[3] Before (and indeed after) the 'race sciences' made their mark on knowledge, race—in England— was largely understood as heritage or *lineage*. Racial difference was familial, national, and environmental difference, albeit difference

---

[1] *R v Elias* (15 December 1998).

[2] See P. Mandler, *The English National Character: The History of an Idea from Edmund Burke to Tony Blair* (New Haven: Yale University Press, 2006).

[3] K. Hall, *Things of Darkness: Economies of Race and Gender in Early Modern England* (Ithaca: Cornell University Press, 1995); C. Hall, K. McClelland and J. Rendell, *Defining the Victorian Nation: Class, Race, Gender, and the Reform Act of 1867* (Cambridge: Cambridge University Press, 2000); K. Wilson, *Island Race: Empire and Gender in the Eighteenth Century* (London: Routledge, 2002).

usually encoded in a system of domination and subordination.[4] In England, those persons originating from outside the British Isles, or even those indigenous to British territory deemed not descended from the 'Anglo-Saxon race' (e.g., the Celts), were often viewed as having a very different character to the English.[5] Indeed, the process of nation-building was and remains partly a process of character-building. As Sara Ahmed has argued, 'the construction of the nation space takes place alongside the production of national character as instances in which "the nation" itself is fleshed out *as place and person*.[6] This process is not fixed or stable—it is a site of political contestation.

In relation to Jews and Jewishness, James Shapiro has argued that notions of English character, as they developed in Elizabethan England, were embedded in a way of thinking that explicitly drew distinctions between English and Jewish character—Englishness was partly about *not* being Jewish.[7] This was largely true of Christian cultures generally; it is hardly contentious to say that Christianity itself developed as a narrative of 'growth out of and away from Jewishness'.[8] These understandings were then somewhat complicated by Protestant theology that identified Jews as the 'chosen people' of a sacred (if superseded) Christian text (the so-called 'Old Testament'). Jewishness implicated racial, religious and national difference;[9] this was further complicated by the understanding of Jews, like Roma peoples, as a 'nation' without a territory: '[Jews] were the ultimate incongruity: a *non-national nation*'.[10] As I

---

[4] D. Goldberg, *Racist Culture* (Malden, MA: Blackwell, 1993), ch. 8; N. Stepan, *The Idea of Race in Science: Great Britain 1800–1960* (Basingstoke: Macmillan,1982); M. Banton, *Racial Theories* (Cambridge: Cambridge University Press, 1998).

[5] Emphasis in original. On English notions of 'the Irish', see M. Hickman, 'Reconstructing Deconstructing "Race": British Political Discourses about the Irish in Britain' (1998) 21(2) *Ethnic and Racial Studies* 288–307, on 'the Celts', see Mandler, *The English National Character*.

[6] S. Ahmed, *Strange Encounters: Embodied Others in Post-coloniality* (London: Routledge, 2000) 99, ital. orig.

[7] J. Shapiro, *Shakespeare and the Jews* (New York: Columbia University Press, 1996). On the relationship between Christianity and English character more generally, see M. Grimley, 'The Religion of Englishness: Puritanism, Providentialism, and "National Character", 1918–1945' (2007) 46(4) *J. of British Studies* 884–906.

[8] J. Boyarin, *The Unconverted Self: Jews, Indians, and the Identity of Christian Europe* (Chicago: University of Chicago Press, 2009) 117.

[9] See also M. Ragussis, *Figures of Conversion: 'The Jewish Question' and English National Identity* (Durham: Duke University Press, 1995).

[10] Z. Bauman, *Modernity and Ambivalence* (Cambridge: Polity, 1991) 85. See also H. Arendt, *The Jewish Writings*, J. Kohn and R.H. Feldman (eds) (New York: Shocken Books, 2007) 69. I am not

explained in Chapter 1, for several centuries (following the earlier expulsion), Jews had formed part of a racialized 'interior' in England. They, along with some others, most notably numerically Irish people, constituted a racialized 'stranger' *within* the nation state long before more recent diasporic populations emerged out of what has become known as 'postcoloniality'.

Following from these observations, I make three key arguments based on my readings of the legal cases. First, many judges in the earlier part of the twentieth century understood 'character' through the prism of 'race' and 'nationality'. In other words, a phrase like 'national character' cannot be understood outside of its racial conceptual framework, and this was very apparent in early-twentieth century legal decisions to do with Jews and Jewishness. James Shapiro has documented this articulation in English culture in earlier centuries,[11] and while its form and subjects change over time, the close relationship between nation, race, and character persists.

Second, the delineation of an 'alien', Jewish character in contrast to an English, Christian one, is evident throughout the century's legal judgments. While the terms of the articulation of race, nation, and character shift, with new ways of explaining difference replacing old ones, the association of Jews with 'alien' character remains alive and well into the twenty-first century. Third, I argue that judicial knowledge about Jews and Jewishness has played an important constitutive role in the making of 'Englishness', and, in particular, English law. In other words, elucidating the character of English law involves racializing processes. Bryan Cheyette has argued,

... race-thinking about Jews was, in fact, a key ingredient in the merging cultural identity of modern Britain ... racialised constructions of Jews and other 'races' were at the heart of domestic liberalism.[12]

---

suggesting that the paradox of a non-national nation is peculiar to Jews (see Gilroy's critique of Bauman in *The Black Atlantic: Modernity and Double Consciousness* (London: Verso, 1993) 213–4, only that 'the Jews' represent one of the earliest peoples embodying this incongruity in Europe. See also Feldman's critique of Bauman's 'totalizing' approach to 'the Jews and Modernity', 'Was Modernity Good for the Jews?' in B. Cheyette and L. Marcus (eds), *Modernity, Culture and 'the Jew'* (Stanford: Stanford University Press, 1998) 171–87.

[11] Shapiro, *Shakespeare and the Jews.*

[12] B. Cheyette, *Constructions of 'The Jew' in English Literature and Society* (Cambridge: Cambridge University Press, 1993) xi.

While Cheyette was referring to a slightly earlier period of British literary history, I suggest that the argument remains persuasive for twentieth- and twenty-first-century legal discourse as well. Although Peter Mandler, in his study of English character, argues that racial aspects of English character were 'decisively marginalised' by the 1920s,[13] my study suggests otherwise. Within legal discourse at any rate, race-thinking in relation to 'character' remains salient.

In tracing how nationality and race were co-dependent in judicial discourse at the turn of the twentieth century, it is important to understand the historical context in which English judges lived and worked. As I explained in Chapter 1, Jews lived openly in England from the mid to late seventeenth century. In addition to a poor and working-class Jewish population, a well-off, and politically and economically influential Jewish community also began to establish itself. By the later part of the eighteenth century, this largely Sephardic community (many of whom arrived via the Netherlands where they had lived following their fifteenth-century expulsion from Spain and Portugal) had been augmented by a number of prominent European Ashkenazi families, mainly from Germany and France. Much of this Jewish community prospered economically in England, despite living under conditions of severe legal discrimination. In time, and once legal barriers were removed (not until the mid nineteenth century: see Chapter 1), several became influential politically, and entered the legal and other professions. While these established Jews, despite their prominence, not to mention the fact that many incorporated Anglican trappings into their religious ritual, were not considered by most English Christians to be part of 'the English race', they nevertheless were tolerated by, importantly married into, and to some extent were respected within, the most elite circles of English power.[14] Their class position required it.

---

[13] Mandler, *The English National Character* 154. Mandler unfortunately ignores throughout his book how English character was partly shaped by having Jewish character as its antithesis.

[14] For one readable account, see C. Bermant, *The Cousinhood: The Anglo-Jewish Gentry* (London: Eyre & Spotiswoode, 1971). For comprehensive histories of the diverse Jewish communities of this period, see T. Endelman, *The Jews of Britain, 1656 to 2000* (Berkeley: University of California Press, 2002) and D. Feldman, *Englishmen and Jews: Social Relations and Political Culture 1840–1914*

At the same time, a slow but steady migration of poorer, eastern Jews came to settle in British cities. By the late nineteenth century, these *ostjuden* were arriving in ever-increasing numbers. Penniless and rural, fleeing war, famine, and antisemitic persecution, the 'intensification' of eastern Jewish immigration precipitated a perceived crisis.[15] While this is not the place to relate this story in detail, for the purposes of this chapter it is important to note that the UK's first legislation restricting immigration and refugees, the Aliens Act 1905, was passed in response to the entry of poor, eastern Jews, as was the introduction of the UK's first 'citizenship' test.[16] The explicit exclusion of Jews of 'bad character' was initially written into the Aliens Bill and only dropped due to pressure from the Liberals.[17] Judicial discourse on Jews and Jewishness during the period thus emerged in this context. Below, I explore a series of cases that I group into early/mid and late(r) twentieth century as I argue there is a shift in discourse between these two periods.

EARLY/MID CENTURY

Horne v *Poland*, in 1922, concerned an insurance claim.[18] Harry Horne had suffered a burglary, and made a claim on a policy he had taken out some years earlier. Lloyd's underwriters were refusing to meet this claim on the basis that a material fact had not been disclosed on the original insurance application—namely, his

---

(New Haven: Yale University Press, 1994). For a poignant and fictional account, see Amy Levy's controversial novel *Reuben Sachs* (London: Persephone, 2001, orig. pub. 1888). See also Arendt's distinction between the 'pariah' and the 'parvenu', *The Jewish Writings*, J. Kohn and R.H. Feldman (eds), (New York: Shocken Books, 2007) 275–302.

[15] 'Intensification' is the word used by B. Williams in '"East and West": Class and Community in Manchester Jewry, 1850–1914', in D. Cesarani (ed.), *Making of Modern Anglo-Jewry* (Oxford: Blackwell, 1990) 20.

[16] See, amongst many others, Endelman, *The Jews of Britain*, ch. 4; Feldman, *Englishmen and Jews*, ch. 11; also, more generally, R. Miles, *Racism after 'Race Relations'* (London: Routledge, 1993), ch. 5. Also H. Wray, 'The Aliens Act 1905 and the Immigration Dilemma' (2006) 33 (2) *J. of Law & Society* 302–23. For one thorough account of parliamentary and press debates see J.A. Garrard, *The English and Immigration 1880–1910* (Oxford: Oxford University Press, 1971), also B. Gainer, *The Alien Invasion: The Origins of the Aliens Act of 1905* (London: Heinmann Education Publishers, 1972). For a discussion of accusations of Jewish criminality at the time, see P. Knepper, 'British Jews and the Racialisation of Crime in the Age of Empire' (2007) 47(1) *British J. of Criminology* 61–79. See also Miles's argument that the racism of the Aliens Act 1905 was masked by the economic framework within which these exclusions played out, *Racism After 'Race Relations'* 143–8.

[17] Garrard, ibid., 45.   [18] *Horne* v *Poland* [1922] 2 KB 364.

Romanian nationality and his original Jewish Romanian name. As Lush J explained:

The plaintiff was born in 1887 in Roumania [sic], where his father was a Hebrew teacher...in order, as he says, to avoid ridicule owing to his foreign name, Euda Gedale, he took the name of Harry Horne.[19]

When he was twelve, Mr Horne came to England, where, in 1917, he married an 'Englishwoman' under his Romanian name. He was also registered under the Registration of Aliens Act in this name.[20] However, when he applied for insurance he did so as Harry Horne, the name by which he was known in England, and 'did not state that he was a Roumanian and had lived in Roumania for many years'.[21]

In finding that indeed there had been a failure to disclose a material fact—his Romanian nationality—Lush J was careful to note that not every foreign status would necessarily be material.

One can easily think of cases in which it could not affect the mind of a reasonable underwriter. The assured might have come here from a state where the business and social habits, the training and education that a child or young person received, and the view taken as to the observance of legal and other obligations might be notoriously exacting, the same as those prevailing here. He might have spent his whole life in the United Kingdom and acquired a recognised position...Each case must depend upon its own circumstances. The circumstances here are that the plaintiff came from Eastern Europe, he and his parents being subjects of a state of whose habits and traditions the underwriters would naturally know nothing.... It is impossible to say that matters such as nationality, caste and early domocil cannot be of importance in judging as to the risk that underwriters run in entering into such a contract. To say that is to say that there are no racial differences, no national differences as regards training and education and the other matters I have mentioned. I say nothing, of course, against the national characteristics of the race to which the plaintiff belongs.[22]

In *Horne* v *Poland*, Jewishness must be distinguished by type— Mr Gedale/Horne is not an English Jew, he is a foreign Jew and his very character bears the marks of both his Jewish and his 'Eastern European' alien origins. It is in fact the business of

---

[19] Ibid., 364–5.   [20] Ibid.   [21] Ibid., 365.   [22] Ibid., 366.

insurance underwriters to know with what sort of Jew they are dealing.[23]

Lush J's reference to English habits, training, education, and observance of the law being 'notoriously exacting' is both the encoding of a pre-existing common-sense and part of an English nation-building project. Harry Horne himself is 'flagged' by such a confusing array of alien signifiers,[24] and yet, the judgment implies, the impossibility of knowing his character would apparently be solved by a declaration of 'Roumanian' nationality on an insurance form. But what are the 'national characteristics' of a 'race'? Perhaps the 'Eastern Europe' designation is sufficient to trigger an appropriate degree of character suspicion. Perhaps the 'reasonable underwriter', the presumptively English Protestant character hovering in the background of this case, would have read the name 'Euda Gedale' as Jewish and then been able to make a more informed decision.

A foreign Jew again came to the attention of the courts in *Glicksman (Pauper)* v *Lancashire & General Assurance Co Ltd*, another 1920s insurance case where the underwriters were refusing to meet a claim, again due to a failure to disclose a material fact.[25] The plaintiffs, Sapsy Glicksman and others, had not disclosed that they had had an application for insurance rejected by another company. According to Viscount Dunedin, in his House of Lords judgment, the plaintiff's 'natural and best language was Yiddish'.[26] Viscount Dunedin, in contemplating the meeting between this 'wretched little ladies' tailor' and an unscrupulous Jewish insurance salesman (a 'Mr Cohen'), could only imagine how distasteful such an *'impar congressus'* must be.[27]

...I am left with the impression, that those,—shall I call them, attractive?—qualities which we are prone to ascribe to the Hebrews, among whom Shylock has always been the prototype, have been quite as satisfactorily developed on the part of this insurance company as ever they were by the little Polish Jew.[28]

---

[23] Note that Lush J remarks that the burden should be on the insurance companies to ask for this specific information, as 'aliens' do not know what constitutes 'material facts'.

[24] Emily Grabham develops the concept of 'flagging' in relation to the body, in ' "Flagging" the Skin: Corporeal Nationalism and the Properties of Belonging' (2009) 15 *Body & Society* 63–82.

[25] [1927] AC 139.   [26] Ibid., 142.   [27] Ibid.

[28] Ibid., 143. I am conscious that Dunedin is Scottish, not English; however, his elite background and education have clearly shaped his understandings of Jews and Jewishness in similar ways.

Here we have a Jewish insurance salesman compared to Shylock—presumably wanting his pound of flesh from the 'wretched' Mr Glicksman who speaks only the inferior foreign language known as a mark of 'the east'[29]—while the latter's Jewishness is inextricably linked to his eastern European origins.

The description of Jewish men as 'little', in this case an entirely irrelevant fact to the appeal,[30] is an often remarked upon phenomenon in the depiction of Jewish masculinity. Gilman has suggested the circumcised penis serves as the prototype for the accusation of diminution.[31] It is obviously also an accusation of effeminacy, an orientalizing belittlement that, accompanied by the unmanly phrase 'ladies tailor', serves to distinguish further the Sapsy Glicksmans from the Viscount Dunedins of this world. The accusation of 'littleness' is also largely absent from, for example, the trusts line of cases where the Jewish man (and occasional woman) is instead invested with the stature of the biblical patriarch, controlling their children's lives from beyond the grave (see following chapter). I am thus arguing here that the particular understanding of Jewishness, and Jewish masculinity in particular, at play in *Glicksman* may be specific to the sort of Jew the English judges were increasingly confronting—the eastern, oriental Jew, the Jew that was most unlike 'the rational man' of the European Enlightenment.[32]

---

[29] S. Gilman, *The Jew's Body* (New York: Routledge, 1991) 12, 34. See also *Hyams v Paragon Insurance Co.* [1927] 27 Ll L Rep. 448 where Salter J, despite finding for the Jewish plaintiff, describes him as 'a Polish Jew, a very poor scholar and an illiterate person', 449.

[30] Note that the Court of Appeal in its decision made no reference to Glicksman's Jewishness, [1925] 2 KB 593.

[31] Gilman, *The Jew's Body*, 160. It should also be noted that the use of ostensibly feminized signifiers in relation to Jewish men is not always a product of racist discourse. One of the first radical Yiddish newspapers was called *Der Polylisher Yidl* – the Little Polish Jew (Endelman, *The Jews of Britain* 139). D. Boyarin makes the argument that Jewish masculinity historically developed in a more 'feminized' way, *Unheroic Conduct: The Rise of Heterosexuality and the Invention of the Jewish Man* (Berkeley: University of California Press, 1997). Similarly, 'littleness' can also be used to signify positive national attributes, as in 'Little England'.

[32] At the same time, the 'feminization' of the Jewish man in English culture generally should not be over-emphasized; just as importantly, Jewish men were often perceived to embody an aggressive, predatory masculinity. As Gilman has shown, the 'eastern Jew' also played an important spectral role in the 'Jack the Ripper' episode, see *The Jew's Body* ch. 4. Note also that the relation between Jewishness and masculinity will be understood differently in different national contexts, for example, see re the United States, D. Itzkovits, 'Secret Temples' in J. Boyarin and D. Boyarin (eds), *Jews and Other Differences: The New Jewish Cultural Studies* (Minneapolis: University of Minnesota Press, 1997) 176–202.

So, while in trusts law, for example, (see Chapter 3), the judges were confronted with familiar Jews and Christian converts, the propertied business class, well known (if often despised) by the English upper class, Viscount Dunedin's 'little Polish Jew', and Lush J's son of a 'Roumanian Hebrew teacher', were differently raced subjects, reflecting how the intersections of class, race, and nationality told a story about a more *alien* Jew, a Jew often characterized by perceived illiteracy and destitution.[33] Insurance cases, often, as in my examples, involving allegations of fraud, highlight these understandings. In yet another of such cases involving Jewish claimants, Lord Chief Justice Hewart asked a jury to try and 'forget that the plaintiff is a Polish Jew and that the defendants were an insurance company, as both might possibly be matters of prejudice'.[34] The jury found for the insurance company.

The apex of the 'eastern' threat can be traced to the earlier decades of the twentieth century; however, the world war two and the post-war years were not periods in which antisemitism abated in England. On the contrary, as various scholars have demonstrated, anti-Jewish sentiment, in both popular and official discourse, intensified during the war and subsisted after its conclusion.[35] One litigant's wartime experience is related in a psychiatric report submitted to the court:

From the first day he was singled out as the only Jew on the camp. The new recruits were told to separate into groups according to religion and he was left standing alone. The flight sergeant asked why he was not in a

---

[33] I am not suggesting 'the judges' always characterized 'the Jews' in this way, rather that these qualities were seen to be characteristic of the eastern Jews in English culture generally during this period: see, e.g., Garrard's review of the evidence before the Royal Commission at the time, *The English and Immigration*, ch. 4, and also J. Steyn, *The Jew: Assumptions of Identity* (London: Cassells, 1999), ch. 4. See also D. Cesarani, 'The Anti-Jewish Career of Sir William Joynson-Hicks, Cabinet Minister' (1989) 24 *J. of Contemporary History* 461–82. For an interesting account of anglo-Jews' attempts to 'naturalize' east-end easterners, see R. Voeltz, ' "...A good Jew and a good Englishman": The Jewish Lads' Brigade, 1894–1922' (1988) 23 *J. of Contemporary History* 119–27.

[34] *Weinstein* v *The Army, Navy and General Assurance Association* [1922] 10 Ll L Rep 558 at 559. In another, similar case, a judge describes Lloyd's as 'almost a national institution', *Silver* v *Mountain* [1922] 10 Ll L Rep 431. See also the finding of fraud against a 'Russian Jew' in *Shoot* v *Hill* [1936] 55 Ll L Rep 29.

[35] See, for example, R. Griffiths, 'The Reception of Bryant's *Unfinished Victory*: Insights into British Public Opinion in Early 1940' (2004) 38(1) *Patterns of Prejudice* 18–36; T. Kushner, *The Persistence of Prejudice: Antisemitism in British Society During the Second World War* (Manchester: Manchester University Press, 1989); G. Macklin, ' "A quite natural and moderate defensive feeling"?: The 1945 Hampstead "Anti-alien" Petition' (2003) 37(3) *Patterns of Prejudice* 277–300; L. London, *Whitehall and the Jews* (Edgeware: Valentine Mitchell, 2003); D. Fraser, *The Jews of the Channel Islands and the Rule of Law, 1940–1945* (Brighton: Sussex Academic Press, 2000).

group and when told that it was because he was Jewish remarked 'that's funny, I can't see any horns'. He was then told in front of the other recruits that his religious duties would be to stand outside the Church of England services every Sunday with a rifle 'to stop the Nazis getting in'. From then onwards he was referred to as 'that fucking Jew' and 'hey, Jewboy, come here' on a daily basis. The other conscripts frequently expressed the view that, as a Jew, he was partly responsible for the war in the first place.[36]

In terms of official policy, nationality continued to play a crucial role, for example in decisions about which Jews to intern during the war;[37] and in determinations over which Jewish refugees would be admitted before and during the war, those from the east remained the least desirable.[38] Even after the war, the legacy of race and nationality persisted in legal discourse on 'the Jew': suspect 'Rumanians' and Poles continued to appear in cases through the 1950s. This is not unexpected for, as Tony Kushner has shown, the disparaging of the 'eastern Jew' persisted unabated in post-war English political culture generally.[39]

In 1951, a contract law dispute arose, according to the judge, 'out of the scramble which took place after the war to acquire and sell surplus equipment at a profit'.[40] Foreign Jews were again 'the villains of the piece'.[41] Although there were four sets of defendants in the case, Cassels J was most disapproving of the Jewish set:

... the man Pyper, ... an adventurer, not overburdened with principle where finance is concerned, and a Mr J.I. Cowan, a mere tool, and Mr Littman, said to be a Rumanian Jew. It was an unattractive combination...[42]

The use of the word 'unattractive' resonates with Viscount Dunedin's sarcastic reference to 'the attractive qualities' of 'the Hebrews' in

---

[36] *R (Gibbs)* v *Sec St Social Security* [2001] EWHC Admin 742, para. 74. This is a quote from a psychiatric report submitted in the case.

[37] Kushner, *The Persistence of Prejudice: Antisemitism in British Society During the Second World War*, ch. 5.

[38] L. London, *Whitehall and the Jews*.

[39] T. Kushner, 'Remembering to Forget: Racism and Anti-racism in Postwar Britain' in B. Cheyette and L. Marcus (eds), *Modernity, Culture and 'the Jew'*. (Stanford: Stanford University Press, 1998) 226–41, as it did also, for example, in Canada, see J.W.St.G. Walker, *'Race', Rights and the Law in the Supreme Court of Canada* (Waterloo: Wilfrid Laurier Press, 1997).

[40] *Hatton* v *Millburn Garage Co.* [1951] 1 Lloyds Rep 379, 381, per Cassels J.

[41] Ibid.   [42] Ibid.

the *Glicksman* case. There is a 'racial aesthetic' in operation explicitly designating 'the Jew' as different, as something unpleasant, particularly when other, non-Jewish, defendants are described as 'honest'.[43]

I do not want to suggest that every judge encountering 'eastern Jews' made negative assumptions about character. Scott LJ, for example, in *Vyner* v *Waldenberg Bros*, remarked that:

[The plaintiff] was a Russian Jew by birth and his native language was still Yiddish. We think there was much difficulty in understanding the questions put and his expressing what he intended to say in some of his answers. The judge, who tried the case very carefully, thought him honest, truthful and accurate, as far as his knowledge went.[44]

It was clearly not necessary to comment on a Jewish litigant's 'unattractiveness'.

In another, slightly later case, this time one involving a complicated dispute over property, Harman J feels he can clearly assess the content of Mr Ryder's character from the mixing of his national and racial origins.[45]

The defendant is a Polish Jew, born in Galacia, and educated in Vienna. He lived until 1938 on the continent, either in Rumania or in Brussels, and though he has been in this country since shortly before the war and was naturalised in 1947, he remains very much a foreigner. He is obviously an impulsive and emotional person, and has espoused Lewis's [a Jewish co-defendant] cause wholeheartedly and immoderately... he allowed himself to be made her catspaw...[46]

Here, Mr Ryder's Polishness, Romanianness, and Jewishness completely overwhelm his Viennese education, his possible sojourn in Brussels, and his subsequent residency in England, which, in a sense, hover in the background as proof of his cosmopolitan rootlessness. In championing his co-defendant's cause in

---

[43] Ibid. One can almost imagine the judges holding their noses, an evocation, perhaps, of the 'foetor Judaicus' (see Chapter 1).

[44] *Vyner* v *Waldenberg Bros* [1945] 2 All ER 547 at 548.

[45] *Loudon v Ryder (No 2)* [1953] Ch 423.

[46] Ibid., 425–6. Note that there was a popular campaign against the naturalization of Jewish refugees in the post-war period, see G. Macklin, ' "A quite natural and moderate defensive feeling"? 299. Ryder was one of the lucky ones to have been naturalized in 1947 at all.

such an un-English manner, Mr Ryder has effectively prejudiced his ability to be heard and taken seriously. His behaviour is also unmanly: he has allowed himself to become a woman's 'catspaw'. He is also clearly unassimilable: 'he remains very much a foreigner'. Harman J effectively rejects Mr Ryder's social 'naturalization', even as his legal status remains intact.

The perceived failure of the eastern Jew to assimilate to English culture was a common refrain during this period.[47] Despite 'naturalization' and the acquisition of civil and political status in the UK, the eastern Jew would never be 'natural' to the environment. It is hardly surprising that Jews from the east, other than the few who could buy their way in, were, more often than not, refused entry to the UK before, during, and after the war. In 1944, a Home Office memo explicitly referred to the 'assertiveness' and 'gregariousness' of Jews as reasons for denying them asylum.[48] Judicial acknowledgement that millions of Jewish Europeans had been murdered by the German government in the 1940s did not begin until the 1970s, and, until that time, judges showed little sympathy for Jewish refugees (see further in Chapter 5).

The growing recognition of the Holocaust, and indeed that term's incorporation into an historical common-sense, instigated a rupture in judicial discourse on Jews and Jewishness. It was no longer possible to identify Jewish people in explicitly racialized terms without invoking the spectre of genocide. The Holocaust's acknowledgment (as opposed to its occurrence) constituted an abrupt end to overt declarations of racial superiority within the official discourse of liberal states. This period also witnessed substantial reforms in English legal education and scholarship (some of this instigated by German-Jewish refugees[49]), as well as a somewhat more diverse legal profession and judiciary. However, that is not to say that the racialization of Jews and Jewishness subsided; but, rather, that such racializations took on a new and different

---

[47] See, for example, T. Kushner, *The Holocaust and the Liberal Imagination: A Social and Cultural History* (Oxford: Blackwell, 1994).

[48] Quoted in Kushner, *Persistence of Prejudice* 206.

[49] See C. Glasser, 'Radicals and Refugees: The Foundation of the Modern Law Review and English Legal Scholarship' (1987) 50 *Modern Law Review* 688–708.

form.[50] It is to the latter decades of the twentieth century's judgments on Jewish character that I now turn.

LATE(R) TWENTIETH CENTURY

By the 1980s, the discourse had shifted. Amongst other developments, including the gradual acknowledgement of the Holocaust as
a powerful symbolic marker, 'race relations' law and culture had
come to dominate the field (see Chapter 6). In relation to questions
of Jewish character, judicial approaches to Jews and Jewishness
took a new turn. In most of these cases, judges no longer referred
to foreign origins but instead used other language to distinguish
Jewishness from Englishness. In certain legal spheres, such as, for
example, child welfare law, the concept of 'ethnicity' gradually took
hold, replacing 'race', although racial assumptions continued to
underpin ethnicity's content (see Chapters 4 and 6). In such contexts, a multicultural liberalism at times prevailed, constructing
Jews as a legitimate minority whose culture required judicial investigation and, perhaps, protection. However, in other contexts,
for example employment law, Jewish parties continued to be held in
disregard, through a series of articulations that, whilst ostensibly
'raceless', succeeded in presenting the Jewish parties as *not* English.
Seide v *Gillette Industries* is one illustration.[51]

Mr Seide was a Jewish employee who became the subject of
remarks from a colleague, Mr Garcia, that were recognized by all
parties as antisemitic and 'clearly to be deplored'.[52] In response to
this situation, the employer transferred Mr Seide to a different
shift. He then became the focus of a complaint by another co-
worker on this new shift, Mr Murray, who accused Mr Seide of
creating a 'provocative atmosphere' by attempting, apparently, to
enlist Mr Murray in his continuing battle with Mr Garcia. Once
again, Mr Seide was transferred, this time to a position at a lower
wage. He then complained to an Industrial Tribunal under the
Race Relations Act 1976, arguing that he had been the victim of
race discrimination. His claim was dismissed, the Tribunal being

---

[50] See also, A. Lentin, 'Replacing "Race", Historicising "Culture" in Multiculturalism' (2005) 39
(4) *Patterns of Prejudice* 379–96.
[51] *Seide* v *Gillette Industries Ltd* [1980] IRLR 427, per Slynn J.   [52] Ibid., 428.

'quite satisfied that there was no racial discrimination on the part of the individuals concerned in the management'.[53] The employer had been 'careful and patient', 'democratic and fair'. The managers 'were not anti-Semitic and they did not succumb to anti-Semitism'.[54]

On appeal, Slynn J reaffirmed the rejection of Mr Seide's claim. In coming to his decision, Slynn J recited facts from the tribunal judgment below. We are told that Mr Murray complained of Mr Seide's 'habit of incessantly humming in a tuneless way', that both Mr Garcia and Mr Murray believed that Mr Seide 'was making too much of the situation and tending to assume that people were saying things about him when they really were not', and that the employer had come to the view that they could not know 'who really was to blame'.[55] Slynn J concluded that the Tribunal's decision—that race was not the 'activating' cause of Mr Seide's final transfer, that, rather, the cause was Mr Murray's discomfort at Mr Seide's inappropriate behaviour—was an entirely reasonable one to take.[56]

Instead, the Jewish employee was constructed as over-sensitive, believing people were talking about him when they were not, refusing to 'let matters rest' and passively resume work on his new shift.[57] The excesses of his behaviour, and the distress he caused Mr Murray, then became good reason for transferring him again, this time resulting in a loss of wages. In contrast to Mr Seide's unmanly paranoia, neurotic obsession with his treatment, and 'incessant humming', the employer was represented as 'careful and patient', 'democratic and fair'—the essence of English masculine virtues.[58]

In another case, also from the early 1980s, an Industrial Tribunal dismissed the complaint of a member of the Musicians' Union.[59]

---

[53] Tribunal judgment quoted by Slynn J, ibid., 430.   [54] Ibid., 428–30.   [55] Ibid.

[56] Ibid. The appropriateness of the *first* transfer, that racism in the workplace should be resolved by transferring the victim, was never addressed.

[57] See also Goodrich and Mills's discussion of the *Quereshi* case—they argue Quereshi's refusal to accept the status quo was constructed as a kind of madness, 'The Law of White Spaces: Race, Culture, and Legal Education' (2001) 51(1) *J. of Legal Education* 15–38.

[58] *Seide*, ibid. For further discussion of 'character' and English masculinity, see J.S. Duncan, 'The Struggle to be Temperate: Climate and 'Moral Masculinity' in Mid-Nineteenth Century Ceylon' (2000) 21(1) *Singapore J of Tropical Geography* 34–47; M. Sinha, *Colonial Masculinity: The 'Manly Englishman' and the 'Effeminate Bengali' in the late Nineteenth Century* (Manchester: Manchester University Press, 1995).

[59] *Garnel* v *Brighton Branch of the Musicians' Union* (13 June 1983).

Mr Garnel alleged that the failure of the Union's Brighton Branch to nominate him to sit on a committee, and his resulting suspension from the Union when he complained about this, were racially motivated. The Tribunal accepted the Union's position that Mr Garnel was 'engendering a feeling of anti-Semitism which did not yet exist', and found that 'if there was discrimination therefore it was not because the applicant was a Jew but because of his own personal behaviour'.[60] According to the Tribunal, Mr Garnel's behaviour in the hearing was 'so intemperate' an adjournment had to be ordered.[61]

On appeal, Browne-Wilkinson J began by noting his 'surprise' at this allegation of race discrimination as 'many of our most talented musicians are, indeed, Jews by race, and that is true of the Brighton Branch'.[62] In reciting the Tribunal's findings, Browne-Wilkinson J repeated the accusation of 'intemperacy' on Mr Garnel's part, and lamented,

It is an unhappy feature in this case that anybody who has come in contact with it, whether in the union or elsewhere, has been accused of untruth, racialism and discrimination.[63]

In contrast to Mr Garnel's 'strange' behaviour, Brown-Wilkinson J described the Tribunal as 'fair, orderly' and 'proper'.[64]

The similarities between the judicial discourse in the cases of *Seide* and *Garnel* are striking. In both decisions, a 'strange', 'intemperate', and 'provocative' Jew is seen to have deserved what he got, a characterization echoing earlier rationales for refusing to admit Jewish refugees fleeing German persecution (see above). My argument is that both Mr Seide and Mr Garnel are as 'unnaturalized' as the explicitly orientalized easterners in the earlier cases, however the focus now is upon their 'strange' behaviour. It is no longer possible to use the shorthand of nationality to signify strangeness; the judges knew the 'Rumanian' and 'little Polish' Jews were alien, it was not necessary to say much beyond noting their eastern

---

[60] Tribunal judgment quoted by the EAT, ibid.

[61] Tribunal judgment quoted by Browne-Wilkinson J, ibid. On 'Englishness' and 'intemperacy', see 'The Struggle to be Temperate: Climate and "Moral Masculinity" in Mid-Nineteenth Century Ceylon' (2000) 21(1) *Singapore J. of Tropical Geography* 34–47. Duncan, J. S.; also D. Herman and D. Cooper, 'Anarchic Armadas, Brussels Bureaucrats, and the Valiant Maple Leaf: Sexuality, Governance, and the Construction of British Nationhood through the Canada–Spain Fish War' (1997) 17(3) *Legal Studies* 415–33.

[62] Ibid., EAT, Browne-Wilkinson J.   [63] Ibid.   [64] Ibid.

status. Now, however, the strange(r)ness of 'the Jew' must be demonstrated through references to distinctly un-English, un-attractive, *conduct*. This 'bad behaviour' is over-emotional, disruptive, and impolite.[65]

In the *Garnel* case, the tribunals add the allegation that the Jewish claimant is failing to understand and accept the English rule of law, an accusation with a long history,[66] and one we can associate with the Jews' 'intractable' refusal to accept Christ.[67] As important as cataloguing the excesses of Jewish character are the ways in which the judges, through their description of law itself as fair, measured, and ruly, praise English character. 'The law' is the perfect English gentleman; the feminized hysterics of 'the Jew' revealed in his very voice, his impulsive, over-emotional, and disruptive 'Jewish voice'.[68] It is no coincidence that 'fairness', one of the alleged and most treasured properties of English law and character, has an explicit racialized etymological lineage.

As Peter Mandler has shown, reverence for 'law' and 'orderliness' was integral to notions of English character, as was the idea of 'the gentleman'.[69] Although Mandler suggests this is no longer the case—indeed, he argues 'character' itself is no longer a viable concept—I would suggest otherwise, as this extract from a *Telegraph* article in 1996 makes clear. Referring to the lawyers acting for Prince Charles and Princess Diana during their divorce proceedings,

It became clear almost immediately that the incompatibility of the Prince and Princess of Wales stretched even to the solicitors they employed. The Prince, as expected, had chosen the bridge-playing Fiona Shackleton... One of the country's most respected family law specialists... She adopts

---

[65] On 'politeness' and English character, see P. Carter, 'Polite "Persons": Character, Biography and the Gentleman' (2002) 12 *Transactions of the Royal Historical Society* 333–54. On pervasive discourses of the 'hysteric male Jew', see Gilman, *The Jew's Body*, ch. 3 on 'The Jewish Psyche'.

[66] See Feldman, *Englishmen and Jews* 259–61; also D. Hirsch, 'Dickens's Queer "Jew" and Anglo-Christian Identity Politics: The Contradictions of Victorian Family Values' in D. Boyarin, D. Itzkovitz, and A. Pellegrini (eds), *Queer Theory and the Jewish Question* (New York: Columbia University Press, 2003) 311–33.

[67] Gilman, *The Jew's Body* 19.

[68] Gilman, *The Jew's Body* ch. 1. See also Harrington and Manji's discussion of Denning's representations of English law in the African context, ' "Mind with mind and spirit with spirit": Lord Denning and African legal education' (2003) 30(3) *J of Law and Society* 376–99.

[69] Mandler, *The English National Character* 12, 68, 166.

a conciliatory approach. Unfortunately, her softly-softly approach is at odds with the more bullish attitude of the Princess's solicitor. Anthony 'Genius' Julius . . . is a Jewish intellectual and Labour supporter, and less likely to feel restrained by considerations of fair play. 'I'd be very worried if I were the Royal Family', says a Cambridge don who taught him. 'He'll get lots of money out of them'.[70]

Within English employment law, at any rate, legal discourse also remains highly dependent on distinguishing between English and other kinds of characters. While the language may appear more behaviour-oriented, focusing on bad conduct rather than a litigant's origins, it is 'character' that remains at stake, as it does in many other areas of law where the assessment of 'character' is an integral part of the legal process.

In *Simon* v *Brimham*, although the judicial language is not so explicit, the result is the same.[71] Here, a Jewish man, Mr Simon, was interviewed by a recruiting agency and told during the interview that the employers were 'Arabs' and that if he was Jewish he would not be hired. Mr Simon was asked his 'religion', refused to answer, and walked out. Although the recruiter testified that he 'suspected' Simon 'might be a Jew', the Tribunal and Appeal Tribunal dismissed Mr Simon's complaint on the basis that all candidates were asked their religion and it was not proper to draw the inference that the recruiter 'knew' Mr Simon was Jewish. The Court of Appeal agreed. If he had not walked out, but had completed the interview and then not been put forward for the position, there may have been a case to answer—here there was not.[72] In other words, his behaviour was equally 'intemperate'—he walked out in a huff when he should have stayed, despite having been told unequivocally that there was no chance he would be hired. Like Mr Seide and Mr Garnel, Mr Simon had violated appropriate codes of behaviour, English codes of behaviour.

I return to the Race Relations Act 1976 cases in Chapter 6. For now, I want to explore how this sense of un-Englishness can also be found in a discussion of Jewish criminality at the end of the twentieth century. *R* v *Elias* involved an appeal, in 1998, of a

---

[70] The item appeared in *The Telegraph* 13 July 1996, and is quoted at slightly greater length in A. Julius, *Trials of the Diaspora* (Oxford: Oxford University Press, 2010) xxxii–iii.
[71] *Simon* v *Brimham Associates* [1987] IRLR 307.   [72] Ibid.

conviction for handling stolen goods.[73] Mr Elias alleged that the
jury had been prejudiced by the Crown counsel's 'racially and
religiously offensive' remarks about him and that, as a result, he
did not receive a fair trial. Potter LJ's decision contains a long
quote from the Crown counsel's closing speech:

I turn just before lunch to start on Mr Elias. He is a completely different sort
of man, isn't he? [different to 'Saunders' the other defendant, who is
described as 'guileless'] Completely and utterly and thoroughly dishonest
to the heart, I suggest to you. The most self-regarding, utterly cynical,
greedy man, you can't believe a word he says . . . A master of deceit . . . I draw
the analogy with Oliver Twist who is seen in the musical where Fagin . . .
goes through all the money and the lolly and the jewels . . . because, like
Fagin, he is in the end keeping his hands on his own material . . . he is very
similar because of course . . . he doesn't actually go out and directly grubby
his hands with the burglars.[74]

Defence counsel complained to the trial judge about this speech,
and while the judge said that he thought Mr Elias 'might be Jewish'
any offence caused 'was because of an unfortunate coincidence',
adding that 'references to Fagin in the handling of cases occurred
almost daily in the courts by way of analogy'.[75] The Court of
Appeal agreed that the 'fusillade of insults' did not exceed 'the
permissible limits of advocacy'. In addition, Potter LJ noted that
while Fagin was an 'offensive racial stereotype' only Mr Elias could
think that this could possibly be an intentional racial slur that
would prejudice a jury. The fact that another defendant, Mr Saunders, had been acquitted was not 'evidence of actual bias'.[76]

While the Crown's speech is obviously problematic, it is the
comments of the judges that are perhaps more interesting. While
the trial judge clearly thinks everyday references to what the
appeal judge calls 'an offensive racial stereotype' is unproblematic,
both courts agree that the 'coincidence' of the literary reference
with a Jewish defendant was merely 'unfortunate'. That the prosecutor used the analogy intentionally, knowing Mr Elias was
Jewish, is inconceivable, as is any possibility that jury members
might be influenced by such a comparison—despite the fact that

---

[73] *R v Elias* (15 December 1998).   [74] Ibid.   [75]Ibid.
[76] *Elias*, ibid. For a sympathetic portrait of the other defendant, see 'Student is cleared over
"Fagin" thefts', *Birmingham Post* (27 March 1998).

the judges (and the prosecutor? and the jury?) might 'suspect' Misha Chaim Baruch Elias was Jewish.

Gray J identified a similarly benign coincidence in the libel action of *Levi* v *Bates*.[77] In this case, Mr Levi, a football entrepreneur well known to be Jewish, alleged that he had been libelled by Mr Bates in several Leeds United programme entries. Although an allegation of antisemitism was not one of Mr Levi's formal charges, Gray J remarked:

...in the course of the hearing there was a debate whether the phrase 'The Enemy Within' would have been understood to hark back to the use of that phrase by the Nazis to describe the Jews. I do not accept that the ordinary member of the Club reading the programme would have understood Mr. Bates' words to be anti-semitic. 'The Enemy Within' is an age-old phrase used by those with power to describe dissidents.[78]

Here, 'ordinary members' are clearly Christian ones, as most Jews would certainly appreciate the antisemitic resonances in the phrase when used in reference to a person well known to be Jewish.

Arguably, the judge's refusal to name what was going in the *Elias* and *Levi* cases, and, instead, to identify unfortunate coincidences, are examples of what David Goldberg refers to as 'racelessness'— eschewing any explicit invoking of race discourse in favour of a refusal to acknowledge specific instances of racism.[79] As both Hirsch and Steyn have observed,[80] in Dickens' *Oliver Twist*, Fagin is usually referred to as 'the Jew'; in twenty-first century 'raceless' Britain, 'the Jew' can be known as 'The Enemy Within'. In 2005, a Labour Party election poster depicted Jewish Conservative leader Michael Howard as a Jewish Svengali character, while another showed Howard, and Oliver Letwin, another Tory politician, also Jewish, as flying pigs.[81] While these posters, too, could be mere

---

[77] *Levi* v *Bates* [2009] EWHC 1495.   [78] Ibid., para 91.

[79] See also Patricia Tuitt's development of how the deployment of 'reasonableness' through racial knowledge results in institutional racism, *Race, Law, Resistance* (London: Glasshouse, 2004), and also G. Dench's elaboration of a discriminatory imperative on the part of liberal states, *Minorities in the Open Society* (New Brunswick: Transaction, 1986).

[80] Hirsch, 'Dickens's Queer "Jew" and Anglo-Christian Identity Politics'; Steyn, *The Jew* 46.

[81] Both these images remain easily accessible on the internet. A Labour politician had compared Letwin to Fagin the previous year: see 'Jewish Fury as Labour Calls Letwin Fagin', *The Telegraph*, 29 February 2004.

'unfortunate coincidences' (and, indeed, the Labour Party more or less made this argument at the time), I would suggest that, as Goldberg has argued, 'racelessness implies not the end of racial consciousness but its ultimate elevation to the given',[82] and these examples embody this spirit. At the same time, it is important not to over-emphasize the phenomenon of 'racelessness', particularly given the fact that Jews in English courts continue to be described as 'Jewish looking and loud-mouthed . . . he had a big nose',[83] or as 'obviously bearing the outward signs of their origins'.[84]

CONCLUDING REMARKS

The cases I draw on here represent Jews and Jewishness in prob-lematic ways. In the earlier part of the century, judges confronting the new Jewish immigrants often found them to be of bad or weak character: 'Shylockian', 'wretched', 'immoderate', 'emotional', and 'unattractive'. Race and nation(ality) were intrinsically linked in this discourse—'Jewish' invariably paired with 'Rumanian' or 'Polish' or 'Russian'. The evaluation of character, an integral component of the legal process, thus took place within an orientalizing and racializing framework.

In the latter half of the century, the reading of 'alien' Jewish character through eastern nationality fell away as 'racelessness' became more pervasive;[85] at the same time, the identification of 'the Jew' with un-English behaviours persists. Jews are, 'Fagin'-like, 'intemperate', 'provocative', and the harm they suffer is self-induced: they 'engender antisemitism where none exists'. While the earlier cases read off all there was to know from the individual's national/racial pedigree, a process no longer 'rational' in the post-Holocaust era, the later judges continue to racialize Jews, but in a way more

---

[82] D. Goldberg, *The Racial State* (Malden, MA: Blackwell, 2002) 236. See also Lentin's argument in 'Replacing "race" '. A similar understanding is developed by Goodrich and Mills in their 'The Law of White Spaces'; however, their analysis is overly dependent on understanding 'race' through the prism of skin colour only.

[83] These are the remarks of a witness not the judge; however they are read into the record by the judge without comment: see *Caton* v *Security Pacific Finance* (28 April 1995), per Hirst L.J.

[84] *Re G (a minor)* [1990] FCR 881, per Purchas L.J. In this case, the court took seriously arguments that it might be against a 'blond' child's interests to be raised in a 'darker' Jewish family: see further discussion in Chapter 4.

[85] This is not to say that 'easterness' no longer operates as a racial mark in the case of others, for example, Roma peoples, some Muslims, and 'east' Asians.

consistent with a post-Holocaust, liberal state. Jewish character remains problematic, but it is no longer possible to 'call a Jew a Jew', the judges must even disavow any knowledge that the litigant/defendant is Jewish, thus enabling them to find only some 'unfortunate coincidences'.

I have also argued that this racialization process is a two-way one. Racialization is not just about 'the other', it is also about 'us'. In this case, racialization involved, at the same time, a depiction of English nationhood and English law as: 'democratic', 'measured', 'exacting', 'fair', 'careful', 'patient', 'orderly', and 'proper'. Thus, while Englishness is infused with all that is good and valued, Jewishness is everything Englishness is not. In the next chapter, I consider a very different source of material to pursue some of these themes—Jews and Jewishness in the law of trusts.

Chapter 3

'IF ONLY I KNEW'[1]: RACE AND FAITH
IN THE LAW OF TRUSTS

In this chapter, I explore questions of alienness and character through a different prism. I use cases in the law of trusts to consider how judges have turned their attention to the following questions: what do the words 'Jew' or 'Jewish', or the terms 'Jewish race' or 'Jewish faith' mean? Can Judaism be compared to Christianity? And, what body is best to issue authoritative pronouncements on such matters? Trust law provides a sharp lens to explore these questions. The cases concern how English courts have responded to attempts by Jewish testators, using specific terms in their wills, to prevent descendants from converting or marrying 'out'. In these decisions, the courts grapple directly with a set of issues they tend to address more spectrally in other areas of law. Judges discuss what Jewishness and Judaism mean, whether religious identity is sufficiently certain to be known and articulated, and who has the expertise, right or authority to make this determination. These questions emerge in relation to the control a testator can exercise post-mortem over their property. Should these Jewish testators be able to control the actions of their children and grandchildren from beyond the grave by insisting in their wills that they marry or reproduce only Jews in order to obtain or keep their inheritance?

Historically, many minority populations have attempted to avoid, in various ways, assimilation becoming erasure. For those with property and wealth, keeping that wealth 'within the family',

---

[1] *Clayton* v *Ramsden* [1943] 1 All ER 16 at 23, per Lord Romer. See also, D. Cooper and D. Herman, 'Jews and Other Uncertainties: Race, Faith, and English law' (1999) 19 *Legal Studies* 339–66.

in this case meaning the wider family of the minority community, has often been one way of attempting to ensure the continuation of the community itself. While from the vantage point of the majority—in this case, Christian—community such measures appear primitive and clannish, it is really only possible to see them in that light if one accepts that Christianity should absorb all other faiths. For the well-off and aspirational sections of the Jewish community in England in particular, pressures to convert were enormous, and had been for several centuries before the cases I discuss here arose.[2] Many Jews were of the view that such pressures should be resisted at all costs (conversion rarely proving to be an entrée into 'Englishness' in any case[3]). Clauses in wills guaranteeing property transmission only to those progeny who remained Jewish and married 'in' were one such tactic. It was only in the mid nineteenth century that such clauses were permitted— Jews and Catholics had been prohibited from disinheriting their converted offspring in specific legislation passed in the early eighteenth century, and not removed until 1846.[4]

For the most part, cases in this area have been resolved, not on policy grounds, but on a doctrinal/conceptual basis.[5] Rather than asking whether the conditions are in the public interest, the courts have asked, instead, the narrower and more formal question: are the terms sufficiently certain and precise to constitute legally acceptable conditions? The emphasis on determining whether certainty, specifically conceptual certainty, exists is not particular to cases dealing with Jewishness. A long-standing concern of trust law is whether testamentary terms are sufficiently clear and detailed for the courts to be able to identify—and operationalize—the testator's

---

[2] On the history of pressures for Jews in England to convert to Christianity, see, amongst others, Jonathan Bush, ' "You're Gonna Miss Me When I'm Gone": Early Modern Common Law Discourse and the Case of the Jews' (1993) 5 *Wisconsin L. Jo.* 1225–85; David S. Katz, *The Jews in the History of England 1485–1850* (Oxford: Clarendon Press, 1994); Michael Ragussis, *Figures of Conversion: 'The Jewish Question' & English National Identity* (Durham: Duke University Press, 1995); James Shapiro, *Shakespeare and the Jews* (New York: Columbia University Press, 1996).

[3] Benjamin Disraeli being the most famous example of this.

[4] See Bush, 'You're Gonna Miss Me' 1271, 1279 and onwards, and also his ' "Include Me Out": Some Lessons of Religious Toleration in Britain' (1991) 12 *Cardozo Law Review* 881–923.

[5] See, for example, D. Hayton, *Commentary and Cases on the Law of Trusts and Equitable Remedies* (London: Sweet & Maxwell, 12th edn, 2005) 171; J.E. Martin, *Modern Equity* (London: Sweet & Maxwell, 18th edn, 2009) 111–13; A.J. Oakley, *The Modern Law of Trusts* (London: Sweet & Maxwell, 9th edn, 2008). None of these texts discuss the history of judicial discourse on Jews and Jewishness in the law of trusts, and I return to this absence in the literature later in the chapter.

intention. Yet, far from detracting, this specific concern enhances the relevance of these cases for my project as judgments discuss the possibility of racial and religious coherence at a level of conceptual detail lacking in many other areas of law I discuss. Through exploring Jews and Jewishness in trust law, it is possible not only to trace the understandings and representations peculiar to this area of law, but also to contrast the judiciary's approach here with its stance towards Jewishness elsewhere.

I consider the cases in two sections—1900–1970s and post-1970s—exploring three central questions that they raise. First, how do the judges conceptualize being a member of 'the Jewish race' or 'the Jewish faith', and has this approach changed over time? Second, what are the implications, in terms of producing knowledge about Christianity, of the courts' conclusion (in the earlier cases) that Jewishness is conceptually uncertain? And, third, who can know the Jew? I suggest—in keeping with my argument in the last chapter—that orientalizing processes are at work here too. However, unlike the cases I discussed in Chapter 2, which largely concerned how poor, eastern immigrants were themselves read and understood by the judges, here the focus is on Judaism itself, rather than Jewish individuals. Also more developed here than in the previous chapter is an analysis of how the judges universalize Christianity.

1900–1970s

At the turn of the twentieth century, the judiciary did not question the certainty of Jewish testamentary conditions. In both *Hodgson* v *Halford* and *Re Joseph*, for example, terms requiring progeny to remain Jewish and to marry 'in' were presumed to be valid—without the need for any discussion.[6] In *Re Joseph*, the term containing the phrase 'professing the Jewish faith' was taken as a self-evident forfeiture clause (i.e. a child forfeits their inheritance by violating the clause), and the case was decided on other grounds. In the *Hodgson* case, a will containing a clause disinheriting any child who married a non-Jew, became a convert, or who might 'forsake the Jewish religion', was held to be perfectly valid.[7] Even as late as 1932, a clause requiring any child who married, without parental

---

[6] *Hodgson* v *Halford* (1879) 11 Ch D 959; *Re Joseph* [1905] 2 Ch 507.   [7] *Hodgson*, ibid., 967.

approval, 'a person not of the Jewish faith or not born of Jewish parents' to 'forfeit' their inheritance was apparently uncontentious.[8] This was consistent with the charitable trust case of *Keren Kayemeth* v *Inland Revenue*, that same year.[9] In that decision, although the House of Lords found that the purposes of the Jewish nationalist agency were not 'charitable' ones, and that Jewish people all over the world could not constitute a 'community', the term 'Jews' itself was not seen to be at all mysterious.

However, in 1939, *Re Spitzel's Will Trusts* suggested a new approach in the line of trust cases.[10] The very same clause inserted in the *Hodgson* and *Re Joseph* wills above was held to be void. Bennett J's reason was that the clause should not be allowed to operate long after named beneficiaries had died (known as 'the rule against perpetuities'). The judge did not refer to the *Hodgson* or *Re Joseph* decisions at all and he did not decide the case on the grounds of uncertainty, or even discuss certainty as an issue. However, as will be seen shortly, two years later he did just that.

The following year, in 1940, *Re Blaiberg* heralded a new era of judicial pronouncements on Jewishness. Solomon Blaiberg died in 1909. He had stipulated in a codicil to his will that 'should any child or grandchild of mine at any time before or after my decease marry any person not of the Jewish faith such child or grandchild shall forfeit and be deprived of any interest or share under my said will'.[11] The parties agreed that the relevant grandchild in question had married outside the faith; twice, in fact. The court was therefore asked to determine whether the codicil's clause was valid. Morton J found that, for the following reasons, it was not:

It seems to me that the question whether or not a person is 'of the Jewish faith' is something which lies in his or her own conscience, and is a matter of belief. It is not altogether easy to see in what sense the words are used, but, supposing, for example, that the marriage had taken place in a synagogue, to my mind that would not establish that the other contracting party was of the Jewish faith. It seems to me that it depends upon whether or not he holds certain beliefs. What the beliefs are which makes

[8] *Levitt* v *Inland Revenue* [1932] SC 629 – albeit this was a Scottish tax case, and not an English trust one.
[9] *Keren Kayemeth Le Jisroel* v *Inland Revenue* [1932] AC 650.
[10] *Re Spitzel's Will Trusts* [1939] 2 All ER 266.
[11] *Re Blaiberg* [1940] 1 All ER 632 at 633, Ch D.

a man of the Jewish faith or not of the Jewish faith I do not know... In my view, the condition... is void for uncertainty.[12]

Perhaps surprisingly, as the precedents were clearly available at the time and cited at the Court of Appeal in another case the following year, Morton J noted that 'no case has been brought to my attention where this phrase "of the Jewish faith"—or indeed a similar phrase referring to any other faith—has been used'.[13] If *Hodgson* v *Halford* and *Re Joseph* had been brought to the attention of the judge, it seems likely that he would have found a way to distinguish them.

As it was, *Re Blaiberg* was not appealed; however Morton J's decision received detailed consideration shortly thereafter in what became the leading case in this area—*Re Samuel*, later known as *Clayton* v *Ramsden*.[14] The facts of this case proved similar to *Re Blaiberg*. Barnett Samuel made a will leaving his estate to his children providing they did not 'contract a marriage with a person who is not of Jewish parentage and of the Jewish faith'.[15] One of his daughters, Edna, married Harold Clayton, whose parents, according to Bennet J, the judge at first instance, had 'no Jewish blood in the[ir] veins'. Bennett J, who had found such a clause void on perpetuities grounds in *Re Spitzel's Will Trusts* two years previously, turned this time to uncertainty. He also introduced the term 'race' into the equation, perhaps unsurprisingly given the times. First, considering the phrase 'Jewish parentage', Bennett J asked whether this phrase implicated religion or race, or both, and, if the latter:

When one speaks of a man's race in this connection, what does one mean? What is meant by a person being of the Jewish race? Does that mean that he is in direct descent, both in the male line and in the female line, from the patriarch Jacob? I do not know. I suppose that it does, because I believe that Jews are Israelites, and that Israelites are persons who are descended from the patriarch Jacob... In this will, there is not a trace of any indication which I can see as to the sense in which this testator used the words 'of Jewish parentage'. There is nothing to indicate whether he

---

[12] Ibid., 636.   [13] Ibid.

[14] *Re Samuel* [1941] 1 All ER 539, Ch.; *Re Samuel* [1941] 3 All ER 196, CA; *Clayton* v *Ramsden* [1943] 1 All ER 16, HL.

[15] *Re Samuel* [1941] 1 All ER 539, 541.

had used them with reference to the race of the parents or whether he had used them with reference to their religion...the condition is void for uncertainty.[16]

Bennett J then moved on to consider the phrase 'of the Jewish faith'. Here, he found that he ought to follow *Re Blaiberg*, although he remarked that Morton J's decision appeared to have been taken without considering relevant precedent.[17] And, so, Bennett J found this phrase, too, void for uncertainty.

Bennett J's decision came to be considered by the Court of Appeal a few months later, in the summer of 1941.[18] In a unanimous decision written by Lord Greene, the Court overturned Bennett J's judgment. Lord Greene refused to accept that judges could not know what a Jew was. Finding that he was able to construe the phrase 'of Jewish parentage' 'without any real difficulty', Lord Greene first concluded that these words 'refer to religion, and not to race'.[19] 'Of Jewish parentage', in this context, simply meant that the person's parents must also have been of the Jewish religion. Whether someone was of the Jewish faith or not was an evidential question, not a question of conceptual uncertainty. He went on to state that it was sufficient for the courts that a witness simply say whether they considered themselves to be of the Jewish faith or not: 'a person who is asked whether or not he is a Jew by religion, or whether he belongs to any other religion will give a perfectly conscientious answer...I should have thought that, *prima facie*, that was enough'.[20] Lord Greene then went on to consider earlier case law, including the *Hodgson* and *Joseph* decisions, to find that authority on this subject was unequivocal—such terms were not uncertain—expressly overruling Morton J's decision in *Re Blaiberg* in the process. Lord Greene also pointed out that if Parliament could apparently 'know' what the phrase 'Jewish faith' meant, for the purposes of employment, charity, and commercial law, for example, then surely the courts, in the area of trusts, could too.[21]

When the case reached the House of Lords, however, the judges there felt otherwise. In what was to become the leading decision on

---

[16] Ibid., 542–3.   [17] Ibid., 544.   [18] *Re Samuel* [1941] 3 All ER 196.
[19] Ibid., 200.   [20] Ibid., 203.   [21] Ibid., 213.

Jewish trust beneficiaries, the Lords reversed the Court of Appeal and upheld Morton J's initial judgment (implicitly restoring the validity of *Re Blaiberg* as well).[22] Taking up Lord Greene's discussion of whether 'Jewish parentage' referred to race or religion, Lord Russell insisted that race, not religion, was in the testator's mind.[23] 'But', he remarked, 'at that point the real difficulty begins.'[24] Lord Romer agreed: 'In my opinion on the true construction of this will the words refer to race and not to religion or faith.'[25] However, this determination was only a first step.

What then did the testator mean by the stipulation that the daughter's husband was to be of Jewish race or descent? It cannot reasonably be supposed that the husband was to show an unbroken line of descent from the patriarch Jacob. If the daughter were compelled to wait for such a husband, she would remain a spinster all her life and the condition would be void as amounting to a total restraint on marriage. It seems far more probable that the testator meant no more than that the husband should be of Hebraic blood. But what degree of Hebraic blood would a permissible husband have to possess? Would it be sufficient if only one of his parents were of Hebraic blood? If not, would it be sufficient if both were? If not, would it be sufficient if in addition it were shown that one grandparent was of Hebraic blood or must it be shown that this was true of all his grandparents? Or must the husband trace his Hebraic blood still further back? These are questions to which no answer has been furnished by the testator... the condition is void for uncertainty.[26]

Lord Russell echoed this focus on blood: 'The testator has given no information or clue as to what percentage or proportion of Jewish blood in the husband will satisfy the requirements that he should be of Jewish parentage.'[27]

Although the testator himself never mentioned the word 'blood', or even, in this case, 'race', the Lords maintained that blood and race were utterly central. The Jewish testator is seen as having blood on his mind, rather than the judges imposing this discourse of racialization. It is as likely as not that by 'parentage', the testator simply meant 'comes from a Jewish family', and that this would be self-evident and not require blood quantum analysis.[28]

---

[22] *Clayton v Ramsden* [1943] 1 All ER 16.   [23] Ibid., 19.   [24] Ibid.
[25] Ibid., 22.   [26] Ibid.   [27] Ibid., 19.
[28] I am not suggesting that Jewish people in this period did not also think in terms of 'blood', only that Barnett Samuel had never used such terms in his will.

Or, the testator might have been implicitly referring to the matrilineal test of Jewishness in Jewish law—again, a 'test' whose answer is usually self-evident.[29] However, for these judges, 'parentage' is defined as racial biology (a rhetorical move we see again in 2009 in the *JFS* case, as I explore later in the book).

Lord Romer then considered the 'Jewish faith' clause, finding this too to be uncertain. Disagreeing with Lord Greene's analysis, Lord Romer said that he could not accept a simple declaration of 'Jewish faith' without first knowing what the phrase meant: 'I should agree entirely with the Court of Appeal as to this if only I knew what was the meaning of the words "of the Jewish faith"'.[30] As I explore further below, it seems somewhat peculiar that Lord Romer throws his hands up in this way, professing extreme ignorance, and making no attempt to enlighten himself.[31] Thus, with Lord Wright dissenting on this clause only, the Lords declared the 'Jewish faith' term too uncertain to be effective. Both clauses, then, were declared void. Despite the Court of Appeal's thorough canvassing of (and adherence to) the prior case law, the House of Lords chose not to mention the cases of *Hodgson* or *Joseph* at all.

Interestingly, in a different case adjudicated in the courts at the same time as the first instance decision in *Clayton* v *Ramsden* (*Re Samuel*), in 1941, the phrase 'a Protestant in religion and a whole hearted believer in the Deity of Christ' was considered by Farwell J.[32] Jessy Mylne, through a legacy in her will, stipulated that beneficiaries must meet this formula. Noting the precedent of *Re Blaiberg*, and relegating its application to 'forfeiture' clauses only, Farwell J found that the clause in question here was one of 'qualification', not forfeiture. The judge found it inconceivable that a court could not determine what such a phrase meant:

[29] A test now struck down as incompatible with English race relations law: see discussion in Chapters 6 and 7.

[30] *Clayton*, 23. Lord Russell also agreed that the 'faith' clause was void. Lord Wright agreed that the 'parentage' clause was void, finding it impossible to determine the degree of 'racial purity' required, but argued that 'Jewish faith' was not any more uncertain than 'Christian faith', which was clearly not uncertain (20).

[31] While Lord Romer was known as a conservative and formalistic judge, and so his decision here may not be so surprising, Lord Wright, who also found the 'parentage' clause uncertain, was known as a liberal on the court. Thus, an explanation of the decision in *Clayton* relying on the doctrinal proclivities of individual judges is not sufficient.

[32] *Re Mylne* [1941] Ch 204.

...whether or not a person is or is not 'of the Jewish faith'...is a matter of the state of a person's mind. In the present case, however, the classes of persons to be benefited include 'retired missionaries or missionaries still engaged as such or continuing Christian workers of any other description' and it is not impossible for the trustees to ascertain whether they are giving effect to the wishes of the testatrix, if they make inquiries as to the preaching and other work of proposed recipients...and so ascertain whether they are Protestants and whole hearted believers in the Deity of Christ...[33]

Thus, unlike the terms in *Clayton* v *Ramsden*, where the majority of the House of Lords assert their own ignorance about the phrase 'Jewish faith', and see this ignorance as determinative, in *Re Mylne*, decided two years previously, the judge feels it would be obvious whether someone held Christian beliefs or not: all that was required was a bit of research. Farwell J's reasoning here is rather contradictory, as he maintains 'Jewish faith' is about 'a person's state of mind' and therefore different to the facts of *Re Mylne*; however he then says that the issue for *Re Mylne* is to determine whether someone is a 'whole-hearted believer in the Deity of Christ', which, presumably, must also be a 'state of mind'. However, my intention in highlighting this decision is not to focus on the judge's questionable reasoning, but rather to demonstrate how the courts understand Christianity, in contrast to Judaism. *Re Mylne* was not an isolated decision, but is consistent with a range of trust cases throughout this period where judges found various forms of Christianity to be wholly knowable.[34] This is further elaborated below, where I discuss *Re Allen*, another Christian case.

The House of Lords decision in *Clayton* v *Ramsden* was followed in a series of subsequent cases over the next twenty or so years. In *Re Donn* v *Moses*, Uthwatt J, expressly relying on both *Re Blaiberg* and *Clayton* v *Ramsden*, held that the phrase 'Jewish faith' was too uncertain to be enforceable.[35] In *Re Moss's Will Trusts*, Vaisey J asserted that '"the Jewish faith", whatever be the sense in which the words are used, is an expression of complete uncertainty, and in the expression "a member of the Jewish faith" I find a double or

---

[33] Ibid., 207–8.
[34] On Catholicism, for example, see *Re Evans* v *Edwards* [1940] Ch. 629. This line of cases is thoroughly canvassed in a later decision, *Blathwayt and Cawley* [1976] AC 397.
[35] *Re Donn* v *Moses* [1944] Ch 8.

perhaps a multiple uncertainty' (he remained true to this approach in *Re Allen*, see below).[36] In *Re Tarnpolsk*, Danckwerts J held a condition containing the phrase 'Jewish race' was void for uncertainty.[37] In *Re Krawitz's Will Trusts*, Vaisey J found the principle in the case law 'well known and well established' and so found the 'faith' clause void, commenting: 'I don't know except in the broadest and most indefinite sense what is meant by practising the Jewish religion or any religion'.[38] And, in *Re Walter's Will Trusts*, in 1962, Plowman J had no trouble concluding a similar clause was invalid.[39]

One of the striking elements of this line of cases, particularly *Re Blaiberg* and *Clayton v Ramsden*, is the judges' preoccupation with 'the Hebraic'. They comment on several occasions about 'the patriarch Jacob', and, while some of their tone could be said to be ironic, they nevertheless insist on viewing Jewishness as a line of historical descent from the ancient Israelites. While the emphasis on the original, Hebraic Jew is an effect of both Christian teachings and wider abstracting tendencies in English law, this particular Jewish figure also plays a different role. As Jonathan Bush has shown, Hebraic references have always been a part of the common law. In deploying the biblical patriarchs in their legal reasoning, the judges are drawing on their 'inherited intellectual categories', one of which has always been 'the Jew'.[40]

But it is also in the mythical construction of the ancient Hebrews that the courts can find the purity of blood they require for their *contemporary* racialization project. This purity is required for two contradictory reasons: first to establish an authentic line of descent— to make Jews meaningful as a racial category; second, to produce the legal problem of racial ambiguity. If there are no original Israelites, Hebrews or Patriarchs, the courts' racial paradigm of Jewishness, along with their response to the testamentary dispositions, crumbles (given the judges have no apparent interest in how Jewish law determines Jewishness). Once having invested these ancient figures

[36] *Re Moss's Will Trusts* [1945] 1 All ER 207 at 209.   [37] *Re Tarnpolsk* [1958] 3 All ER 479.
[38] *Re Krawitz's Will Trusts* [1959] 3 All ER 793 at 796.
[39] *Re Walter's Will Trusts* (1962) 106 Sol Jo 221.
[40] Bush, 'You're Gonna Miss Me' 1277. See also, E.M. Reisenover, 'Anti-Jewish Philosemitism: British and Hebrew Affinity and Nineteenth Century British Antisemitism' (2008) I (1) *British Scholar* 79–104.

with 100 per cent pure Jewish blood, it is clear that any Jews centuries later must have fluid that is rather diluted. Thus, if the testator does not explicitly give the recipe required, the courts must find uncertainty. In *Clayton v Ramsden*, Lord Wright asks about the quantum of blood: 'Is it to be 100 per cent, or will 75 per cent, or 50 per cent, be sufficient?'[41] As Deborah Cohen has argued in a different context, the 'racial ambiguity' of 'the Jew' causes English Christians anxiety: 'In the case of Jews, racial categories should be viewed as much as a product of uncertainties as certainties.'[42]

It is, perhaps, not coincidental that this discourse about racial purity arose first in these cases in the late 1930s, and that by the mid 1960s it was almost entirely replaced. However, the connection between blood and ancient Israel is one not seen in other areas of law during the mid twentieth century, perhaps reflecting the class dimension of these trust cases in contrast to others I discuss elsewhere in this book. In other words, in deciding whether or not to give effect to the terms constructed by relatively wealthy Jewish testators, the judges had before them the wills of many second, third, and even fourth generation English Jews—as opposed to the more recent 'eastern' immigrants found in many other areas of legal concern. The fact that many of the beneficiaries disputing these inheritance clauses were married to Christians and raising Christian children, as many assimilated Jews were, would also have troubled any judicial attempt at neat racial classification. Jewish racial purity, or 'parentage', thus becomes impossible to determine as no English Jew clearly can be traced through an unbroken line to the Hebraic patriarchs. Despite Judaism's own, historical self-classifications, based on *matrilineal* not patri- archal continuity, the courts' persistent inability/unwillingness to agree the 'amount' of race legally required left Jewishness, as a

---

[41] *Clayton v Ramsden*, 20. Jerome Friedman argues the idea of 'race' as blood quantum first arose in sixteenth-century Spain, through the 'pure blood laws', in response to the many Jews who were converting to Christianity, and the anxiety caused by these 'New Christians' entering mainstream Spanish life, see 'Jewish Conversion, the Spanish Pure Blood Laws and Reformation: A Revisionist View of Racial and Religious Antisemitism' (1987) 18(1) *Sixteenth Century Journal* 3–30. On the other hand, Deborah Cohen suggests that, in England, a racial move from 'tribe' to 'blood' did not occur until the mid nineteenth century, see 'Who Was Who?: Race and Jews in Turn-of-the-century Britain' (2002) 41(4) *The Journal of British Studies* 472–3.

[42] Cohen, ibid., 481.

juridical category, indefinable (arguably, this is now also a result of the *JFS* case: see Chapters 6 and 7).

Aside from their concern with degrees of 'Hebraic blood' for the 'parentage' clauses, *Clayton v Ramsden* and its progeny show a similar inability to define what is meant by 'the Jewish faith'; indeed, more dramatically, they claim that it is impossible to define. Implicitly, and sometimes explicitly, the judges compare Judaism with Anglicanism, finding the former amorphous and non-institutional: 'the requirement that a person shall be of Jewish faith seems to me too vague to enable it to be said with certainty that a particular individual complies with the requirement'.[43] What is striking is how keen many of the judges prove to be to emphasize their own ignorance and their refusal to draw on extrinsic evidence to address this, despite such evidence about Judaism being in plentiful supply in other courts during this same period.

This self-reflexive stress on judicial ignorance is interesting. It contrasts with judicial practice in the Christian trust cases where judges simply draw on their own common sense (see *Re Mylne* and *Re Evans* above, and *Re Allen* below). In the Jewish trust cases, on the other hand, the courts place themselves in the paradoxical position of having to determine what a term means—or, more precisely, having to ascertain whether the testator has identified what he/she means—while simultaneously professing their own ignorance of the subject. As a consequence, this lack of clarity is projected onto the Jewish testator. Meanwhile, the obvious experts as to what the clauses might mean remain unheard.[44]

Returning to the line of cases, one decision during this period, *Re Wolffe's Will Trusts*, distinguished the *Clayton* case and others on the basis that they were about 'conditions subsequent', or forfeiture clauses.[45] In other words, if the child married out, they would forfeit an inheritance they had already been awarded. In *Re Wolffe*, Harman J found the clause was a 'condition precedent': here, as the grandchild needed to marry within the 'Jewish faith' *in order to*

[43] *Clayton*, 329, per Lord Russell.

[44] In many family law cases throughout this period, the courts were availing themselves of outside Jewish expertise. Some of these include: *Spivak v Spivak* [1930] All ER Rep 133; *Har-Shefi v Har-Shefi* [1953] 2 All ER 373; *Joseph v Joseph* [1953] 2 All ER 710; *Cheni v Cheni* [1962] 3 All ER 873; *Brett v Brett* [1969] 1 All ER 1007.

[45] *Re Wolffe's Will Trusts* [1953] 2 All ER 697.

inherit, it was a term of 'qualification' not forfeiture. According to Harman J, the phrase 'Jewish faith' was sufficiently certain for a condition precedent since these, doctrinally, attracted a lesser level of scrutiny. However, the judge may have indicated his opinion of the other line of cases when he remarked:

...no testator would ever guess that in the eye of the law one could not marry a Jew, and it is only by a reasoning from the peculiar doctrine which covers conditions subsequent that a position is reached where it is impossible to say whether a man is a Jew or of Jewish parentage. Those who select scholars for Jewish charitable scholarships have no difficulty at all...I find it very difficult to believe that if a man married a woman of pure Zulu parents, anyone can say that she is a Jewess of Jewish parents, at some point there comes a limit on these things.[46]

The distinction between conditions precedent and subsequent was further elaborated that same year by the Court of Appeal in *Re Allen*, a case about the certainty of the phrases 'Church of England' and 'adherent to the doctrine of that Church'.[47] Henry Allen had converted from Catholicism to the Church of England, and stipulated that his progeny should do the same in order to inherit. At first instance, Vaisey J had found both phrases void for uncertainty. He had not felt bound by *Clayton* v *Ramsden*, but rather was clear that the phrases 'Church of England' and 'adherent to the doctrine of' were too vague and indeterminate: 'there is so much uncertainty, so much vagueness, so much room for doubt, so much room for difference of opinion and so much room for differing interpretations'.[48]

The Court of Appeal overturned Vaisey's judgment later in 1953.[49] All the judges were clearly concerned with the implications of finding 'the Church of England' uncertain. Evershed MR based his decision on the distinction between conditions precedent and subsequent, remarking that if the clause in *Clayton* had been one of qualification rather than forfeiture, the House of Lords would have come to a different decision.[50] Birkett LJ was more direct:

If the question which calls for an answer in this appeal were being asked for the first time in the courts, I should have thought that the answer

---

[46] Ibid., 700–1.   [47] *Re Allen* [1953] Ch 116.   [48] Ibid., 124.
[49] [1953] Ch 810.   [50] Ibid., 822.

could be given without very much doubt or hesitation. 'Is this man a member of the Church of England?' would seem to me to be a question which could be answered quite simply 'Yes' or 'No'. It would certainly be surprising to be met with the reply that the words were so vague and uncertain that no reply could be given... when a testator uses the words 'a member of the Church of England', he must not be assumed to be speaking as a learned theologian or an ecclesiastical historian, with special meanings in his mind, or with refinements and reservations. He must be assumed to be an ordinary man using ordinary language... The Church of England is an institution bound into the national life by a thousand links, legal and historical. It seems to me to be a very strange conclusion that when millions of people, drawn to that church by ties of piety or feeling or history, claim to be and are recognised to be members of that church, this court should say that the words employed by the testator are so uncertain in their meaning to be void.[51]

In contrast to how the judges understand the Jewish testators as engaging in a mysterious discourse by using the phrase 'Jewish faith', here a Christian one is 'an ordinary man using ordinary language' (recall also the 'ordinary man' of the 'The Enemy Within' case in Chapter 2). The Church of England is thus rendered ordinary itself, normalized and universalized in a way that Judaism could never be, despite the latter's centuries-old 'historical link'; indeed, an English history considerably longer than the Church of England's (see Chapter 1). To find the phrase 'Church of England' uncertain would be, as Romer J put it in his judgment in *Re Allen*, 'a shock to the public conscience'.[52]

As with *Re Mylne*, *Re Evans*, and a host of other decisions about various forms of Christianity, in *Re Allen*, the Court of Appeal was not prepared to admit that they could not know, with sufficient certainty, England's established church. While, technically, they manoeuvred around the *Clayton* decision by distinguishing the types of terms involved, their discourse makes it abundantly clear how well they understood the nation's faith while, elsewhere, continuing to profess their ignorance of Judaism. Eventually, however, the somewhat dubious distinction between conditions

[51] Ibid., 822–7.
[52] Ibid., 834. Romer J did, however, find the 'adherent' phrase to be uncertain and dissented on this point. If Lord Greene had still been on the Court of Appeal, one wonders what he would have made of this case.

precedent and subsequent was taken up by more judges in the Jewish trust cases, and clauses were upheld on the basis they were conditions precedent. The judges in both *Re Selby's Will Trusts* and *Re Abraham's Will Trusts* cited *Re Allen* for authority to uphold conditions they defined as precedents, both judges remarking that the phrase 'Jewish faith' was far from 'meaningless'.[53]

1970S AND BEYOND

These matters were finally more or less resolved in October of 1975. In *Re Tuck's Settlement Trusts*, Whitford J had to consider whether clauses requiring that a successor baronet be 'of the Jewish faith' and 'married to an approved wife' in order for the trust income to be paid, were void for uncertainty.[54] An 'approved' wife was defined in the settlement as 'a wife of Jewish blood by one or both of her parents and who has been brought up in and has never departed from and at the date of her marriage continues to worship according to the Jewish faith'. Should there be any doubt as to the status of the wife, the testator stipulated that any dispute would be resolved by the Chief Rabbi, whose decision would be conclusive. During the litigation, it was accepted by all parties that the wife in question was not 'approved'.

According to Whitford J,

When he was made a baronet, the settler considered this honour not merely an honour to himself but to the Jewish race of which he was proud to be a member, and he wanted to try to impose conditions which would ensure that that dignity should remain in the hands of successors of Jewish faith born of parents of Jewish blood . . . [55]

In his judgment, Whitford J reflected on 'the strange situation' whereby the same phrase could be sufficiently certain in one instance (as a condition precedent) and uncertain in another (as a condition subsequent). He found, in this case, that both types of clause were present. In distinguishing *Clayton* v *Ramsden*, Whitford J relied

---

[53] *Re Selby's Will Trusts* [1965] 3 All ER 386; *Re Abraham's Will Trusts* [1969] 1 Ch 463. See also, *Re Meres' Will Trusts* (4 May 1957), where a condition rendering 'coloured persons and Jews' ineligible for medical research fellowships at Cambridge was held to be void for uncertainty (with no reported reasons), and *Re Lysaght* [1966] Ch.191, where a legacy to the Royal College of Surgeons excluding 'Jews and Roman Catholics' was held to be perfectly certain (it was struck down on other grounds).
[54] *Re Tuck's Settlement Trusts* [1976] Ch 99.   [55] Ibid., 104.

on the 'Chief Rabbi' provision—clearly a new innovation by trust lawyers and an attempt to respond to the case law precedents. This clause, he said, provided for an authoritative interpretation of Jewishness and was sufficient to render the clause enforceable.[56] At the same time, Whitford J remarked that he saw nothing problematic in the phrase 'of Jewish blood':

... the words 'of Jewish blood' do not, to my mind, involve any conceptual difficulty in themselves. What is intended by 'Jewish blood' is to my mind quite plainly this, that one has to look to see the racial descent. When the settlor speaks of a person 'of Jewish blood', he speaks of a person who is a member of that group, now spread throughout the world, who are descended from the ancient Jewish people, and whose religion is Judaism.[57]

While Whitford J's formulation gives little actual guidance, and there is a return to the Hebraic, its tone is akin to the one used by the judges in the Christian cases: there is a common-sense at play here. Rather than professing ignorance of the testator's mysterious imaginings, Whitford J insists that the testator's meaning is plainly obvious. This common-sense, combined with the 'rabbinical recourse' clause, was sufficient in Whitford J's view to circumvent the *Clayton* decision: 'there can never be any doubt or difficulty over the question whether any given wife is an approved wife; the Chief Rabbis [sic] decide'.[58]

The Court of Appeal upheld Whitford J's judgment in 1978, although for somewhat different reasons.[59] Lord Denning simply refused to follow what he seems to have regarded as obiter in *Clayton* v *Ramsden* concerning the phrase 'of the Jewish faith'. These words, Lord Denning suggests, were easily understood and simply required the production of relevant evidence about religious practice; there was nothing uncertain about them.[60] Second, while Lord Denning 'deplored' the conceptual dichotomy between conditions subsequent and precedent, he acknowledged that this was settled law for now, and he must be bound by it. Third, he agreed with Whitford J that the 'Chief Rabbi' provision was crucial and, on the basis that contracting parties could always

---

[56] Ibid., 118.   [57] Ibid., 116.   [58] Ibid., 118.
[59] *Re Tuck's Settlement Trusts* [1978] 1 All ER 1047.   [60] Ibid., 1052.

refer disputes to a third party without ousting the jurisdiction of the court, valid:

... the courts may get bogged down in distinctions between conceptual uncertainty and evidential uncertainty, and between conditions subsequent and conditions precedent. The testator may want to cut out all that cackle, and let someone decide it who really will understand what the testator is talking about... who better to decide these questions of 'Jewish blood' and 'Jewish faith' than the chief rabbi?.[61]

However, despite Lord Denning's desire to avoid 'cackle', Lord Russell and Eveleigh LJ took the view that the clauses in *Re Tuck's* were conditions precedent and enforceable on that basis alone.

In 1959, Nathan Tepper died, leaving a will stating that, in order to inherit, progeny must not marry out.[62] In coming to his decision on the will some thirty years later, Scott J described this area of trust law as 'bedevilled by authority'.[63] Although he found that the condition in question was a 'subsequent' one, and recognised that *Clayton* v *Ramsden* was the leading case, Scott J refused to concede that he was bound to find the clause uncertain.

A decision by another court, even a court as august as the House of Lords, is not binding on the question of whether in Nathan Tepper's will a sufficiently certain meaning can be attributed to the expression 'the Jewish faith'.[64]

In remarking that there was evidence that Nathan Tepper was 'a devout Jew', Scott J adjourned the hearing so that further evidence could be adduced as to the nature of Tepper's observance. There is no further reported decision in this case, and it appears that no further Jewish trust case has come to court since. However, it is worth drawing attention to *Halpern* v *Halpern*, a dispute about a will where the judge expressly drew a distinction between the plain meaning of the phrase 'Jewish law' as opposed to Islamic law: '"The principles of the glorious Shar'ia law" would seem to be a very uncertain phrase.'[65] Perhaps little has been learned after all.

---

[61] Ibid., 1054.   [62] *Re Tepper's Will Trusts* [1987] Ch 358.   [63] Ibid., 364.
[64] Ibid., 377.   [65] *Halpern* v *Halpern* [2007] All ER (D) 38, para. 33.

FINAL THOUGHTS

I have traced the shifting language about Jews and Jewishness in English trust law. Judges, at the turn of the twentieth century, had no qualms about finding restrictive testamentary clauses containing the words 'Jew' or 'Jewish' valid. However, by the 1940s, with little explanation, this had changed. The judiciary now professed their ignorance as to the meaning of these words, and chose to find such clauses uncertain and therefore of no effect. In doing so, they developed an understanding of Jewishness that contained both theological/biblical and racial assumptions, although the latter were projected onto the testators, who themselves never mentioned Hebraic patriarchs or blood quanta. In contrast to Jewish race and faith, the clarity of Christianity and the Church of England, on the other hand, was understood to be self-evident. Eventually, by the 1970s, the courts were happy to accept clauses giving up interpretive authority to the Chief Rabbi. Some deference to Jewish religious authority was already an intrinsic part of legal decision-making elsewhere, particularly in family law, as I noted in Chapter 1.

I also argued that, in contrast to the previous chapter, with its cases largely concerned with poor Jewish immigrants, in the area of trust law judges do not indulge in any obvious orientalization of individuals. However, until the 1970s, they remained concerned with alienness and character—but, in this case, of Judaism itself. Thus, the references here are to Abraham and Jacob, not Shylock or Fagin. At the same time as the judiciary was engaging, or not, with Judaism, they were also asked to determine the character of Christianity in similar cases. Here, they insisted on the knowability of Christianity—particularly the Church of England—to everyone, of its common-sense meanings and the clear motivations of its adherents. The ways in which Judaism (and other faiths) suffer in the comparison is evident in a number of cases in other legal areas, particularly in cases involving children, as I go on to explore in Chapter 4.[66]

---

[66] For example, in *Holy Law South Broughton Burial Board* v *Failsworth Urban DC* [1927] All ER Rep 628, where a Jewish cemetery was found to be not contiguous with its overseeing synagogue and so similarly not exempt from tax as a Christian one would be (with no recognition given to how

The trust cases also reveal a tension between two ways of understanding Jews and Jewishness. In one, judges see the alienness of individuals as self-evident, as written on their bodies; they exhibit racialized characteristics immediately recognizable to the court. This kind of understanding was much in evidence in the previous chapter. Recall how Harry Horne should have written his Hebrew name and 'Roumanian' on his insurance form as though this would have resolved all ambiguity. In the trust cases, however, Judaism is something mysterious and even unknowable. While it remains a 'racial matter', in the sense of how judges are obsessed with Hebrew blood, I do not suggest that the judges are racializing individuals. Rather, they adopt an orientalizing gaze towards Judaism, one that sees it as intrinsically foreign to them, despite its longevity within England's borders. And, interestingly, within many trust law textbooks, the 'Jewish history' of this area of law has been entirely erased.[67]

Finally, it is worth considering the outcome of the mid-twentieth century trust decisions. People inserted these conditions into their wills in order to ensure the continuity of Jewish families and the Jewish community. The cases came to court because a child or grandchild of Jewish parents had converted or married 'out' and was thus challenging their exclusion from inheritance. By refusing to uphold the testator's conditions for inheritance, the courts were effectively breaking these familial and communal ties and, in many cases, sanctioning the loss of Jewish identity. This process, the judicial authorization of Christian conversions, most particularly Protestant conversions—as we see also in terms of a conversion out of Catholicism in *Re Allen*—is something I go on to discuss more fully in the next chapter.

Jewish synagogues rarely owned sufficient city land to attach a cemetery at this time); in *Springfield Synagogue* v *Gladwin* [1957] 2 RRC 338, where dwelling, educational and meeting space attached to a synagogue were not uses 'to which a church hall would normally be put'; and in *Gillett* v *North West London Communal Mikvah* [1982] RA 346, where a mikvah was deemed to be about private ritual and not 'the community' (and thus not exempt from certain taxes like a 'church hall'). In a more recent case, *R* v *Leeds City Council* [2005] EWHC 2495, the court held that bussing Jewish children to the nearest Jewish school was not an appropriate state expenditure; the fact that Christian schools were dotted all over the city, thus limiting the cost of transporting children to them, was deemed to be irrelevant.

[67] See, for example, Hayton, *Commentary and Cases on the Law of Trusts*; Martin, *Modern Equity*; Oakley, *The Modern Law of Trusts*.

Chapter 4

'SHE IS AND WILL FOREVER REMAIN A JEW':[1] CHILD WELFARE AND THE COURTS

This chapter continues to explore themes of Christianity, 'race', and orientalizing processes by considering judicial representations of Jews and Jewishness in English child welfare cases.[2] In order to help elucidate the arguments, I also include a discussion of some cases involving Muslim, Jain and Sikh children. In contrast to the previous two chapters, which considered the development of the case law more historically, here I focus upon decisions involving consideration of children's religious and cultural identity over the last twenty years.[3] I do this because I wish to consider more contemporary judicial pronouncements on matters of Jews and Jewishness, and to trace their (dis)continuities with the mostly older ones discussed in the previous chapters.

The decisions in this chapter tend to involve litigation between parents, or between parents and local authorities, surrounding adoption, residence, or 'specific issue orders', the latter involving, for example, decisions about whether to circumcise a child or not. Cases where courts calculate a child's cultural welfare offer rich material for my project as the judges decide what is best for that

---

[1] *Re P* [2000] 15 Fam 476, CA, 494, per Ward LJ.

[2] This chapter is a revised version of '"It is Difficult for a White Judge to Understand": Orientalism, Racialisation, and Christianity in English Child Welfare Cases' [2009] 21(3) *CFLQ* 283–308, co-authored with Suhraiya Jivraj. While the chapter's emphasis, and some of its content, departs from that publication, my thinking remains indebted to Suhraiya's work in this area.

[3] Examples of older child welfare cases on Jews and Jewishness include: *Re G (an infant)* [1962] 2 QB 141, and *Guery v Guery* (9 June 1982).

child presently and in the future. Where parents, guardians, experts, and/or local authorities dispute a child's cultural identity, legal decision-makers intervene to demarcate the boundaries, direction, and pace of this trajectory.

Some of these decisions, or related ones, are analysed in a different way elsewhere. In the socio-legal literature on religion, for example, scholars tend to focus on arguments to do with human rights and religious freedoms, particularly in relation to respecting the rights of ethnic minority groups to bring up their children according to the beliefs and practices of that culture or religion.[4] These themes are also explored in academic work that considers the relevance of concepts of multiculturalism, tolerance, diversity, children's rights, and belonging, amongst others.[5]

A further literature, in the law and healthcare field, implicates issues of religion and ethnicity through a consideration of decisions defined as being about medical ethics.[6] These scholars turn their attention to how parental cultural affiliations impact on their children's wider healthcare needs. Marie Fox and Michael Thomson, for example, differentiate between the religious and cultural identity issues of parents and their children, arguing that both female and male circumcision is a harmful practice with little redeeming value.[7] Other writers in the medical law area tend to take a similar position

---

[4] A. Bradney, *Religion, Rights and Laws* (Leicester: Leicester University Press, 1993) and *Law and Faith in a Sceptical Age* (London: Routledge, 2009); R. Ahdar, 'Religion as a Factor in Custody and Access Disputes' (1996) 10 *International J. L. Policy & the Family* 177–99; S. Poulter, *Ethnicity, Law and Human Rights* (Oxford: Oxford University Press, 1999).

[5] See J. Eekelaar, 'Children Between Cultures' (2004) *18 International J. of Law, Policy and the Family* 178–94; M. Freeman, 'Whose Life is it Anyway?' (2001) 9 *Medical Law Rev* 259–80; P. Hayes, 'Giving Due Consideration to Ethnicity in Adoption Placements—A Principled Approach' (2003) 15 *Child & Family Law Q* 255–68; R. Jones and W. Gnanapala, *Ethnic Minorities in English Law* (Stoke-on-Trent: Trentham Books, 2000); Y. Ronen, 'Redefining the Child's Right to Identity' (2004) *International J. of Law, Policy and the Family* 147–77; S. Van Praagh, 'Faith, Belonging, and the Protection of Our Children' (1999) XVII *Windsor Yearbook of Access to Justice* 154–203.

[6] For example, M. Fox and J. McHale, 'In Whose Best Interests?' (1997) 60 *Modern Law Review* 700–9; H. Gilbert, 'Time to Reconsider the Lawfulness of Ritual Male Circumcision' (2007) *European Human Rights Law Review* 279–94.

[7] M. Fox and M. Thomson, 'Short Changed? The Law and Ethics of Male Circumcision' (2005) 13 *International J. of Children's Rights* 161–81; M. Fox and M. Thomson, 'A Covenant with the Status Quo? Male Circumcision and the New BMA Guidance to Doctors' (2005) 31 *J. of Medical Ethics* 463–9; see also M. Thomson, *Endowed: Regulating the Male Sexed Body* (London: Routledge, 2008), especially ch. 2. See also K. Green and H. Lim, 'What is This Thing about Female Circumcision?: Legal Education and Human Rights' (1998) 7 *Social & Legal Studies* 365–88. While Green and Lim's piece is about female circumcision, a topic I do not address in any way here, their focus on the 'western-centred universalism', at p. 366, inherent in much of the anti-female circumcision discourse, is similar to how I approach understanding anti-male circumcision discourse, as discussed further below.

in terms of focusing on how non-Christian beliefs and practices (often termed 'rituals') potentially harm children. Caroline Bridge, for example, calls male circumcision 'a mutilatory assault on an infant', and cites Margaret Brazier as 'insightfully pointing out' that 'foreskins can be removed at parental will [yet] I cannot have my little boy given a discreet cross tattooed on his arm to signify my Christian faith'.[8]

Unlike much of the socio-legal literature, however, my interest here is not in framing the questions as ones of 'minority rights' or 'religious dilemmas'[9] or even about 'childhood' or children's rights per se, nor do I choose to consider a practice like circumcision purely in terms of consent, harm, and injury. Rather, the cases I consider here provide a lens to illustrate the circulation of a set of pervasive discourses: in keeping with the book's focus as a whole, I do not seek to advance a normative project about what the courts *should* do when confronted with such disputes.[10]

First, I argue that judges deploy three distinct yet, occasionally, overlapping approaches to characterizing Jewishness: as belief and ritual practice; as racial genetic marker; and as culture and environment. The first approach prioritizes a child's intellectual capacity to understand the meaning of belief and ritual; the second prioritizes a 'racial' or ethnic lineage, similar to the mid-twentieth century trust law cases; and the third applies a more context-oriented perspective in order to determine a child's cultural identity.

Second, I argue that, within these judicial texts, a way of thinking can be identified that is, at times, orientalist, racialized, and Christian. I argue that this way of thinking leads to particular forms of decision-making with significant implications for both the children and their parents/guardians. Following from my discussion in the previous two chapters, in the cases here there is evidence of the orientalizing and racialization of both Jewish individuals and Judaism itself. I further argue that the orientalism, racialization, and Christian universalism in these cases are relevant

---

[8] The quote from Brazier is from a conference paper, 'Children's Interests: Community Norms' (1997), quoted in C. Bridge, 'Religion, Culture, and Conviction—The Medical Treatment of Young Children' (1999) 11 *Child and Family Law Quarterly* 1–16.

[9] Bridge, ibid.

[10] But see Eekelaar, Hayes, and Ronen, n. 5 above. Nor do I seek to advance a normative position about circumcision itself.

to contemporary debates about 'western values' and civilizational missions. Although I will refer to a number of legal judgments, my main focus is upon seven cases where more extensive discussion of non-Christian identity took place. I set them out briefly below in the order in which I discuss them in the text.

BRIEF BACKGROUND TO THE CASES

In *Re P,* a child, known as 'N' in the judgments, with Down's Syndrome and other disabilities, was born, in 1990, into a large, orthodox Jewish family.[11] Seventeen months later, for various reasons, the parents felt unable to cope with having N at home and asked the local authority to temporarily place her with an orthodox Jewish family. A home conforming to the parents' wishes was not available, and, with great reluctance, they agreed to place N with Christian carers. The child remained with the carers for four years, having regular contact with the birth parents. In 1994, against the birth parents' objections, the foster family applied to court for a residence order, which was granted. The foster family was thus given some rights with respect to religious and educational matters. In 1998, the birth parents' application to have this order varied was refused, and in 1999 this refusal was confirmed by the Court of Appeal. Both judgments contained extensive discussion of what weight to attach to N's alleged 'Jewishness'.

At this same time, another case was making its way through the system. *Re J* concerned a seven-year-old child with a 'Turkish Muslim' father and an 'English Christian' mother.[12] The parents were separated, and the mother had been granted a residence order. The father wished to have the boy circumcised (amongst other requests) and the mother objected. In May 1999, Wall J found for the mother, and in November 1999, the father's appeal was rejected. The extent of the boy's 'Muslimness' was a key factor in both judgments, as was, ostensibly, the medical case against circumcision.

---

[11]   *Re P* [1994] 2 FCR 1093; *Re P* [2000] 15 Fam 476.
[12]   *Re J* [1999] 2 FLR 678, [2000] 1 FLR 571, CA.

In *Re B*, Jonathan Bradley, whose case became the subject of press reports and a television documentary,[13] challenged the validity of his own adoption as a baby by a Jewish couple.[14] He argued that the couple had mistakenly been led to believe he was a Jewish baby, when in fact his birth mother was Christian and his birth father Muslim. Although the courts had great sympathy for Jonathan's predicament, his claim failed on public policy grounds, as adoption orders are almost never set aside.

In *Re G*, a seven-year-old boy, identified by the name of 'Tarquin' in the judgment, was the subject of a bitter dispute between a Christian grandmother and a Jewish aunt and uncle.[15] The detailed facts surrounding the case are quite complicated and, for the most part, are not relevant to my discussion. I will return later to consider a small portion of the judgment where Tarquin and his family's 'Jewish appearance' are the subject of judicial discussion.

A Muslim mother and Sikh father were in dispute in *Re S*, in 2001.[16] The parents had divorced, and the mother wished to change their child's Sikh names, including by deed poll, so that he would be accepted within the Muslim community of which she was a part. She also wished the boy to be circumcised, for the same reason. The father opposed both applications. Here, the judge, Wilson J, took a different approach to both *Re P* and *Re J*. In terms of the name change, Wilson concluded that it was in the child's best interests to have his names informally changed from Sikh to Muslim ones, but that it was not in his interests for this to be done officially by deed poll. In relation to circumcision, Wilson J, with virtually no discussion or debate, authorized it.

In another judgment of Wilson J's, *Re C*,[17] a child with 'Jewish, Irish Roman Catholic and Turkish-Cypriot Muslim elements' was placed for adoption. Both birth parents, according to the judgment, had 'learning disabilities'. A prospective adoptive couple was found by the local authority—this couple was Jewish. It is somewhat unclear from the judgment whether the birth parents

---

[13] M. Whitfield, 'Arab's son loses adoption plea' *The Independent* (18 March 1995); C. Dyer, 'Pitching a tent in no-man's land' *The Guardian* (15 March 1993); *Jon's Journey*, Cicada Films, shown on *Everyman*, BBC (22 May 1994, dir. Liz Gray).

[14] *Re B (adoption)* [1994] 2 FCR 1297, [1995] 3 All ER 333, CA.

[15] *Re G* [1990] FCR 881.   [16] Re *S* [2001] 3 FCR 648.

[17] *Re C* [2002] 1 FLR 1119.

fully consented to this particular couple adopting the child, but in fact the case came to court because the child's official guardian issued proceedings to judicially review the local authority's decision to place the child with a Jewish couple. The guardian's objection was that placement with the couple was not appropriate. Wilson J disagreed, commenting in his judgment extensively on the nature and qualities of Jewishness.

The final case I add to this mix is *S (Children)*.[18] Here, a separated Muslim mother and Jain father were in dispute over their children's future religious upbringing. The mother, who had a residence order, wished both children to be given a Muslim education, and wanted to have their son circumcised, a practice explicitly prohibited in Jainism. In this case, the judge did not authorize the circumcision, but in terms quite different to those used in *Re J*.

APPROACHING NON-CHRISTIANITY

Belief, Ritual, and Cognitive Processing

One way that judges approach minority cultures containing religious dimensions is to insist that true faith entails theological understanding accompanied by observant practice. Belief is manifested through practice and the latter provides the evidence for the former. According to this judicial narrative, theological understanding is about knowing the *meaning*—as in significance—of a particular form of spiritual belief. To be Jewish, it is not enough to 'know God'; one must understand what knowing God means to Jews as distinct from anyone else. To be Muslim, it is not enough to have an affective appreciation of Muslim culture; one must be able to explain its terms in rational discourse. Consistent with the ethos of the welfare paradigm, most judges implicitly and explicitly depict childhood as a state of cognitive immaturity and thus discount any subjective feeling or agency even older children might have. Instead, the judges assume that children are not capable of being truly religious; they do not possess the requisite degree of rational autonomy to knowingly profess religion in this sense.[19]

[18] *S (Children)* [2004] EWHC 1282.
[19] For an alternative view, see R. Coles, *The Spiritual Life of Children* (Boston: Houghton Mifflin, 1990).

In *Re P*, the case about the young child with Down's Syndrome placed with Christian foster parents, both Wall J at first instance, and Butler-Sloss LJ on appeal, appeared to have a clear sense of what 'being Jewish' entailed, and the relationship between any such Jewishness and the best interests of the child. Wall J expressed the 'critical question' thus: 'does N's welfare require the displacement of her right to be brought up by her parents in their religion and way of life?'.[20] In other words, a child has a prima facie right to her parents' religion, but welfare calculations can outweigh this right. In coming to his decision that, in fact, her welfare did outweigh any presumed religious rights, Wall J placed great emphasis on the effect of N's learning disability that would leave her always with a mental age of between seven and ten. Relying on expert evidence, he concluded that:

N. will never have any real appreciation of her Jewish heritage, and that her understanding of her religion will be limited to a rudimentary perception of God as Creator and as a Beneficent Being and that in addition she will have a capacity to participate in (and no doubt enjoy) certain rituals without any full understanding of their significance.[21]

Thus, N's learning disability meant that 'being Jewish' had no *and could never have* meaning to her; it would have no meaning because 'being Jewish' necessitates a 'real' appreciation and an understanding of theological frameworks as well as knowing the 'full' theological significance of specific 'rituals'.[22] Jewishness, within this understanding, is, presumably, a knowledge acquired over time; if a child cannot understand the *why* of religion, they are not fully *of* that religion. Jewishness is a 'heritage' only in so far as it is a legacy of some sort. If the legacy is not properly treasured, invested in as religious education or training, if a child is unable to understand the theology (and as N is presumed by the experts to have an intellectual age of between seven and ten the judge must assume that children under ten are not able to achieve this understanding), then Jewishness becomes a fossilized relic. In so far as N is concerned, Jewishness is akin to a mysterious

[20] *Re P* [2000] Fam 15 476, 483. All quotes from Wall J's decision are taken from Butler Sloss LJ's appeal court judgment.
[21] Ibid.
[22] Many medical ethics cases about the treatment of infants also take this approach, see, e.g., *NHS v A* [2007] EWHC 1696.

historical artefact the significance of which is now unknown. Jewishness may offer N aesthetic or sensory pleasures, but it is not cognitively processed by her.

On appeal, Butler-Sloss LJ put it thus:

No one would wish to deprive a Jewish child of her right to her Jewish heritage. If she had remained with a Jewish family it would be almost unthinkable, other than in an emergency, to remove her from it. I have no doubt, like the judge [Wall J], that the Orthodox Jewish religion provides a deeply satisfying way of life for its members and that this child, like other Down's syndrome children, would have flowered and prospered in her Jewish family and surroundings if she had continued to live with them. But in the unusual circumstances of this case her parents were not able to accommodate her within the community.... she was deprived of her opportunity to grow up within the Jewish community.[23]

And, later in the judgment:

They [the parents] have asserted in their evidence and through their counsel on this appeal their fervent belief that N's home is with them and within the Orthodox Jewish community. She was born a Jew and remains a Jew wherever she may live and however she may be brought up.[24]

In these passages, Butler-Sloss LJ makes clear that being Jewish may be a child's 'heritage right' but, if so, it is a right that requires a mediator, the parents, to implement in order to have effect. Implementation apparently requires: (1) full-time immersion in 'the community' (clearly the birth parents' non-residential contact is insufficient); and (2) according to Wall J, a level of intellectual engagement with the theology and ritual that amounts to far more than mere 'enjoyment'.

In *Re P*, one cannot help concluding that Butler-Sloss LJ is effectively saying that since N has not been brought up within the Jewish community, and does not have the intellectual capacity to understand the nature of Judaism, this child, who once may have been Jewish, or at least born with a heritage right to be Jewish, is Jewish no longer. Her birth parents effectively deprived her of her heritage right by placing her in care. Although, according to the reported facts of an early decision in the litigation,[25] the parents

---

[23] *Re P*, 486.   [24] Ibid., 491.   [25] *Re P*, 1093.

were desperate to ensure that N was placed with a Jewish family, the local authority was unable to find a suitable one. She thus entered a Christian home with the parents' very reluctant consent and with their understanding that the placement would be temporary. According to Hale J's earlier (and more nuanced) judgment in this saga, when N was first placed with the foster carers the birth parents visited often, bringing with them kosher food for N to eat (this seemed to end with the initial residence order in 1994).[26]

Nevertheless, as a result of this chain of events, N lost her right to be Jewish, while her parents' 'fervent' attempts to 'get her back' are pathologized as selfish and out of control.[27] A child's heritage or religious rights must, then, not be fundamental if they can be so simply and permanently alienable by the parents. This seems a 'child welfare' and human rights issue that the court conveniently ignores; a parent's inability to care for a child can result in the permanent loss of that child's heritage right. N's Down's Syndrome and other disabilities add a further complication: if she had been a so-called 'normal' child, would the court have used the same discourse? Is there a disability rights issue here that the courts are also ignoring? If the child had been a circumcised boy, with a permanent mark of Jewishness on his penis, would the courts have gone about arriving at their decision any differently?

While these questions are complicated ones, for my purpose here it is crucial to recognize, as the courts neglect to do, that N has not been received into some secular state of 'non'-religion: she has, arguably, been placed on the road to conversion through having been removed from the Jewish community and placed in a Christian home. While the foster family is reported as being 'non-practising Catholics', Wall J's 1998 judgment makes clear that they had applied previously to the court to have N baptized. In his 1998 decision, Wall J rejected this application (with no explanation). Clearly the foster carers are not entirely 'non-practising', and, in any event, a child raised by self-identified Christians, deprived almost entirely of contact with her Jewish birth parents, may,

---

[26] Ibid.

[27] For further analysis of this discourse in the context of the father's history as a 'survivor of the Holocaust', see Chapter 5.

arguably, lose whatever residual Jewish identity she may have had over time.[28]

In the same year as they considered Jewishness in *Re P*, several of these same judges considered the significance of Muslimness in *Re J*. At first instance, Wall J, in reaching his decision that the father's wish to have his son circumcised should be denied, came to a number of preliminary conclusions. These included: that J was a Muslim in Islamic law but that this was not in any way binding in English law; that while the mother was 'nominally Christian', her household was 'essentially secular' (the Official Solicitor had presented evidence that the mother had been baptized and 'thinks of herself as a Christian' but that the child had a 'mixed heritage' and an 'essentially secular lifestyle'); and that neither parent had Muslim friends or a Muslim 'circle'.[29] Using strong rhetoric, and drawing on expert medical evidence as well as the literature of an anti-circumcision organization called 'Norm',[30] Wall J also noted that the medical case against circumcision was very strong:

The medical benefits arising from circumcision ... are highly *contentious*... There is a *powerful body of medical opinion* which puts strongly in issue any suggestion that male circumcision prevents or reduces the risk of urinary tract infection, penile cancer, or sexually transmitted disease. Equally *contentious* is the suggestion that it reduces the incidence of cervical cancer in women ... The procedure for a child of J's age carries small but identifiable *physical and psychological risks.* It is an *invasive* procedure... There is evidence that ... there is a consequential *loss of sexual sensory pleasure* during sexual intercourse ... [This] is *an issue for society*, not the health professionals [emphasis added].[31]

In terms of the legal framework governing his decision-making, Wall J noted that there was a legal presumption that a child's religious upbringing should be in the religion of the parent with

---

[28] Most family law texts ignore the complex issues in this case, e.g.: S. Harris-Short and J. Miles, *Family Law: Text, Cases and Materials* (Oxford: Oxford University Press, 2007); L. Herring, *Family Law* (Harlow: Pearson, 2009); J. Masson, R. Bailey-Harris, R. Probert, *Cretney: Principles of Family Law* (London: Sweet & Maxwell, 2008). In contrast, B. Hale, D. Pearle, E. Cooke, and D. Monk, *The Family, Law & Society: Cases and Materials* (Oxford: Oxford University Press, 2009) contains some critical discussion: 395–6.

[29] *Re J*, 682.

[30] An organization whose website contains links to sites unmasking an alleged 'trade in foreskins', see: http://www.norm-uk.org/where_do_foreskins_go.html. Last accessed 21 May 2010.

[31] *Re J*, 693.

the residence order (the mother here), and that the relevance of religion was ultimately subservient to the welfare principle. He also, somewhat reluctantly, concluded that the courts could not interfere with circumcision where both parents were agreed on it.

In bringing 'the law' to bear upon 'the facts' as he saw them, Wall J relied heavily on the fact that neither the residential carer (the mother) nor the child's immediate environment were Muslim and that one of the 'risks' of circumcision was that J could 'be picked on or teased by his peers' (an old argument familiar from anti-gay custody cases)[32] and that this constituted one of the 'psychological effects' of the procedure.

Although born a Muslim, it is clear to me that J is going to have an essentially secular upbringing in England. He is not going to mix in Muslim circles, and his main contact with Muslims and the Muslim ethos will be his contact with his father. J is therefore not going to grow up in an environment in which circumcision is part of family life; or in which circumcision will be in conformity with the religion practised by his primary carer; or in which his peers have all been circumcised and for him not to be so would render him either unusual or an outsider. To the contrary, circumcision in the circles in which J is likely to move will be the exception rather than the rule. Circumcision is an effectively irreversible surgical intervention which has no medical basis in J's case. It is likely to be painful and carries with it...risks... As I have already made clear, he is not going to be brought up as a Muslim child...[33]

Although the father had presented evidence that he defined himself as a 'secular Muslim', and that his son's circumcision was important not for religious reasons but for 'identity' ones, the judge ignored these arguments. Instead, Wall J acknowledged that although J was 'born a Muslim', meaning something presumably similar to N's 'heritage right' to be a Jew in *Re P*, he was not going to be 'brought up as a Muslim child'. By virtue of his parents' separation and his primary carer being his Christian mother, J too had presumably lost his birthright to be a Muslim child.

Like the courts' approach in *Re P*, the space outside the minority community is marked as 'secular'. Not only does J's Christian

---

[32] And one thoroughly discredited in that context by Helen Reece, 'Subverting the Stigmatization Argument' (1996) 23 *J. of Law and Society* 484–505.

[33] *Re J*, 699.

mother literally transform into a 'secular' one in the judgment, but, according to Wall J, 'England' will not provide J with contact with Muslims; J will get that only through his father, who, being Muslim, is presumably not 'of' England but, rather, provides the child's 'Turkish side'.[34] There is an assumption that the boys that J will mix with throughout his childhood will be neither Muslim nor Jewish as they will be uncircumcised: 'The evidence does not disclose that there are any other Muslim children at J's school.'[35] This explains why to allow J to be circumcised would be to 'render him either unusual or an outsider' amongst his presumptively Christian peers.[36]

J's father's Muslimness, and therefore circumcision, becomes solely associated with his Turkish origins, an eastern, Islamic world outside England's Christian borders. Wall J states, 'in Turkish society, a Muslim male child's peers will all be circumcised'.[37] His father, who, as it happens, also lives in England, will have the opportunity to 'provide information'[38] *about* Muslimness in much the same way that the child N's birth parents (should they be allowed any contact with her, which eventually they were not) could tell N stories about Jewishness. For J, Muslimness becomes collapsed into nationality in the phrase 'the Turkish side of his inheritance', a phrase the judge repeats several times.[39] The inevitable development of the child's Christianness is never explicitly articulated.

On appeal before Thorpe and Schiemann LJJ, and Butler-Sloss P, Wall J's first decision was described by the appeal court as 'characteristically thorough', 'important', 'significant', 'concise', and 'impregnable'.[40] Most of Thorpe LJ's leading judgment was a reproduction of passages from it and thus the court happily rejected the appeal. Schiemann LJ chose to pose the question on appeal as: 'whether to authorise the infliction of pain, the permanent loss of foreskin and the exposure to the small risk of serious physical and psychological damage'.[41] The question could have been posed differently, for example: whether to authorize that this child should not carry a significant mark of Muslimness?

---

[34] Ibid.   [35] Ibid., 682.   [36] Ibid., 699.   [37] Ibid., 697.
[38] Ibid., 699.   [39] Ibid.   [40] *Re J*, 573.   [41] Ibid., 576.

The key passage in Thorpe LJ's judgment (with which both Schiemann LJ and Butler-Sloss P agreed) reads:

Some faiths recognise their religion as a birthright derived from either the child's mother or the child's father. Some recognise religion by some ceremony of induction or initiation. But the newborn does not share the perception of his parents or of the religious community to which the parents belong. A child's perception of his or her religion generally depends on involvement in worship and teaching within the family. From this develops the emotional, intellectual, psychological and spiritual sense of belonging to a religious faith... the realities of child development [are that] fear, pain, despair or a sense of betrayal may all be transient in the temporal sense but still inflict emotional and psychological trauma that will burden a child for life.[42]

A number of assumptions underlie this passage. First, as with Jewishness in *Re P*, Muslimness is about *religion*, and religion is about *perception* not *right*: it requires theological knowledge and ritual participation in order to 'be'. The father's arguments about culture and identity—what could be called *ethnicity*—are noted but not considered by Wall J at first instance, and entirely marginalized on appeal. Circumcision, rather than being understood as a cultural practice, is characterized as a matter of belief. As a 'newborn' (never mind the child in question here was much older) cannot have beliefs, circumcision is wrong to perform.

Second, religion, thus defined, is a private, family concern. If it is not taught within the family, it effectively does not exist as living matter to which the courts should attend. The 'public' is implicitly defined as nominally non-religious, secular; the hegemonic Christianness of the public remains unspoken.[43] If, as Jakobsen and Pellegrini (and others) argue, 'religious and secular formations are profoundly intertwined',[44] then this apparent relegation of religion to the privatized family is a rhetorical move to which we should attend. The approach in *Re J* is thus entirely consistent with *Re P*, discussed above, and exemplifies a similar invisibilizing of dominant Christianity in the public sphere.

---

[42] Ibid., 575.

[43] See also Davina Cooper's argument in *Governing Out of Order* (London: Rivers Oram, 1998), ch. 6.

[44] 'Introduction', in *Secularisms* (Durham: Duke University Press, 2007) 11.

Related to this, in *Re J*, Thorpe LJ refers to the 'realities of child development', which he recites as a form of common sense (and in the absence of child development 'experts').[45] First using the term 'newborn', he states that a child, 'will' be burdened for life by the trauma of undergoing circumcision.[46] The court could have looked at the issue differently: the trauma of having *not* been circumcised could 'burden' a Muslim boy for life. Or, perhaps: a Christian child will be 'burdened' for life by being circumcised. However, J is never represented as Christian; his 'mother's side', what the judges presumably think of as the 'English side of his inheritance', is unmarked, or marked as 'secular'. He thus becomes 'a' child, rather than a Christian child.

The appeal judges also strongly endorse Wall J's view that all cases of disputed male circumcision should be resolved by the courts. Circumcision, the judges agree, is one of the 'exceptional' issues that require judicial scrutiny when parents are in conflict. According to Butler-Sloss P, it is akin to sterilizing a child, or changing its surname.[47] While the courts recognize that refusing to authorize the sterilization of a child may protect their rights to future reproductive choice, they fail to recognize that refusing to authorize circumcision could impair a child's ability to exercise future choices with respect to ethnicity and/or religion. J, for example, should he ever wish to join a devout Muslim community, may feel that he has to consider having an arguably more invasive, painful procedure as an adult. As Peter Edge has suggested:

How are we to characterise the recipient of circumcision? Are they a hyper-autonomous individual, a holder of rights against the world, or are they an integral, organic, part of broader communities, both religious and familial? This is not a manifestation of the argument as to whether circumcising children for community reasons treats them as means not ends. We can treat the child as the end, but construct circumcision quite differently if we see it as something whereby 'his culture, religion and family is enhanced' [quoting Bridge, 1999], as opposed to something carried out upon him for the benefit of others.[48]

---

[45] *Re J*, 575.   [46] Ibid.   [47] Ibid., 577.

[48] P. Edge, 'Male Circumcision after the Human Rights Act 1998' (2000) 5 *Journal of Civil Liberties* 320–37. For quoted Bridge piece, see 'Religion, Culture, and Conviction—The Medical Treatment of Young Children' (1999) 11(1) *CFLQ* 1–16.

The retention of foreskin is an act of commission—it can orient a child towards the majority Christian culture. Thus a judicial decision not to authorize a boy's circumcision could, in itself, arguably be considered a normative religious edict with far-reaching future consequences. What the judges, and many academic commentators, fail to grapple with is that the rejection of male circumcision, draped as it is in the language of medical and psychological health, is as much a normative ethno-religious choice as is the act of circumcision itself. While recent scholarship on male circumcision wishes to protect an unconsenting child from the intentional infliction of pain, and this is a worthwhile aim, these writers choose to ignore the surrounding context of power in which these decisions get played out—namely, a nation state with an established Christian church and active participation in a long European history of anti-Islamic and anti-Jewish thinking within which the denunciation of circumcision has played a major role.[49]

These approaches also reinforce the understanding of Jewishness and Muslimness as a narrow form of religious faith—predominantly as belief evidenced by practice—as they implicitly or explicitly assume the child in question 'has no religion',[50] only the parents do.[51] A decision not to circumcise such as that in *Re J* follows inevitably from a particular way of characterizing what being Muslim means: if a child cannot understand what it means to be Muslim then certainly they should not be circumcised. To acknowledge meanings of Muslimness or Jewishness wider than the ability to cognitively process theological principles would be to

---

[49] See, for example, S. Gilman, *The Jew's Body* (New York: Routledge, 1991) and J. Katz, *From Prejudice to Destruction: Antisemitism, 1700–1933* (Cambridge: Harvard University Press, 1980). On the antisemitic history of anti-circumcision discourse in England, see, amongst others, J. Shapiro, *Shakespeare and the Jews* (New York: Columbia University Press, 1996); M. Ragussis, *Figures of Conversion* (Durham: Duke University Press, 1995); D. Katz, *The Jews in the History of England 1485–1850* (Oxford: Clarendon, 1994). In contrast to this historical work, M. Fox and M. Thomson, in their consideration of circumcision as purely an issue of 'religion', even go so far as to assert that a 'long history' of the *acceptance* of circumcision exists in North America, the UK, and Australia, 'Older Minors and Circumcision: Questioning the Limits of Religious Actions' (2008) 9 *Medical Law International* 283–311.

[50] H. Gilbert, 'Time to Reconsider the Lawfulness of Ritual Male Circumcision' (2007) *European Human Rights Law Review* 289.

[51] Thomson, *Endowed: Regulating the Male Sexed Body*, 22. See also Green and Lim's discussion of 'the child' in feminist anti-female circumcision discourse, 'What is This Thing about Female Circumcision?: Legal Education and Human Rights' (1998) 7 *Social & Legal Studies* 376–8. Consequences such as that an uncircumcised male will not be accepted as properly Jewish by many orthodox Jewish communities are also ignored by anti-circumcision writers. This could affect their burial choices, amongst other things.

place circumcision in its wider cultural context and to do this complicates any simple anti-circumcision argument.

A focus on the child's lack of consent not only masks the impositions taking place on the child's body by virtue of a failure to circumcise; such arguments also facilitate the extension of Christian universalism by relegating circumcision to a pre-modernity practice of unreason and pain. Particularly in a post-9/11 world of 'clash of civilizations' discourse, this focus on circumcision, like the similar obsession with 'the veil' or 'forced marriage',[52] as barbaric practices that become associated with non-Christian cultures, is problematic.[53] In the case of circumcision, a secularized, modern 'healthcare' argument can thus be read as racializing, orientalist and Christian,[54] as can the related argument that circumcision is, at root, a barbaric ritual having no place in a civilized society, made by European enlightenment rationalists over 200 years ago.[55] I am not suggesting this is the only way that circumcision has been read in the west; however, my argument is that contemporary denunciations of it in England evoke an older discourse and that this is problematic in this current era.

I also do not dispute that the courts have a duty to arrive at a child welfare calculation in these kinds of cases. Nor do I wish to argue that *Re P* or *Re J* were wrongly decided. What I wish to highlight is *how* judges go about finding their way; what gets valued, and not, what gets normalized, and not, what gets sacralized, and not; in other words, the choices that get made, the work

---

[52] S. Motha, 'Veiled Women and the *Affect* of Religion in Democracy' (2007) 34 *Journal of Law and Society* 139–62 and 'Liberal Cults, Suicide Bombers, and Other Theological Dilemmas' (2008) 5 *Journal of Law, Culture and the Humanities* 228–46; S. Razack, 'Imperilled Muslim Women, Dangerous Muslim Men and Civilised Europeans: Legal and Social Responses to Forced Marriages' (2004) 12 *Feminist Legal Studies* 129–74; R. Reddy, 'Gender, Culture and the Law: Approaches to "Honour Crimes" in the UK' (2008) 16 *Feminist Legal Studies* 305–21; A. Vakulenko, 'Islamic Dress in Human Rights Jurisprudence: A Critque of Current Trends' (2007) 7(4) *Human Rights Law Review* 717–39.

[53] See G. Anidjar, *Semites: Race, Religion, Literature* (Stanford: Stanford University Press, 2008) 51–2; also T. Asad, *Formations of the Secular: Christianity, Islam, Modernity* (Stanford: Stanford University Press, 2003) 106–15.

[54] There is also a different argument to make—which I am not able to pursue here. Following Gilman, in *The Jew's Body*, one could argue that anti-circumcision scholars' focus on the 'lack' of foreskin from circumcision, and its consequences for masculinity, replicate a much earlier discourse about Jewish (lack of) masculinity.

[55] See Katz's study, *From Prejudice to Destruction*, which contains a comprehensive discussion of how 'reason' was deployed in Enlightenment disparaging of Jews and Jewishness, with reference specifically to circumcision, see pp. 39, 112, 158, 169. For Elizabethan anti-circumcision discourse, see Shapiro, *Shakespeare and the Jews* 113–30. For the nineteenth century, see Gilman, *The Jew's Body* 90–94.

these choices do, and the pervasive discourses that inform these acts of choice. In this section, I have argued that judges in these cases deploy a 'cognitive processing' approach to non-mainstream Christian cultures that prioritizes a secular-seeming rationality, in terms of the child's capacity to truly understand beliefs and practices narrowly defined as 'religious'.[56] I have also highlighted how this very partial picture of Jewishness and Muslimness both facilitates anti-male circumcision arguments and is informed by an implicit Christian normativity that can, effectively, result in a judicially authorized conversion. This is a different argument to the one made by Green and Lim in their important work on female circumcision, but it may be worth returning to their prescient warning:

. . . as the number of non-religious circumcisions rapidly declines in the west, all the ingredients are present for male circumcision to shift from the realm of the 'normal' and the 'culture-free' to being constituted as a fixed and barbaric practice of the west's local others.[57]

In the Blood

Other child welfare and adoption cases take a different approach to that of emphasizing belief/practice. In these judgments, Jewishness, Muslimness, and other minority identities, are biological markers that cannot be overcome by any amount of theological understanding. They become conceptualized predominantly as genetic material, handed down in a blood line (assumed by the judges to be a patriarchal one). This process of racialization, conceiving of Muslimness and Jewishness as inherited from a birth parent, is also articulated to the language of 'ethnicity', when judges suggest traditions and practices are shared in community with others of the same 'race'; an individual's cognitive ability, and therefore theology, whether knowledge or belief, becomes subject to this racialization process.

The decisions in Jonathan Bradley's case (*Re B*) also exhibit a similar mixing of religion, race, and ethnicity. At first instance,

---

[56] This rationality is also applied to Christians who stray too far into the realm of the 'miraculous', see e.g., *NHS v A* [2007] EWHC 1696, or away from 'forgiveness', see *Re R (a minor)* [1993] 2 FLR 163.

[57] Green and Lim, 'What is This Thing about Female Circumcision?' 382.

Stephen Brown J used the concept of 'serious' and 'unique' 'embar-
rassment' to describe Jonathan's predicament.[58] This presumably
meant that it was rather shameful to have been 'born' a Muslim
Arab, and have been raised as a Jew. However, adoption law,
according to the judge, was settled in this area—there could be
no remedy for a person in Jonathan's position: 'despite having
sympathy for the extraordinary situation in which Mr B finds
himself, I do not believe that his circumstances provide any ground
for setting aside the adoption order'.[59] While the appeal court
agreed that precedent and good public policy tied their hands as
well, it is worth considering one particular passage in their decision more closely.

On appeal, Simon Brown J began his decision with the following
paragraph:

My sympathy for B. is profound. It is difficult to imagine a more ill-
starred adoption placement than that of a Kuwaiti Muslim's son with an
orthodox Jewish couple. B. was brought up believing himself a Jew,
against a background of deep prejudice and hostility between Jews and
Arabs, discovering only in adult life that ethnically he belongs to the
opposing group.[60]

For Simon Brown J, Jonathan is Kuwaiti, Muslim, and Arab. As I
will discuss further later, his English, Catholic mother is nearly
invisible in the judgments. While Simon Brown J's move from the
facts of a 1960s adoption case in Liverpool to the fact of eternally,
'opposing' groups of Jews and Arabs was no doubt facilitated by
Jonathan's own case presentation,[61] the judge's language choice
of 'ill-starred', 'profound', 'ethnic', and 'opposition' reveals a particular racialized way-finding to which I wish to draw attention. As
Anidjar has discussed, 'the Jew' and 'the Arab', and the apparent
perennial war between them, are central to the imaginings of
western Christendom.[62] While Jonathan Bradley's legal submission no doubt contributed to the polarization evident in the judgment, the judge's recirculation of this discourse is more than the

---

[58] [1994] 2 FCR 1297, 1304, 1301.   [59] Ibid., 1304.   [60] [1995] 3 All ER 333, 341.
[61] It appears from the various sources that Jonathan's main driver in the litigation was to facilitate
his application for Kuwaiti citizenship.
[62] G. Anidjar, The Jew, The Arab: A History of the Enemy (Stanford: Stanford University Press,
2003), see also his Semites.

simple repetition of an argument made by a litigant. For the court, a person's genetic inheritance, and the historical narrative embedded in it, is key to knowing who they really are.

In Jonathan's case, the language of ethnicity obscures the judge's *racial* categorizations. This has the effect of eradicating the possibilities of mixed ethnicity and multiple religious identifications, leading to a decision that divests Jonathan of all his potential Jewish *and Christian* identities. For Simon Brown J, Jonathan has always been and will forever be an Arab Muslim (or Muslim Arab),[63] despite his full-time Jewish upbringing, his formal conversion to Judaism,[64] and his Christian mother. In a reversal of the bodily dysmorphia argument, Jonathan is not 'wrong' in his body, but in his mind. He has been led to believe he was Jewish when he is, in fact, the 'opposite'. His mind must transition to align with his body which has been misunderstood, and, therefore, misraced. Jonathan's supposed Arabness trumps not only his Jewishness, but also his Christianness and Englishness, which remain unthinkable in the judgment through the virtual erasure of Jonathan's English, Catholic mother. Unlike Jonathan's Kuwaiti father, his English mother is seemingly unable to 'pass on' her religious and racial markers to her son.

To return for a moment to *Re P* and *Re J*, there, as I argued earlier, we are witnesses to quiet conversions. The child N is forever lost to Jewishness; she is now Catholic. There is no room in the theological/practice approach for Jewishness as ethnicity or culture; it is simply faith (and even pure faith is not enough, as the intellectual bases for the faith must be properly understood). In *Re J*, the child, although 'born a Muslim', is Muslim no longer. The court effectively sanctions not only the child's effective conversion to Christianness, but also makes any future choice to return to Islam far more difficult for him (as his lack of circumcision may be a mark of unbelonging). In *Re B*, Jonathan Bradley, despite living for more than two decades as an observant Jew, is judicially 'converted', rhetorically if not legally, this time to Islam, in a

---

[63] Note the impossibility of being a Jewish Arab or Arab Jew in this formulation.

[64] Upon discovering Jonathan's parentage, the Bet Din had insisted on Jonathan's conversion before allowing him to have his bar mitzvah.

different way—through a process of racialization. His paternal genetic material tells the truth about who he is.

Another adoption case, *Re G*, can be read to highlight a similar, racialized understanding.[65] Although evidence is presented to the court noting that Tarquin's parents did not participate in any Judaic belief or practice, and, indeed, his mother may not have come from a Jewish family at all (we are not informed), nevertheless, Purchas LJ confidently states:

> ...I cannot close my eyes to the fact that in spite of the protestations of the grandmother this basically was a Jewish family. It is perfectly true that the dead father did not go to the Synagogue, or anything of the sort, but the grandfather, the grandmother's husband, was a Jew and his brother, who is also now dead, was, as I understand it, also a practising Jew.[66]

The judge finds that the (now dead) family patriarchs (ignored for the purposes of determining Jewishness in Jewish law of course) were Jewish; therefore, the child is Jewish. Purchas LJ therefore resolves the 'ethnic problem' of the case (a phrase he repeats four times) through applying a racial lineage. This is even despite the judge's apparent approval of expert evidence suggesting Tarquin would find it hard to fit into the 'darker' Jewish family, who 'bear the outward signs of their origins', as he was 'fair of complexion'.[67] So, although Purchas LJ may be uneasy with the fact that Tarquin may not be sufficiently Semitic-looking (and this disturbs his racial aesthetic), he nonetheless finds that the child's patriarchal racial lineage is a Jewish one; this, together with his welfare interests overall, entail him remaining with the 'darker' Jews rather than the Christian grandmother (whose 'complexion' remains unmarked and therefore unremarked upon).

In tracing this discourse of racial lineage, it is worth returning again to *Re P* (the very first case I discussed), and Ward LJ's judgment, which took a somewhat different turn than Butler-Sloss LJ's in one respect: he explicitly references 'blood'.[68] Ward LJ refers to the case as a 'blood-tie' case, agrees that N has a 'Jewish

[65] *Re G (a minor)* [1990] FCR 881.
[66] Ibid.
[67] Ibid.   [68] *Re P* [2000] 15 Fam 494.

birthright', but concludes that 'the psychological tie outweighs the blood tie'.[69]

... here the primary contention is that by the tie of blood the further knot of religion is firmly attached to N. At the heart of the appellants' submission is their conviction that the knot should also bind the court. Therein lies the error: religion is but one factor—though I do not doubt that it may be a weighty factor—to be placed in the scales which, when the balance is struck, will determine what N's welfare demands. Thus it is submitted that N's birthright is to be Jewish and to live her life in the practice, enjoyment and ultimate fulfilment of her Jewish faith. I accept that as her birthright. She is and will forever remain a Jew in this life and hereafter whatever this court may determine.[70]

Ward LJ thus decouples race and religion. Unlike Butler-Sloss LJ, Ward LJ believes N is and will always be a Jew by race (even, apparently, after she is dead); race cannot be undone by the court—it is in the blood. However, race and religion are separate—one can, presumably according to Ward LJ, be a Jew by race, and a Christian by religion and the latter is something the courts can authorize in the interests of the child.

In *Re S*, Wilson J also decouples race/ethnicity and religion.[71] He decides that the boy, a child of a Muslim mother and a Sikh father, should have his Sikh names changed to Muslim ones, but not by deed poll. He should be brought up as a Muslim, as that is the residential carer's (the mother's) community, and that also requires his circumcision. Wilson J confidently states that:

A child cannot be brought up in two faiths simultaneously so, admirable though Sikhism is, he cannot be brought up as a Sikh. That however in no way precludes his becoming aware of his Sikh identity.[72]

This 'half-Sikh identity', Wilson J concludes, is a 'genetic identity' that the mother was attempting to 're-write'.[73] So, like Ward LJ's judgment in *Re P*, the child in *Re S* is seemingly racially or ethnically Sikh through carrying his father's 'Sikh genes' (as N was a Jew in *Re P*), but he can and *should* become a Muslim by faith, like his mother.

---

[69] Ibid., 497.   [70] Ibid., 494.   [71] Re *S* [2001] 3 FCR 648.
[72] Ibid., 660.   [73] Ibid.

However, unlike the judges in the first set of belief/practice cases, Wilson J also believes it is the court's duty to facilitate the child's 'half-Sikh identity', and so he concludes that an official name-change would 'contribute to a comprehensive elimination of his half Sikh identity'. Thus, maintaining, as best as possible in the circumstances, both elements of the child's identity (as the judge understands them) is crucial to the child's welfare in the long term. This is not the conclusion reached in *Re J* (the first circumcision case), where the judges' championing of the case against circumcision overwhelmed their ability to balance these 'identity' issues. In both *Re J* and *Re P*, the courts did, in effect, authorize the 'comprehensive elimination' of the children's Muslim and Jewish identities.

However, Wilson J's judgment is, at the same time, indebted to an orientalist discourse. He confidently comments upon the violence of non-Christian others. 'It is difficult', Wilson J writes, 'for a white judge to understand, let alone articulate' the shame the Muslim family must have experienced (from the daughter marrying out to a Sikh man) and what sorts of acts could result from such humiliation.[74] While a 'shame' discourse clearly emanated from the mother's legal submissions, Wilson J went on to offer further comment:

One of the great strengths of Islam is the loyalty which it draws from its members. But every strength has its downside; and on the evidence of this case there is in some quarters a concomitant intolerance, the strength of which, even in East London only ten miles from where I speak, is astonishing. Analogous problems are reflected in today's news of ugly clashes between Muslims and Hindus in Bradford.[75]

Where the judge speaks from, the court, is, implicitly, a white space of (again unspoken) Christian (secular) tolerance and rationality— 10 miles away, in East London, is an 'astonishing' non-white space of racial/religious extremism, a space that is difficult for a 'white' judge to even understand.[76] The judge's whiteness is visibilized here (unusually), and this succeeds in racializing the 'Islam'

---

[74] Re S [2001] 3 FCR 648.　　[75] Ibid., at 651.

[76] Note that London's east end was historically subject to such depictions, see Judith Walkowitz's work, for example, perhaps most intriguingly, in terms of intersections of gender, race, class, and religion, 'The Indian Woman, the Flower Girl, and the Jew: Photojournalism in Edwardian London' (1998–1999) 42 *Victorian Studies* 3–46. See also P. Knepper, 'British Jews and the Racialisation of

of his remarks, as Wilson J distances himself from what must be darker 'East London'; further, a white judge cannot be Muslim, presumably. A false antimony is thus established between whiteness and Muslimness, while, Christianity, the more obvious religious suspect to contrast with 'Muslim' or 'Hindu', remains, again, unspoken.

Once again, a civilizational discourse rears its head—the English courtroom versus the 'intolerant, ugly clashes' of inner city tribals, 'only ten miles' from where the judge 'speaks'. As Asad has argued: 'to make an enlightened space, the liberal must continually attack the darkness of the outside world that threatens to overwhelm that space'.[77] The judge's confident knowledge of Islam's 'great strengths' recalls Said's elucidation of orientalism as a self-conscious knowing and speaking about the orient/east.

In this section of the chapter, I have highlighted how the judicial discourse in these cases privileges a logic in which ethnicity, religion and sometimes nationality are determined by blood ties passed on to a child from its (birth) parents. Thus, religion, or rather Jewishness, Muslimness or Sikhness, becomes emptied of theological content (in contrast to the first belief/practice approach) and ethnicized into a lineage of shared tradition and practices. At the same time, and in common with the cases in the first section of the chapter, this racialized discourse is firmly embedded in an orientalist, 'civilizational' way-finding.[78]

The Significance of Culture and Personal Identity

Another judgment of Wilson J's exemplifies a somewhat different approach to understanding religion and ethnicity, one that appears on first reading to rely neither on genetic inheritance nor theological understanding and practice. In *Re C*, Wilson J authorizes the adoption by a Jewish couple of a two-year-old girl who, according to the

---

Crime in the Age of Empire' (2007) 47(1) *British J. of Criminology* 61–79. On white, Christian representations of Chinese communities in the east end, see S. Auerbach, *Race, Law, and 'The Chinese Puzzle' in Imperial Britain* (New York: Palgrave Macmillan, 2009), particularly ch. 6.

[77] Asad, *Formations of the Secular*, 59.

[78] See also Lord Denning's echoes of this discourse in *Mandla* v *Dowell Lee* [1982] 3 All ER 1108: 'Jews are not to be distinguished by their national origins. The wandering Jew has no nation. He is a wanderer over the face of the earth. The one definable characteristic of the Jews is a racial characteristic' at 1113, see further Chapter 6.

judge, has a mixed genetic heritage that included Jewish, Christian, Muslim, Scottish, and Turkish-Cypriot elements.[79] Both birth parents had learning disabilities, and it is unclear from Wilson J's judgment whether they ultimately approved of this adoption or not. However, the official guardian objected to it strenuously, and she was the one who applied to the court to prevent it.

The guardian's argument, as presented by the judge in his decision, was that the prospective adopters were, in effect, too Jewish.

The crux of the guardian's primary argument is that, contrary to the guidance, the local authority, including for this purpose the panel, have labelled C as Jewish and have ignored the other elements of her background. C's mixed heritage requires, so she argues, placement in an essentially secular family, in other words in a religiously neutral environment, from which exposure to the different elements of her background can evenly be developed.[80]

Given this argument, Wilson J felt compelled to investigate the adopters' Jewishness and, in a section headed 'The Level of Mr and Mrs A's Jewishness', the judge listed over twenty items relevant to this investigation.[81] Concluding this lengthy section, he stated: 'I accept that Mr and Mrs A have quite a strong Jewish identity, but with a low level of specifically religious observance...'[82] Wilson J went on to find that the guardian's argument, that the A's home was, in effect, too Jewish, and that C had been inappropriately labelled as Jewish by the local authority when her birth home was a 'secular' one, was 'inflexible and doctrinaire'; that the guardian's search was for 'the lowest common denominator'.[83]

In considering further the relevance of the birth home and the wishes of the birth parents, Wilson J found that the former was characterized by 'poverty, physical but in particular intellectual and emotional', and that it contained a 'religious void', which the guardian 'paradoxically' was seeking to replicate.[84] In relation to the weight that should be accorded the birth parents' views, Wilson J offered the following:

---

[79] *Re C* [2002] 1 FLR 1119, para. 3.   [80] Ibid., para. 36.
[81] These ranged from where the As had been married (in a United Synagogue), to who comprised their circle of friends, to their practices on Friday night, and at Christmas.
[82] Ibid., para. 32.   [83] Ibid., para. 37.   [84] Ibid., para. 38.

Parental wishes much be analysed in context. How considered are the wishes? Upon what are they founded? How deep do they run? In answering these questions there is no escape from some reference to the tragic barrenness of the parents' lives and the superficiality of their thoughts. Although they have occupied their present accommodation for almost 2 years, there is no carpet in the living room and it is entirely empty apart from a television set and one plastic garden chair... The room is testament less to lack of money than to lack of purpose... even the making of an appointment with their solicitors seems to overwhelm them... The mother describes herself as Church of England but it is unclear whether she has ever attended a church service, still less whether Anglican teaching holds any meaning for her. When on 18 June she indicated opposition to the placement on the basis that C was Church of England, it is hard to discern any meaning behind that label; and the father's contribution at that time was to say that C had a 'London religion'.[85]

The judge thus builds up the case for the As, first by noting yet playing down their degree of religious observance, second by playing up their middle-class multicultural milieu, and, finally, by finding that the birth parents lived poor, tragic, barren, and super-ficial lives, and thus their views on their own religion and culture, much less that of the prospective adopters, were irrelevant.[86] The intriguing complexity of the father's response—that C had a 'London religion'—is instead offered as evidence of his lack of intellect.

So, in *Re C*, a more hybrid approach to Jewishness is apparent, part theology/ritual practice, part 'cultural' or perhaps ethnic. Wilson J takes the former approach to the learning disabled birth parents; he interprets their words as demonstrating a lack of cognitive ability to understand religion. Like N, the learning disabled child in *Re P*, they cannot 'know' religion, and thus they cannot have any: their lives are 'tragically barren' and their thoughts 'superficial'. Their own subjective experience and under-standing—their 'London religion'—is ridiculed. Wilson portrays the birth parents as leading uncivilized lives—they have no carpet,

---

[85] Ibid., para. 42.
[86] The mother had said that if she had had a son, she would have had him circumcised, ibid., para. 44.

no furniture, they cannot make business appointments, their existence is without purpose.

At the same time, the Jewishness of the proposed adoptive parents is treated in a more nuanced way than one usually finds in these judgments. Although the facts clearly indicate some level of orthodox Jewish practice (i.e., keeping kosher, a religiously Jewish marriage), Wilson J prefers not to dwell on these. The judge describes the As' beliefs as 'liberal Jewish', but there is no further explication of what that might mean. He notes the As' live in a non-Jewish area and do not observe Shabbat; they are willing to observe Christmas; and they undertake not to batmitzvah the child—perhaps tests of their adaptability to Christian England. In considering religious observance alongside wider cultural practices, Wilson J thus evinces an understanding of the complexity of Jewishness—as religion, as ethnicity, as culture—largely absent in the other decisions I have discussed. But he does this in the context of rebutting the guardian's claim that the couple are too Jewish.

Re S (Specific Issue Order) takes a somewhat similar approach. While here, Baron J, relying on expert evidence, found that circumcision was 'relatively safe',[87] and unlike the judges in *Re J*, she spent no time elaborating its potential abusive effect on children, she nevertheless refused to authorize it. Arguing that it was in the interests of the children to 'have the best of both worlds', and that circumcision now might impinge on the boy's later choices to be Jain, Baron J found that it would be best to wait until the boy was 'Gillick competent' and could make his own choice.[88] The fact that circumcision at this later age would not violate Islamic law also influenced her decision.

Baron J appears fully committed to the possibility of mixed identity and the court's duty to facilitate this, and also seems to have a more expansive understanding of children's cognitive abilities to appreciate ethno-religious worlds:

...K's understanding of his dual heritage is well established. Therefore, obviously, both Muslim and Hindu elements of his identity will

---

[87] *S (Children)* [2004] EWHC 1282, at para. 72.   [88] Ibid., para. 83.

require validation if he is to grow up with a proper knowledge of his true self.[89]

However, the belief/practice approach creeps into her judgment too; she dismisses the religiosity of the parents as they do not evidence sufficiently serious ritual practice. She remarks that the father, 'assert[s] his religion when his adherence is patchy'.[90]

While both *Re C* and *Re S (Specific Issue Order)* are problematic decisions in some respects, both the judges in these cases do manage to think somewhat more complexly about the character of non-Christianness, and it is striking how few judges do.[91] They rely neither on belief/practice, nor on racial genetic ancestry. Wilson J and Baron J are both committed to the possibility of mixed identity, which they believe it is the court's duty to facilitate. Wilson J's judgment in *Re C* goes some way in this direction; however, it is limited by his insistence that while ethnicity can be mixed because it is 'genetic', a child cannot be brought up believing in two different religions and so religion cannot be legally 'mixed' in this way.

CONCLUDING REMARKS

I have focused on a number of English child welfare-related cases in order to explore several interlocking and also divergent themes. In doing so, I made two main sets of arguments. The first proceeded by tracing the different yet overlapping approaches judges take to coming to terms with children's non-Christian cultural back-grounds: I identified these as belief/practice; racial/genetic ances-try; and cultural context-oriented. I do not argue that these three approaches are analytically or normatively distinct, but rather that considering the cases through this sorting mechanism illuminates particular dimensions of the judgments to which I wish to draw attention.

---

[89] Ibid., para. 71.   [90] Ibid., at para. 59.

[91] This more generous approach to Jewishness is apparent in some of the cases in another legal area relating to children—the education law field dealing with children with 'special needs', for example, see *R* v *Sec St Ed, ex parte E* [1996] ELR 312 and *A* v *SENT, LB Barnet* [2004] ELR 293; most recently, see *R (JW)* v *The Learning Trust* [2010] ELR 115; although, here, too, some decision-makers adopt a far less nuanced approach: see *G* v *LB Barnet and SENT* [1998] ELR 480 and *R* v *LB Hackney, ex parte GC* [1995] ELR 144.

So, for example, an understanding of 'Jewish', 'Muslim', or 'Sikh' as 'religion' narrowly defined through the prioritization of belief/ practice and cognitive processing can result in the de facto conversion of non-Christian children to Christianity, which itself remains invisible; if spoken of at all, it is called 'secularism'. Those cases that prioritize blood and genetic ancestry exhibit a racialized logic that the first set of cases largely do not. Here, 'Jewish', 'Muslim', or 'Sikh' are de-theologized, and, instead, ethnicized, resulting in a complex relationship between the 'religious' and the 'racial'. While, through the language of ethnicity, the children's authentic heritage is judicially identified as being 'in the blood', it is possible, according to some of the judges, to de-couple race and religion. Thus, a Jew by virtue of her 'blood' (per Ward LJ in *Re P*), or a Sikh by virtue of his 'genetic[s]' (per Wilson J in *Re S*), can become Christian, or Muslim, by religion, but they will never lose their racial make-up, they will always and forever remain Jewish or Sikh by race. In *Re B*, Jonathan *is* an Arab, and, as an Arab, and, by extension, a Muslim, his adoption by a Jewish couple was a tragedy.

The final set of cases, those emphasizing the child's wider cultural context and personal identity, exhibit an attempt to overcome the rigidities of the other approaches. Both Wilson J and Baron J, in *Re C* and *Re S (Specific Issue Order)* respectively, demonstrate a more sophisticated understanding of non-Christian worlds, one that adopts a broader concept of 'culture'. However, even here, and particularly in *Re C*, a different problem is encountered—and this brings me to my second set of arguments.

While each child welfare discourse has its own (at times overlapping) logic, almost all the judgments exhibit aspects of orientalist thinking and Christian universalism. This is evident both in terms of how Jewish individuals are characterized (i.e., in *Re P*), as I explore in Chapters 2 and 5, but, more extensively, in how Jewish and other non-Christian practices are rendered alien, and cruel and/or primitive. This rendering is different to what we have seen in the trust cases (Chapter 3), where Judaism was a mysterious and unknowable element in the blood. Here, there is no uncertainty on the part of the courts. And, while all the judges share a common framework—namely a normative Christianity—in the child welfare cases, Christianity becomes defined as secularism, it is rarely, in itself, the subject of story-telling or enquiry. Unlike the trust cases, where courts were compelled to address the meaning of the 'Church of England', here Christianity is invisibilized, submerged under the language of secularity. At the same time, conversions to Christianity are judicially facilitated.

Finally, I have drawn parallels between some of the language in these decisions and contemporary 'clash of civilizations' discourse. Whether it is through how anti-circumcision arguments are mobilized to advance the path of western reason against barbaric ritual, or through how a judge might sit back and reflect on the warring tribes of non-Christian, racialized aliens, I argue that there is a kinship between legal narrative in child welfare cases and an orientalist, civilizational discourse at this particular moment, one to which we should attend. Missions to 'improve others' are not just about 'over there', but also about 'right here'. Underlying some of these legal decisions is a project of conversion, of bringing 'reason' to bear on primitive cultures 'at home', that resonates with judicial discourse on Jewish intemperacy vs English/Protestant civility (Chapter 2), with decisions refusing to allow Jewish testators to disinherit their Christian children (Chapter 3), and with the consequences of the *JFS* case (see Chapters 6 and 7). In the next chapter, I change gear somewhat by considering 'the Holocaust'; however, I will come back there as well to ideas about England and Englishness.

Chapter 5

'WE LIVE IN THE AGE OF THE HOLOCAUST OF THE JEWS'[1]

In this chapter, I continue exploring themes of racialization and alienness, but also return to considering how judges engage in processes of myth-making (see Chapter 3). However, in contrast to other chapters in the book, my focus here is not on cases that explicitly mention Jews and Jewishness, but rather on ones that take note of 'the Holocaust', as I will argue doing so is essential to developing a fuller picture of the relationship between Jewishness and English case law. I focus predominantly on the deployment of Holocaust references in cases having little obvious relationship to Nazi policy, or mass killings of any kind as I am particularly interested in routine reiterations of the Holocaust in judicial discourse and the relationship between these reiterations and judicial representations of Jews and Jewishness. Thus, cases *explicitly* about the events the Holocaust is usually intended to describe, war crimes and 'denial' trials in particular, receive little attention in these pages.[2]

Rather, this chapter tells two overlapping yet diverging stories; first, I offer a history of the term 'holocaust' in a range of English legal cases over the course of the last 100 years; second, I consider how 'the Holocaust' circulated in judicial discourse once that

---

[1] *R v Howe* [1987] 1 AC 417, Lord Hailsham.
[2] But see D. Bloxham, *Genocide on Trial: War Crimes Trials and the Formation of Holocaust History and Memory* (New York: Oxford University Press, 2003); L. Douglas, *The Memory of Judgment: Making Law and History in the Trials of the Holocaust* (New Haven: Yale University Press, 2001); R.J. Evans, *Telling Lies About Hitler: The Holocaust, History and the David Irving Trial* (London: Verso, 2002); D. Fraser, *Law After Auschwitz* (Durham: Carolina Academic Press, 2005); M.M. Hill, and L.N. Williams, *Auschwitz in England: A Record of a Libel Action* (London: MacGibbon & Kee, 1965).

phrase proliferated. I consider the many meanings of the word 'holocaust', and the phrase 'the Holocaust' in English twentieth- and twenty-first century legal cases. I explore how the term 'holocaust' circulated and disappeared, when and in what contexts 'the Holocaust' emerged, and how we can understand the work 'the Holocaust' does in legal judgments.[3]

In mapping this terrain, I am conscious of the many debates that swirl around the politics of the phrase 'the Holocaust': the questions of 'analogy', 'scope', 'uniqueness', 'evil', 'banality', and 'rationality';[4] the claims of big business and industry associated with it;[5] the rejection, by some, of the phrase altogether;[6] as well as the reasonably well-trodden ground of (un)representability, ethics, and law 'after the Holocaust'.[7] My intention here is to bracket these debates, although many of the issues they concern will arise during the course of my exploration. While it is true that by writing a chapter that under-scores the phrase 'the Holocaust' I may contribute to its problematic iconography, I am not overly concerned with this danger.

In a British context, as I go on to explore, the phrase has arguably not achieved such iconic status. Critics such as Tim Cole, for

---

[3] As is reasonably well known, the etymology of the term 'holocaust' derives from *holokauston*, the Greek translation of *olah* in the Hebrew Torah, where it was used to denote a sacrificial offering to God. The Greek *holocaustos* was translated by early Christian theologians into the Latin *holocaustum*. The word then became embedded in Christian writings, leading Georgio Agamben, for one, to state that 'the semantic history of the term is essentially Christian': G. Agamben, *Remnants of Auschwitz: The Witness and the Archive* (New York: Zone Books, 1999) 28. There is some debate about whether the word's contemporary usage need always signify *religious* sacrifice. Agamben, for example, insists that the term implies 'an unacceptable equation between crematoria and altars; it also continues a semantic heredity that is from its inception anti-Semitic', and so he rejects its use altogether, ibid., 31. Others, however, disagree with this assessment, arguing that etymology is not determinative of contemporary meaning, P. Novick, *The Holocaust in American Life* (New York: Houghton Mifflin, 1999); J. Petrie, 'The Secular Word HOLOCAUST: Scholarly Myths, History, and 20th Century Meanings' (2000) 2(1) *Journal of Genocide Research* 31–63. My concern in this chapter is not with this debate, and my arguments do not depend or rely on how one resolves the question of meaning in relation to the word.

[4] H. Arendt, *Eichmann in Jerusalem: A Report on the Banality of Evil* (New York: Penguin, 1963); Z. Bauman, *Modernity and the Holocaust* (Cambridge: Polity, 1989); D. Goldhagen, *Hitler's Willing Executioners: Ordinary Germans and the Holocaust* (New York: Knopf, 1996); L. Herman, *Engaging the Disturbing Images of Evil: How Do Those Born After Remember Auschwitz?* (Saarbrücken: VDM Verlag, 2009).

[5] T. Cole, *Selling the Holocaust: From Auschwitz to Schindler: How History is Bought, Packaged, and Sold* (New York: Routledge, 2000); N.G. Finkelstein, *The Holocaust Industry: Reflections on the Exploitation of Jewish Suffering* (London: Verso, 2000).

[6] Agamben, *Remnants*.

[7] Fraser, *Law After Auschwitz*; S. Friedlander (ed.), *Probing the Limits of Representation: Nazism and the 'Final Solution'* (Cambridge: Harvard University Press, 1992); R. Lentin, *Representing the Shoah for the Twenty-First Century* (Oxford: Berghan Books, 2004); G. Rose, *Mourning Becomes the Law* (Cambridge: Cambridge University Press, 1996); D. Seymour, *Law, Antisemitism and the Holocaust* (London: Routledge/Cavendish, 2007).

example, may be excessive when they suggest that 'western culture' in general is 'saturated' with the Holocaust.[8] And, even if we do perceive such 'saturation', we would do well to question its terms. In Britain at any rate, heeding Dominic La Capra's warning, against an 'over-critique' of Holocaust memorialization, might not go amiss.[9] However, rather than taking a position in this debate, it is primarily for reasons of clarity that I use 'the Holocaust' in this chapter solely to refer to the phrase's literal deployment by judges. When I wish, myself, to refer to the German-led systematic mass killing of Jewish Europeans, it is a variant of this phrase that I use here.[10]

In considering this material, I am interested, first, in discovering the legal history of the Holocaust—in other words, in conducting the first genealogical investigation of the term in English case law. This aim of the chapter addresses the questions of when and how 'holocaust' appeared in cases prior to the entrenchment of 'the Holocaust'. This is partly a descriptive endeavour; however, it is vital to my main concern which is to consider the work the Holocaust does once it makes its appearance. And so my second, but primary, aim is to explore how the Holocaust acts, or more to the point does not act, as a mnemonic device in legal discourse. How does it, or indeed does it at all, perform the work of remembering? What is the quality of these memories, and what is their purpose in the present moment of legal decision-making? And if, as I shall suggest, the Holocaust's role as a mnemonic device is far from straightforward, what work is it doing apart from or instead of instigating Holocaust remembrance?

I argue that when the Holocaust is referred to in contemporary judgments it tends to be spliced in as a form of stock footage, and suggest that this routinized, mechanical, and mindless (here I mean without awareness, not without thought) manoeuvre succeeds in limiting rather than contributing to any substantive comprehension of the events the phrase is intended to describe.

---

[8] Cole, *Selling the Holocaust*.

[9] D. La Capra, 'Representing the Holocaust: Reflections on the Historians' Debate' in S. Friedlander (ed.), *Probing the Limits of Representation* 108–42. See also his *History and Memory after Auschwitz* (Ithaca: Cornell, 1998) and *Writing History, Writing Trauma* (Baltimore: Johns Hopkins University Press, 2001).

[10] I explain why I prefer this phrase in D. Herman, ' "I Do Not Attach Great Significance To It": Taking Note of "the Holocaust" in English Law' (2008) 17 *Social & Legal Studies* 427–52.

This conclusion echoes La Capra's distinction between 'acting out' and 'working through':

I would like to argue that one crucial—perhaps *the* crucial—historical issue is whether (and how) the Holocaust is attended to, or whether attention is diverted from it in a manner that decreases chances that it will be worked through to any conceivable extent.[11]

The effect of this judicial failure to 'work through' the Holocaust is three-fold.

First, the past is misremembered; contemporary, routinized judicial deployments of the Holocaust work to construct a mythical British past where Jews were deserving victims and their persecution understood and alleviated. The actual UK social and legal history of judicial indifference, along with state policies of internment, deportation, and collaboration (in the Channel Islands), is erased, as is the legal history of orientalization and racialization of Jews and Jewishness I discuss in other chapters.[12] Second, this myth of Holocaust consciousness is often deployed to facilitate the denial of contemporary claims of persecution. According to this narrative, Jews were the paradigmatic case of 'the deserving' to which some other groups' experience does not measure up. Third, the mythological representation of past, 'Holocaust' Jews as 'deserving' serves to obfuscate the present: for example, the fact that contemporary Jewish claims of discrimination, under the UK Race Relations Act 1976, for example, invariably end in failure (see Chapter 6). While some Jews might have been deserving in a mythological past, contemporary ones are not. Indeed, I suggest that the deployment of the Holocaust by the judges may reinforce particularly English understandings of Jews and Jewishness. Far from acting as a mnemonic device to recall atrocity, the Holocaust can in fact act as a racializing aid to remembering what it is English judges find 'unattractive' and alien about 'the Jew'.

---

[11] LaCapra, 'Representing the Holocaust' 109. See also E.L. Santner, 'History Beyond the Pleasure Principle: Some Thoughts on the Representation of Trauma' in S. Friedlander (ed.), *Probing the Limits of Representation*, 143–54.

[12] On collaboration, see D. Fraser, *The Jews of the Channel Islands*. On the internment of Jewish refugees in England during the war, see D. Cesarani and T. Kushner, *The Internment of Aliens in Twentieth-Century Britain* (London: Frank Cass, 1993).

I begin by tracing a holocaust history in English case law, exploring the uses of 'holocaust' in the early and middle parts of the twentieth century, to the eventual near disappearance of 'holocaust' in favour of 'the Holocaust' in the 1990s. The next section of the chapter returns to a selection of the decisions, considering the tensions, contradictions, and accomplishments of 'the Holocaust' in these judicial pronouncements.

A HISTORY OF THE CASES

1906–1970

In relation to non-legal sources, Jon Petrie has thoroughly traced the extensive use of 'holocaust' in a range of international materials, demonstrating that the word's primary common usage, in the early part of the twentieth century, was to refer to disasters or a loss of sorts in the context of a disaster.[13] As Petrie documents, 'the Holocaust', deployed to signify the mass killings of Jewish Europeans, gradually emerged in Israel and the US in the 1950s and 1960s. By the 1970s, it had come to dominate there as a descriptor of these killings.[14] A search for 'holocaust' in English case law suggests a similar early trajectory but a different later one.

One of the first judicial uses of the term in the twentieth century came in 1906, where it was deployed to describe the potential damage a wayward cat might do to a litigant's 'rabbits, ducks, chickens and pigeons'.[15] Two cases from the 1920s suggest that both a body of precedent itself, and legal instruments the courts were compelled to scrutinize, could constitute 'holocausts' of their own,[16] as in this flowery example: 'some limit should be put to the holocaust of testamentary dispositions which are immolated upon the alter of judicial nescience'.[17] Three 1940s cases continue these uses. In one, the war itself is referred to as a holocaust;[18] two further decisions describe both 'earlier authority', and 'a century

---

[13] J. Petrie, 'The Secular Word Holocaust: Scholarly Myths, History, and 20th Century Meanings' (2000) 2(1) *J. of Genocide Research* 31–63.

[14] Ibid.   [15] *Peden* v *Charleton* (1906) 13 SLT 773.

[16] *English and Scottish Law Life Ass. Assoc.* v *Carmichael* (1920) S.C. (H.L.) 195 (HL); *Reid's Trustees* v *M'George* (1929) IH (2 Div); see also *Ward* v *Van de Loeff* [1924] All ER Rep 542.

[17] *Reid's*, ibid.

[18] *Anglo Iranian Oil Co Ltd* v *Owners of the Thorsholm (The Thorsholm)* 1942 WL 30983.

of judicial pronouncements' as 'holocausts', meaning, in the context of these cases, a disaster, and a bonfire.[19]

At the same time, in the late 1930s and early 1940s, several decisions begin to take some note of the situation for Jews on the Continent, mostly in the context of property and contract cases involving Jewish German refugees. In one early judgment, the events unfolding for Jewish Europeans are described as a set of 'disabilities',[20] while, later, one judge speaks of the 'Nazi oppression' of the Jews.[21] Other judgments, mostly to do with the expropriation of property, make clear reference to Jews being placed in 'concentration camps'.[22] However, a number of cases involving Jewish refugee parties during the wartime period make little or no reference to German anti-Jewish policies at all.[23]

It is certainly arguable that judges during the early years of the war would not have understood the scale of killing and could not be expected to refer to it. For example, Peter Novick argues that while knowledge of the scale and systematization of killing was available to the Allied nations by 1942, for a number of understandable reasons this information was not processed by most who heard of it and tended to be greeted with disbelief.[24] However, English judicial discourse after the war, and continuing through the 1950s, showed little greater awareness, despite a flurry of death camp publicity and photographs at war's end.[25]

As an exemplar of this kind of judgment, I will focus in more detail on one, *R* v *Sec of State for Foreign Affairs, ex parte Greenberg*, a case about 4,500 Jewish passengers on a boat violently apprehended near Palestine by the British a few weeks before the judge

---

[19]   *Campbell's* v *Campbell's* (1949) IH (1 Div); *Angus's Executrix* v *Batchan's Trustees* (1949) SC 335.

[20]   *Friedlander* v *Lloyds Bank Ltd* (1935) 52 Lloyd's Rep 233.

[21]   *Unger* v *Preston* [1942] 1 All ER 200.

[22]   *Ellinger* v *Guiness* [1939] 4 All ER 16; *Oppenheimer* v *Louis Rosenthal Co* [1937] 1 All ER 23; *May* v *May* [1943] 2 All ER 146; *Re D* [1943] Ch 305.

[23]   *The King* v *Home Secretary, ex parte L* [1945] KB 7; *R* v *Ketter* [1939] 1 All ER 729; *Bendit* v *Dickson* [1945] KB 1331.

[24]   Novick, *The Holocaust in American Life*, ch. 1. See also M.R. Marrus, *The Holocaust in History* (London: Penguin, 1987) 163. But see also R. Bolchover, *British Jewry and the Holocaust* (Cambridge: Cambridge University Press, 1993).

[25]   Just one of many such examples is the following quote from a page 4 article in *The Times* in 1945: '... for sheer ghastliness nothing has equalled the description given in evidence today of the gas chambers and burning ghats of Auschwitz, which were used as the chief instruments of Nazi policy for the mass extermination of the Jews', in Special Correspondent, 'Burning Pits of Auschwitz' (2 October 1945; Issue 50262; col. E).

issued his decision.[26] Sabine Greenberg was one of six representative passengers on behalf of whom D.N. Pritt, the noted left-wing lawyer, retained by the Jewish Agency, applied for a writ of *habeas corpus*. The claim alleged that Greenberg and others were being unlawfully detained by the British Government on three ships at sea. In his decision denying the writ, Jenkins J found against the Jewish claimants without a single reference to any difficulty that might have led to their flight to Palestine. I quote at length from the judgment as there are a number of points I wish to pick up:

The circumstances in which these persons find themselves in their present situation are briefly these. The question of the immigration of Jews into Palestine has for many years been the subject of acute controversy, and His Majesty's Government and the Government of Palestine have found it necessary to impose certain restrictions on immigration. Those restrictions are strenuously objected to by many of the Jews, and it has become the common practice for the champions of unrestricted immigration to organise parties of Jews from Europe and to send them to enter Palestine, if they can, in defiance of the regulations restricting immigration. These six persons were members of a party of illegal immigrants which set sail from the south of France bound for Palestine in a ship called the 'President Warfield,' with the intention either of getting into Palestine by stealth, or, if intercepted, of embarrassing the authorities who would then have on their hands a further 4,500 people to be dealt with somehow. When the 'President Warfield' was nearing Palestine, it was intercepted by His Majesty's ships... a deportation order was made in respect of the immigrants in the ship under the Palestine Defence (Emergency) Regulations, 1945. Pursuant to that deportation order, the immigrants were transferred to the three British ships I have mentioned and were taken in those ships to Port de Bouc in the south of France, arriving there on or about July 29, 1947. Port de Bouc was selected because it was in the south of France, and the south of France was the place from which these illegal immigrants had set sail. On arrival at Port de Bouc the immigrants were invited, and, indeed, pressed, to land in France. The French authorities were ready for them to land, but they refused to do so. Finally, an ultimatum was given that, unless they landed by 6 p.m. on August 22, the ships would sail and they would be disembarked at Hamburg in Germany. Substantially all the 4,500 or so people

---

[26] *R* v *Sec of State for Foreign Affairs, ex parte Greenberg* [1947] 2 All ER 550. I have consulted a number of documents pertaining to this case in the National Archives, CO 537/2403.

on board the ships refused to land, with the result that the ships set sail and are now on their way to Hamburg...

...

It seems to me that these immigrants, having been given the warning and the choice, deliberately elected to go on in the ships to the next destination of which they had been informed. Therefore, in my opinion, it would be possible to dispose of this case really on the short ground that, whatever the position was at any point of time before arrival at Port de Bouc, there can now be no question of illegal restraint, since the immigrants remained in the ships of their own free will after they had been invited to land at Port de Bouc. For these reasons a case for a writ of habeas corpus has not been made out.[27]

And, so, the three ships made their way to Hamburg, where these 4,500 people were forcibly removed and transferred by rail to a UK-administered detention camp in Poppendorf. Those who were ill were treated by 'German doctors and German nurses', provision which, according to a report in *The Times*, 'seems adequate for present purposes'.[28] They did not remain there long, many of them eventually finding their way to the new state of Israel.

We know a great deal about the fate of these passengers because *The President Warfield* was, in fact, renamed *The Exodus* by its Jewish nationalist crew. The ship's journey, its detention, the passengers' ultimate arrival at Hamburg, and their placement in camps, caused such an international outcry that *The Exodus*'s journey has been recorded in historical sources, and in popular culture, as a key catalyst leading to the end of British rule in Palestine and the creation of Israel.[29] While Jenkins J obviously could not be aware of the events that would follow his ruling, he must have been very aware of the passengers' journey before the legal case reached him. *The Times*, for example, covered the story extensively in July and August 1947 (Jenkins J ruled in *ex parte Greenberg* on 27 and 29 August). The coverage in *The Times* pitted disruptive 'Jews' against 'patient' and 'honourable' British soldiers carrying out 'distasteful'

[27] *Ex parte Greenberg*, 551–556, Jenkins J.

[28] 'Settling in at Poppendorf' (9 September 1947) *The Times*.

[29] R. Gruber, *Exodus 1947: The Ship that Launched a Nation* (New York: Random House, 1999); A. Halamish, *The Exodus Affair: Holocaust Survivors and the Struggle for Palestine* (Syracuse: Syracuse University Press, 1998); D.C. Holly, *Exodus 1947* (Annapolis: Naval Institute Press, 1995, rev., orig. 1965); Y. Kaniuk, *Commander of the Exodus* (New York: Grove Press, 1999). Most famous, of course, is Leon Uris's highly fictionalized novel *Exodus*, and the film adaptation.

duties.[30] The stories of the refugees' journey were often placed next to ones condemning 'Jewish terrorists' in Palestine, including one about a plot to bomb London. For example, on 8 September 1947, a story entitled 'Plot to bomb London—Zionists under arrest' was placed immediately above one entitled 'Ocean Vigour at Hamburg—Disembarkation delayed' (the *Ocean Vigour* was the ship to which the refugees had been transferred for their journey to Hamburg).

Perhaps the most striking aspect of Jenkins J's decision was his failure to mention that the ship's passengers were Jewish (this fact is contained in the case headnote only) or that any catastrophic events had recently occurred in Europe. There was no mention of war, much less of any specific experience undergone by Jewish people. These silences suggest Jenkins J deliberately chose to deem these facts irrelevant to the legal issue before him. The judge referred to the passengers as 'illegal immigrants' throughout the judgment and their 'champions' as 'the Jews'. He remarked that 'many of the Jews' had organized 'parties of Jews from Europe' whom they sent to Palestine and that controversy over such journeys had gone on 'for many years'.[31]

Jenkins J's use of the phrase 'illegal immigrants' was deliberate, and followed the Government's use of the term in court. D.N. Pritt, as well as affidavit evidence presented to the court, referred to the claimants as 'displaced Jews', a phrase Jenkins J chose not to repeat.[32] In his oral argument, Pritt also made reference to the passengers' background, which he referred to as 'their tragic experience of life in Europe in the last seven or eight years'.[33] However, once the judge chose to deem this context irrelevant, it became entirely unremarkable that he took no interest in the prospect of the passengers being sent to Germany, which Jenkins J referred to merely as the ship's 'next destination', which the 'immigrants' intended to go on to 'of their own free will'.

While *ex parte Greenberg* could be analysed as an exemplar of how adherence to legal formalism results in the marginalization of extrinsic 'political' factors, I would argue that it represents more

---

[30] I.e. 'Lessons of Hamburg' *The Times* (10 September 1947).
[31] The stories about the ship in *The Times* highlight Jewish 'plotters'.
[32] See documents in National Archives, CO537/2403.   [33] Ibid., CO537/2403, 277798, p. 30.

than this. It is not that Jenkins J ignores the extrinsic factor of the mass killings of Jewish Europeans, and simply focuses on the 'legal' question; it is that he attempts to set out a history, identifies the claimants' strategy, ignores references made in court to the mass killings, so obviously expresses distaste with the stubbornness of the 'illegal immigrants' and the illegal activity of their Jewish 'champions', and explicitly says he is going to dispose of the case on the 'short ground'. Legal formalism, to the extent it is evident, is thus, I would argue, an ideologically driven route adopted consciously, informed and shaped in itself by 'extrinsic' projects of racialization.

The case of *ex Parte Greenberg* was not an isolated example of such judicial indifference to the mass killings. Other cases dealing with Jewish refugees during this period similarly edited out the facts of the situation leading to the refugees' escape, offering unexplained euphemisms as contextual asides. Judges, during these years, might refer to the 'exile' of the Jewish litigant, or use the phrase 'the troubles' to describe the circumstances leading to the refugees' flight.[34] While one judge mentioned 'persecution', another, Harman J, described a Jewish woman as having 'failed to emerge from the ghetto of Krakau'.[35] As late as 1959, in a divorce case, a Jewish wartime refugee was said to have come to England in the 1930s 'as a result of political developments in Czechoslovakia'.[36] Again, in several cases, the events that motivated Jewish Germans to leave Germany are simply ignored altogether.[37] At the same time, 'holocaust' continued to be used in commercial cases throughout the 1960s.[38]

This period in my Holocaust chronology is thus characterized by a lower case deployment of holocaust to reference a disaster or onslaught of some sort, and no reference to the Holocaust to signify the mass killings of Jewish Europeans by the German

[34] *Igra v Igra* [1951] P 404; *Evans & Barrs v Kramer* [1957] EGD 350.

[35] *R v Owen* [1957] 1 QB 174; *Loudon v Ryder (No. 2)* [1953] 1 All ER 1005. See further discussion of this last case in Chapter 2.

[36] *Pachner v Parker (formerly Pachner)* [1960] 1 All ER 159.

[37] Ie: *Adrema Werke Maschinenbau GmbH v Custodian of Enemy Property and the Administrator of German Enemy Property (No.1)* [1956] RPC 301.

[38] *Sadler Bros v Meredith* [1963] 2 Lloyd's Rep 293; *Garnac Grain v HMF Faure & Fairclough* [1966] 1 QB 650. Outside of legal discourse, the continued use of the term in commercial and other contexts during this period is confirmed by Petrie's research: see 'The Secular Use of the Term Holocaust'.

state. However, these killings went virtually unacknowledged by English judges in any other way throughout the 1940s and 1950s. Indeed, the case of *ex parte Greenberg* evinces total indifference to these millions of deaths, while slightly later cases euphemistically make small references to vague troubles or ignore the events altogether. It is also worth remembering that, in a number of other cases where Jews appeared in English case law during this immediate post-war period, the judges' discussion of the Jewish litigant's character was often highly derogatory (see Chapter 2), and, in others, Jewishness was deemed to be an unknowable concept (see Chapter 3).

1970–1986

By the early 1970s, a new willingness to acknowledge the extent of the wartime killing is apparent amongst some of the judiciary. The word 'extermination' is used in relation to Jews for what appears to be the first time,[39] and in *Meyer* v *Meyer*, Bagnall J, in a case about the validity of a divorce under German law in the Third Reich, couples 'extermination' with the phrase 'the final solution'.[40] However, until the mid 1970s, there is no reference to 'the Holocaust' whatsoever. In 1975, the House of Lords decision in the combined cases of *Oppenheimer* and *Nothman* constituted a brief, and isolated, rupture in this silence.[41] In order to fully appreciate the rhetorical shifts represented by this judgment, it is worth retracing a set of decisions in a series of 'Nazi law' cases leading up to *Oppenheimer* and *Nothman* that I have thus far left unexplored.[42]

The case *The King* v *Home Secretary, ex parte L* was amongst the first in which English judges were faced with the validity of the 1941 German decree depriving Jewish Germans living outside of

---

[39] *Szechter* v *Szechter* [1970] 3 All ER 905. Jocelyn Simon P's (whose mother, I believe, was from a Jewish family) decision is, in my view, a very empathetic judgment to which I cannot begin to do justice here. The litigants, an academic and a poet, who, as a baby, had been thrown from an Auschwitz-bound train, have written about their histories in N. Karsov and S. Szechter, *Monuments are not Loved* (London: Hodder and Stoughton, 1970).

[40] *Meyer* v *Meyer* [1971] 1 All ER 378, Bagnall J. This is another example of a more nuanced, knowledgeable judgment.

[41] *Oppenheimer* v *Cattermore/Nothman* v *Cooper* [1976] AC 249, HL.

[42] See also D. Fraser, '"This is not like any other legal question": A Brief History of Nazi Law before U.K. and U.S. Courts' (2003–4) 19 *Connecticut J. of International Law* 59–125; J.G. Merrills, 'One Nationality or Two? The Strange Case of *Oppenheimer* v. *Cattermole*' (1974) 23 *International & Comparative Law Quarterly* 143–59; J.G. Merrills, '*Oppenheimer* v. *Cattermole*—The Curtain Falls' (1975) 24 *International & Comparative Law Quarterly* 617–34.

Germany of their German citizenship.[43] Needless to say, the main people affected by this decree were Jewish refugees who had fled for their lives. *Ex parte L* involved two Austrian brothers, who, by virtue of the Anschluss and subsequent German laws in 1938, suddenly found themselves to be German citizens. They quickly left Austria for France, where they remained until 1941, when, as a result of the decree of that year, they lost their German citizenship. According to the case headnote, the brothers, 'who were Jews within the meaning of that decree', were then 'minded to go to South America'. They left Europe by sea, and, when the ship docked in Trinidad, the brothers were apprehended by the British as 'enemy aliens'. They were then transported to Britain, and immediately interned. They remained in internment until their application for a writ of *habeas corpus* was heard in 1944.

In a short judgment, like several discussed earlier not once mentioning that the brothers were Jewish, nor even that they had fled for their lives, Viscount Caldecote refused to recognize the validity of the 1941 decree on the basis that doing so would allow enemy states to plant saboteurs who could easily divest themselves of 'enemy' status: 'such changes of nationality are not recognised for very obvious reasons'.[44] The brothers were, in English law, Germans and therefore 'enemy aliens'.

The case of *ex Parte L* went on to play a significant role in subsequent ones dealing with the 1941 decree. In 1948, the Lowenthals, Jewish refugees from Germany who had settled in England, were denied the right to seek damages for infringement of a patent, a right denied to all nationals of enemy states.[45] According to the UK Government, the 1941 decree depriving them of their German nationality was not effective. Romer J agreed, relying on *ex Parte L*:

If such damages were to be permitted in time of war enemy agents might acquire facilities which could be used in a way very much to the prejudice of this country.[46]

The Lowenthals, like the brothers in *ex parte L*, were to remain 'enemy aliens' in British law. Until the 1970s, statements finding

---

[43] *The King* v *Home Secretary, ex parte L* [1945] KB 7.   [44] Ibid.
[45] *Lowenthal* v *Attorney-General* [1948] 1 All ER 295.   [46] Ibid.

the German wartime law invalid on grounds of national security, rather than any opprobrium for the decree itself, remained salient. As Griffiths, Macklin, and Kushner have all argued, and as the case law appears to confirm, the aftermath of the war, and increasing knowledge of German atrocities, did not result in a wave of compassion for Jewish refugees in England.[47] The judges in the cases of *ex parte L* and *Lowenthal* had no concern that their decisions might compound the profound racism already experienced by these litigants, indeed there was no recognition that any substantial suffering had occurred. These Jews were Germans because to say anything else would be to expose the British state to potential terrorism.

By the 1970s, however, as I have shown above, judicial notice had been taken of a German policy of 'extermination', and this was reflected in a final set of decisions on the 1941 decree. In the tax cases of *Nothman* and *Oppenheimer*, the government was pursuing two Jewish refugees, both naturalized British citizens, for taxes owed on income. The income involved various reparations-related pensions from Germany. The Inland Revenue alleged that, as British citizens, Nothman and Oppenheimer should pay the tax assessed on this income. The litigants argued that their German citizenship had remained intact and that, as dual citizens, they were owed relief under the double taxation agreements between the UK and Germany.

At first instance, in 1971 and 1972, Goulding J found for Nothman and Oppenheimer, arguing that the 1941 decree depriving them of their German citizenship was invalid on grounds of public policy.[48] As in the previous enemy alien cases, Goulding J maintained that an attempt to remove citizenship during a time of war could not be recognized. However, deploying a new discourse of moral opprobrium, he also added some obiter comment on the nature of the Nazi regime:

---

[47] R. Griffiths, 'The Reception of Bryant's *Unfinished Victory*: Insights into British Public Opinion in Early 1940' (2004) 38 *Patterns of Prejudice* 18–36; G. Macklin, ' "A quite natural and moderate defensive feeling"?: The 1945 Hampstead "Anti-alien" Petition' (2003) 37 *Patterns of Prejudice* 277–300; T. Kushner, *The Persistence of Prejudice: Antisemitism in British Society During the Second World War* (Manchester: Manchester University Press, 1989).

[48] *Nothman* v *Cooper* [1971] 50 ATC 526; *Oppenheimer* v *Cattermole* [1972] Ch 585.

...it would be an odd thing if the victorious end of a war, which in its later stages was presented as a crusade against the barbarities of the National Socialist regime, should lead *ipso facto* to the recognition, hitherto denied, of the Nazi's oppressive laws against the Jews.[49]

When the cases reached the Court of Appeal in 1973, the judges rejected the 'public policy' argument on the grounds that, once the war ended, and the 'enemy alien' problem was no longer salient, German law must be recognized.[50] The Court thus found the decree depriving Nothman and Oppenheimer of their German citizenship valid, although, in doing so, they took some notice of the fact that the decree might have been morally, if not legally, wrong.

...the question whether or not the person is a national or citizen of the country must be answered in the light of the law of that country however inequitable, oppressive or objectionable it may be.[51]

By 1976, when the House of Lords reached their decision in the cases, the terms of discourse had changed again. The Lords found the decree invalid on human rights grounds.[52] According to Lord Hodson, the 1941 decree was 'notorious' and could not be recognized by English courts:

The courts of this country are not in my opinion obliged to shut their eyes to the shocking nature of such legislation as the 1941 decree if and when it falls for consideration.[53]

Lord Cross argued that the deprivation of citizenship and property on purely 'racial grounds' is 'so grave an infringement of human rights that the courts of this country ought to refuse to recognise it as law at all'.[54]

The strongest and most detailed condemnation of German policy was left to Lord Salmon:

The expense of transporting large numbers of men, women and children, in all 6,000,000, even without heat, food or sanitary arrangements must have been considerable. So no doubt was the expense of erecting, equipping and staffing concentration camps and gas chambers for their extermination. Evidently, the Nazis considered it only natural that the confiscated

---

[49] *Oppenheimer* (1972) 595.   [50] *Oppenheimer* v *Cattermole* [1973] Ch 264.
[51] Ibid., Buckley J.   [52] *Oppenheimer* v *Cattermore/Nothman* v *Cooper* [1976] AC 249.
[53] Ibid., 265.   [54] Ibid., 278.

assets of those who had been lucky enough to escape the holocaust should be used to finance it . . . [55]

Lord Salmon concluded that 'the barbarity of the Nazi legislation . . . is happily unique' and found that 'the 1941 decree was so great an offence against human rights' that it could not be recognized in English courts.[56]

However, for Mr Oppenheimer and Ms Nothman, the decision did not end here. Although the 1941 decree was declared invalid, and thus their dual citizenship should have been recognized, the Lords found that a 1949 German law required that Jewish German refugees reapply for German nationality if they wished to have it reinstated. As neither litigant had reapplied under the terms of this statute, the loss of their German citizenship remained intact. Thus, despite the lofty remarks of the judges, Ms Nothman and Mr Oppenheimer were left having been stripped of their German citizenship—although, now, they were themselves to blame,[57] with no acknowledgment made of the fact that many Jewish German refugees found the idea of being made to apply for German citizenship repugnant on a number of grounds.

Nevertheless, Lord Salmon's 1976 reference to 'the holocaust' in connection with the killing of 6,000,000 Jews appears to have been the first such use of holocaust in English case law. It was perhaps just a 'coincidence' that it is the only Jewish judge in the House of Lords who speaks of 'the holocaust' in this way. In any event, while there continued to be references in subsequent cases to various kinds of holocausts—in the *Hunter* case, for example, the reference was to the Birmingham pub bombing, and, in *Hayward* v *Thompson*, to an onslaught of media attention[58]—there were none to 'the Holocaust' until more than ten years after Lord Salmon's remarks.

The series of decisions in *Oppenheimer/Nothman* thus stands out rather as an anomaly in this legal history of the Holocaust. Yet, I would argue that the three court judgments in the case represent a struggle, evident in the 1970s more generally, to come to terms with the legacy of the mass killings of Jewish Europeans, a struggle that was not apparent in the case law prior to this period. The moral condemnation of German killing policies common to all

---

[55] Ibid., 281.   [56] Ibid., 282–3.
[57] See also Fraser, '"This is not like any other legal question"'.
[58] *Hayward* v *Thompson* [1982] QB 47; *Hunter* v *Chief Constable of West Midlands* [1982] AC 529.

three levels of decision-making in the case was unprecedented, and, as I shall shortly show, Lord Salmon's recitation of the 6,000,000 figure, his references to deportation, transportation, and gas chambers, were, in fact, never to be seen again (other than in 'denier' trials) and were, at the time, anything but banal. If, as La Capra argues, what is important in recalling the Holocaust is to substantively engage it, *Oppenheimer/Nothman* possibly represents the English judiciary's high-water mark in this regard.[59]

Cases Post-1986

In the mid 1980s, 'the Holocaust' appeared for the first time in two reported cases. One was a minor reference in a National Front-related defamation decision;[60] however, in the second, Lord Hailsham, in a criminal case about the doctrine of duress, remarked:

We live in the age of the Holocaust of the Jews, of international terrorism on the scale of massacre, of the explosion of aircraft in mid-air, and murder sometimes at least as obscene as anything experienced in Blackstone's day.[61]

The idea that the phenomenon 'the Holocaust of the Jews' constituted an 'age' was unprecedented in English case law. That it appears here as stock footage in an entirely unrelated case about criminal duress is, however, indicative of subsequent developments, as I go on to show. Lord Hailsham's juxtapositions are also revealing in terms of how the Holocaust comes to be inserted into a series of seemingly unrelated evils, where the mass killing 'of the Jews' is equivalent to an aircraft explosion or an individual's murder. Nevertheless, Lord Hailsham's remarks appear to be the first mention of 'the Holocaust' as an incontrovertible fact, as taken for granted and indisputable.

And, yet, for nearly another ten years, this appears to remain the only such notice that English judges take (in reported decisions) of 'the Holocaust'. Indeed, some cases continue to deploy the older uses, as for example, in a 1988 insolvency case, where the judge refers to 'the holocaust of ordinary creditors'.[62] Even as late as 1994, in another case about a disaster at sea, the judge, quoting the

---

[59] La Capra, *Representing the Holocaust.*   [60] *Verrall* v *Guardian Newspapers* (26 June 1986).
[61] *R* v *Howe* [1987] 1 AC 417.
[62] *Re Tucker* [2000] BPIR 859 (decided in 1988); *Dormeuil Freres* v *Feraglow* [1990] RPC 449.

plaintiff's lawyer, remarks that, 'it is hardly possible to imagine anything more horrific than the holocaust on Piper Alpha'.[63] However, within a very few years, these older usages had entirely disappeared to be replaced by an explosion of references to 'the Holocaust' in a diverse range of judgments.[64]

In 1997, the first of several cases referring to 'the Holocaust' in refugee appeals occurred. Simon Brown J, noting the origins of the Refugee Convention, remarked that:

... those displaced from their homelands by the horrors of the Holocaust years, and were still unable to return, were particularly deserving of refugee status.[65]

In 1999, the *Pinochet* judgment contained two references to 'the Holocaust'.[66] Also in that year, an animal rights-related harassment case elicited this comment from the judge:

I do not attach great significance to it, but the fact is that Mr Zwirn is Jewish and references to 'burning' and 'gas' and the 'holocaust' are, perhaps, understandably, more painful to him than they might be to others. I have no reason to suppose that the defendants or any of the persons concerned have used that sort of language with that deliberate intention because their contention, no doubt, is that animals killed for their fur are often gassed and that carcasses are disposed of by burning and it is a short step to call that a holocaust in relation to the animals.[67]

In 2000, two cases covering ground that, at the outset of this chapter, I noted I would sideline, war crimes and 'denial' prosecutions,

---

[63] *McFarlane* v *EE Caledonia Ltd* [1994] 2 All ER 1.

[64] A consideration of the more general history and cultural politics of the Holocaust in Britain is beyond the scope of this chapter, although this story inevitably forms a backdrop to the legal history I explore here. The comparatively late adoption of the capitalized phrase 'the Holocaust' in the UK generally can be explained by a number of overlapping historical, colonial, socio-political, religious, geographical, and demographic factors, including those discussed by: O. Almog, *Britain, Israel and the United States, 1955–1958: Beyond Suez* (London: Frank Cass, 2003); N.J. Ashton, ' "A Special Relationship Sometimes in Spite of Ourselves": Britain and Jordan, 1957–73' (2005) 33(2) *J. of Imperial and Commonwealth History* 221–44; D. Cesarani, *Justice Delayed: How Britain Became a Refuge for Nazi War Criminals* (London: Mandarin, 1992); M. Haron, 'Britain and Israel, 1948–1950' (1983) 3(2) *Modern Judaism* 217–23; T. Kushner, *The Holocaust and the Liberal Imagination* (Oxford: Blackwell, 1994); T. Lawson, 'The Anglican Understanding of Nazism 1933–1945: Placing the Church of England's Response to the Holocaust in Context' (2003) 14(2) *Twentieth Century British History* 112–37.

[65] *Adan* v *Secretary of State* [1997] 2 All ER 732.

[66] *R* v *Bow Street, ex parte Pinochet* [2000] 1 AC 147. Once uttered by Lord Phillips, who refers to two American cases about restitution claims 'in respect of the holocaust', and then by Lord Millett: 'war crimes and atrocities of the scale and international character of the Holocaust are crimes of universal jurisdiction'.

[67] *Zwirn* v *Gravett* (15 October 1999).

received widespread popular attention.[68] The Court of Appeal upheld the conviction, under the War Crimes Act 1991, of Anthony Sawoniuk for murders of local Jewish people committed in what is now Belarus in the early 1940s.[69] Although the decision makes several references to Nazi policies of 'extermination', the judges do not refer to the Holocaust at all. And yet, that same year, in the approximately 200-page trial judgment in *Irving* v *Penguin Books*, the Holocaust is constantly invoked; this is unsurprising as the case specifically addressed the question of whether or not David Irving was a 'Holocaust denier'.[70] But what is interesting about this judgment for my purposes here is how the Holocaust, within a relatively short space of time, had become so entrenched in English legal discourse that it could be coupled with 'denier' in such a common-sense manner.

This proliferation of 'the Holocaust' in English cases is evident in a number of other decisions since the mid 1990s. In the *Briody* case, for example, a litigant's medical negligence claim for post-traumatic stress disorder was compared (by her lawyer) to the suffering 'of Holocaust and torture victims';[71] and in both *Krotov* and *European Roma Rights*, the Holocaust was deployed by the judges as part of an asylum-denying discourse (I return to this below).[72] Other cases invoking 'the Holocaust' include ones concerning: the human rights of council tenants; libel; family law; wills and probate; a 'holocaust restitution claim'; and an action seeking permission to dig up King Harold's possible remains, where we learn that a forensic scientist has had experience examining the bones of Holocaust victims.[73]

In *R* v *Kirk*, a case with facts similar to the *Zwirn* decision (see above), a package sent by an animal rights activist to a

---

[68] See also sources in n. 2, and Fraser's discussion of the earlier *Gecas* case, *Law After Auschwitz* 264–75.

[69] *R* v *Sawoniuk* [2000] 2 Cr App R 220.

[70] *Irving* v *Penguin Books* (11 April 2000); [2001] All ER (D) 257 (refused leave to appeal).

[71] *Briody* v *St Helen's and Knowsley Health Authority* [2000] 2 FCR 13.

[72] *Krotov* v *Sec of State* [2004] EWCA Civ 69; *European Roma Rights Centre* v *Immigration Officer at Prague Airport* [2003] 4 All ER 247.

[73] *Harrow LBC* v *Qazi* [2003] 2 FCR 43; *Re P* [2000] 15 Fam 476; *Glatt* v *Glatt* (10 December 1999); *AG* v *Trustees of the British Museum* [2005] EWHC 1089; *Re Holy Trinity* [2004] 2 All ER 820. Although 'the Holocaust' was not specifically referred to in *Al Almeri (FC)* v *RB Kensington & Chelsea* [2003] EWCA Civ 235, a refugee housing case, the judge did invoke the film *Sophie's Choice* and mention the phrase 'gas chambers'.

scientific laboratory was found to be 'obscene'. Written on the cover of the package were words suggesting the recipients were carrying out acts similar to those of 'Dr Mengele' at 'Auschwitz'. The package also had a swastika drawn on it. In upholding the jury's finding of obscenity relating to these words and image, the judge commented that such a conclusion 'needs no explanation', despite the fact that the defendant had no intention of insulting 'holocaust survivors'.[74]

Ken Livingstone, then Mayor of London, was another who claimed to have no such intentions when he likened a Jewish journalist to a 'German war criminal'.[75] In overturning a tribunal's decision to impose a four-week suspension as mayor on Livingstone for his exchange with the journalist, Collins J referred to 'the holocaust' towards the end of his judgment in a passage condemnatory of Livingstone's refusal to apologize for his remarks. He noted that 'those who had survived the holocaust' would have been particularly offended by Livingstone's accusation and this should have been acknowledged in an apology.[76]

Most recently, the Holocaust was mentioned in a case relating to the publication of a comic entitled 'Holohoax',[77] and in a decision originating in Northern Ireland about two former Republican fighters (who had served extensive jail terms) who applied for jobs at a community centre for homeless people.[78] This latter case progressed to the House of Lords, where the Court found that the two men, who had been denied employment based on their previous histories of violence, had not suffered discrimination on grounds of political belief. The Lords defended the right of the community centre to express not only its fears for its users but also its abhorrence of past violence and to do this through a denial of an employment opportunity. Making no attempt to place the reference in any context, Lord Roger remarked:

The parallel with Jewish refugees who lost relatives in the Holocaust is striking. In the 1960s, it would surely have been unthinkable for

---

[74] *R v Kirk* [2006] EWCA Crim 725.

[75] *Livingstone v Adjudication Panel for England* [2006] All ER (D) 230.

[76] Ibid., para. 45. Collins J went on to find that Livingstone was not acting in his capacity as mayor at the time of the exchange, and that, even if he had been, he was exercising a protected speech right.

[77] *R v Sheppard* [2010] All ER (D) 204.   [78] *McConkey v Simon Community* [2009] UKHL 24.

Parliament to legislate, say, to force such a Jewish restaurateur to serve a German professor who had spoken in support of Hitler's anti-Semitic policies during the Nazi regime...[79]

Leaving this peculiar example to one side (and the all too common refusal to recognize that such a restaurateur might have also been 'German'), the analogy remains as yet another Holocaust abstraction: a deployment of 'the Jew' that creates a parallel between the experience of Jewish refugees and a community centre's employment policies and between former IRA soldiers and a Nazi ideologue—one that results in a denial of employment to ex-prisoners based on their former histories of violence.

Finally, I want to mention the Supreme Court's decision in the *JFS* case, where 'the Holocaust' made one appearance. I examine in detail the three decisions in this case in the next two chapters. For the purposes of this one, I simply wish to note the following comment of Lady Hale's:

No parliament, passing legislation to protect against racial discrimination in the second half of the twentieth century, could possibly have failed to protect the Jewish people, who had suffered so unspeakably before, during, and after the Holocaust.[80]

While Parliament's intentions vis-à-vis race relations legislation were not as clear cut as Lady Hale suggests (as I show in Chapter 6), it is the routinized appearance of 'the Holocaust' here (in a case that has nothing to do with it) that is noteworthy. For Lady Hale does nothing with this knowledge other than to find a *Jewish* school has violated *English* law. What purpose is the abstracted victimhood of 'the Jewish people' serving here? I return to this question below.

In tracing the emergence of 'the Holocaust' in English case law, it becomes clear, leaving Lord Salmon's dicta in *Oppenhiemer/ Nothman* to one side, that the phrase—as referring to the mass systematic killing of Jewish Europeans by the German state—did not enter the English judicial lexicon until the mid 1980s, where its utterance by Lord Hailsham in a criminal law case appeared strangely incongruous and out of place. It then took another ten years for 'the Holocaust' to re-emerge as a taken-for-granted

---

[79] Ibid., para. 32.   [80] *R(E)* v *Governing Body of JFS* [2010] IRLR 136, SC, para. 67.

phenomenon, references to it 'needing no explanation'.[81] Of equal interest in this most recent period is the fact that the older, generic uses of 'holocaust' become scarce after 1988, and disappeared entirely after 1994.

It was not until the mid 1990s, then, that English case law witnessed the entrenchment of the Holocaust as a signifier of the mass killings of Jewish Europeans in the early 1940s. And yet, the splicing in of this trope, now almost formulaic in its appearance, occurred within a process of mechanical routinization unapparent in the 1970s cases more than 20 years earlier. At the same time, the Holocaust begins to do other, problematic work in these more recent judgments. I pursue both these arguments by returning in more detail to a selection of the contemporary cases.

THE FATHER IS A SURVIVOR OF THE HOLOCAUST: *Re P* AND OTHERS

I first return to a case I considered in Chapter 4—*Re P*, a family law judgment in 2000, led by Butler-Sloss J, concerning the welfare of a fostered child.[82] Briefly, the court decided that a disabled child, born into an orthodox Jewish family but raised by Catholic foster parents from an early age, should remain with the foster carers. Here, I am not interested in analysing the decision in this case or in exploring the court's construction of the child's best interests (but see Chapter 4). For the purposes of this chapter, what I wish to attend to is the Holocaust language deployed by Butler-Sloss J as she proceeds to judgment. She summarizes the birth family's background as follows:

N is the fourteenth child of an orthodox Jewish rabbi and his wife. The father is 64 and was headmaster of a Jewish school. The mother is 54. Two of the 14 children still live at home, aged 12 and 9. The father is a survivor of the Holocaust and was detained in concentration camps with his family, many of whom died. No doubt as a result of his experiences, he has a morbid fear of illness and hospitals.[83]

---

[81] *R v Kirk* [2006] EWCA Crim 725.   [82] [2000] 15 Fam 476.
[83] Ibid., 479. I have discussed elsewhere the use of the word 'detained', and the reference to the father's 'morbid fear', see D. Herman, '"I do not attach great significance to it": Taking Note of "the Holocaust" in English Law' (2008) 17 *Social & Legal Studies* 427–52.

At the same time, we learn little factual detail about the foster family, other than that there are also a number of children and that they are 'non-practising Roman Catholics'.[84] Nor do we discover any traumatic histories the foster parents might have. Which thus leaves the question: why does she mention that the Jewish father is a 'survivor' at all?[85]

Perhaps this can only be made sense of in light of a number of other remarks the judge makes:

This is clearly not a case where the parents have made repeated and unreasonable applications. It is none the less a case where the emotions run extremely high and the parents have an added religious dimension to the incentive to get the child back to them. They were unable to accept the decision in 1994 and the decision in 1998. There is no reason to suppose that they will accept the decision of this court. They have been unable to indicate that they will not make a further residence application. They have asserted in their evidence and through their counsel on this appeal their fervent belief that N's home is with them and within the orthodox Jewish community. She was born a Jew and remains a Jew wherever she may live and however she may be brought up. Her place-ment with the foster parents is, as I have already set out under the part dealing with contact, unacceptable to them and they seem unable to recognise that this issue is decided and cannot be relitigated.[86]

In describing the Jewish parents as 'unable to recognise' English legal decisions, Butler-Sloss J appears to suggest that the parents are either stubborn, wilful, irrational, or perhaps some combination of these. The representation of Jews and Jewishness as foreign to English law is a common refrain in judicial discourse, as I have discussed in detail in Chapter 2. Butler-Sloss J also splices in another familiar trope, albeit one originating in the court below, suggesting that the Jewish parents are to blame for their own misfortune: 'they tended to blame others for the decisions which they made'.[87] All of this language suggests to the reader that the Jewish parents' psychic investment in attempting to maintain their

---

[84] *Re P*, 480.

[85] Family law texts make no mention of this aspect of the case, see B. Hale, D. Pearle, E. Cooke, and D. Monk, *The Family, Law & Society: Cases and Materials* (Oxford: Oxford University Press, 2009); S. Harris-Short and J. Miles, *Family Law: Text, Cases and Materials* (Oxford: Oxford University Press, 2007); J. Herring, *Family Law* (Harlow: Pearson, 2009); J. Masson, R. Bailey-Harris, R. Probert, *Cretney: Principles of Family Law* (London: Sweet & Maxwell, 2008).   [86] *Re P*, 491–2.

[87] Ibid., 483.

child's Jewish identity is evidence of their emotional instability; and, perhaps further, a manifestation of their selfish refusal to recognize their own culpability in creating the situation in which they now argue for victimhood status (see also discussion of race relations cases in Chapter 6).

Perhaps this, then, is the purpose ultimately served by us knowing that 'the father is a survivor of the Holocaust'; that he is scarred, damaged, and over-emotional, unable to know what is best for his daughter. But, then, if he was simply 'detained' for some time, while some of his family unfortunately 'died', why is he so 'fervent'? Butler-Sloss J manages to both downgrade the severity of the mass killings while at the same time implicitly suggesting the father is overly passionate because of them.

Butler-Sloss J's depiction of the Jewish father—the 'survivor of the Holocaust'—must also be read alongside how she chooses to describe the foster parents. Although there are many passages in the judgment that suggest the foster parents are equally overcome by emotion, Butler-Sloss J affirms Wall J's view that their 'level of intensity' was something 'impressive',[88] definitely 'not selfish',[89] and she chooses to 'commend' their 'devotion'.[90] Butler-Sloss J's admiration for and intense empathy with the foster parents is apparent throughout her judgment, ultimately culminating in her decision not only to deny the birth parents' application, but to limit their contact with the child as well. In terms of this latter move, it is perhaps telling that the birth parents contact with the child, deemed 'beneficial' for the child in uncontradicted evidence,[91] is turned by Butler-Sloss J into something that has not 'yet' had an 'adverse affect'.[92]

If, in Butler Sloss J's recitation of facts, we learn something about the fervency of Jews, and little, explicitly, about the passion of Christians,[93] that in itself is nothing new. English case law, as I have discussed elsewhere throughout this book, is replete with such racializations. But, in the context of the themes of this particular chapter, I want to emphasize here what Butler-Sloss J's

---

[88] Ibid., 480.   [89] Ibid., 484.   [90] Ibid., 492.   [91] Ibid., 487.   [92] Ibid., 488.

[93] Other than those of Butler-Sloss J herself: 'I have never really reflected very much on what I think; I tend to feel what I do, rather than intellectualize it. I am instinctively a Christian': E. Butler-Sloss, 'Matters of Life and Death' in C. Chartres (ed.), *Why I Am Still an Anglican: Essays and Conversations* (London: Continuum, 2006) 55. See also her lecture, 2006.

discourse accomplishes in terms of both routinization and racialization. On the one hand, the montage she puts together in 'the survivor' passage serves both to trivialize and distance herself from the father's wartime experiences. In this sense, the Holocaust appears in 'stock footage' format—its insertion engenders passivity and indifference. It does not trouble, challenge, or provoke in any way. On the other hand, 'the survivor' passage, when read in conjunction with Butler-Sloss J's other remarks about the respective litigants, works to construct the Jewish parents as racial others. This racialization process is not innocent; it engenders judicial passion, it strips away empathy, and it facilitates the severing of the birth parents' link to the child.

Butler-Sloss J is not alone in her treatment of the Holocaust. In the recent case law, where, in the 1990s, English judges suddenly took note of it, the Holocaust's appearance was, for the most part, a repetitive reference that, in Barbara Zelizer's terms, could be construed as a 'remembering to forget'.[94] To return to my opening quote, this routinization is evident in Lord Hailsham's reference to 'the Holocaust of the Jews' to make a point about the incidence of violence in a duress case.[95] In *Harrow* v *Qazi*, Lord Scott makes a banal reference to the Holocaust in a case about a council housing tenancy.[96]

The work performed by references to the Holocaust in contemporary refugee cases in particular serves both to mythologize the past and erect an obstruction that the claimants are unable to overcome. In *Krotov*, a refugee claimant soldier who had deserted the Russian army due to atrocities in Chechnya was told by the judge that 'even in the midst of the horrors of the Nazi Holocaust' soldiers could opt not to participate in such activities.[97] In *European Roma Rights*, Simon Brown J was not persuaded that the persecution of Roma peoples in the Czech Republic amounted to the 'spectre of a fresh Holocaust'.[98]

---

[94] B. Zelizer, *Remembering to Forget: Holocaust Memory Through the Camera's Eye* (Chicago: University of Chicago Press, 1998).

[95] *R* v *Howe* [1987] 1 AC 417. Particularly when we know that Lord Hailsham was an outspoken opponent of the War Crimes Bill, counselling against it partly on the grounds that it reeked of 'Old Testament revenge', see D. Cesarani, *Justice Delayed* 254. Lord Hailsham was also vehemently opposed to the Race Relations Act 1976: see Chapter 6.

[96] *Harrow LBC* v *Qazi* [2003] 2 FCR 43.   [97] *Krotov* v *Sec of State* [2004] EWCA Civ 69.

[98] *European Roma Rights Centre* v *Immigration Officer at Prague Airport* [2003] 4 All ER 247. I have come across two decisions involving Jewish refugee claimants. In one, *R (Bodzek)* v *Special Adjudicator*

Although 'the Holocaust' was not uttered, the use of 'the Holocaust Jew' as an example appeared in *Shah*, another refugee case,
where Lord Hoffmann, in constructing parallels between the 'social
groups' of 'Pakistani women', and 'Jews', began a passage with
the words: 'Suppose oneself in Germany in 1935'.[99] Using a Jewish
shopkeeper as his example, Lord Hoffmann went on to discuss the
various ways in which Jews were subject to persecution in the 1930s,
explaining, for the purposes of his argument, how the German state
was complicit in acts of violence during this period. The passage is
not long, but it is noticeably detailed and nuanced, and it is deployed
in order to assess the culpability of the Pakistani state in the
oppression of women. However, Lord Hoffmann's efforts are reproduced to opposite ends in another refugee case two years later. Lord
Berwick, rejecting the claim of the Roma appellant, dismissed an
argument put before him as 'a variation of the case of the Jewish
shopkeeper described by Lord Hoffmann'.[100] In *Fornah*, Auld J also
quoted Lord Hoffmann's remarks in *Shah*—again, in the service of
denying the refugee's claim.[101]

My argument in this section has been that references to the
Holocaust in contemporary English cases contribute to processes
of myth-making and/or racialization. Taken-for-granted, routine
references to the Holocaust suggest an 'everyone knows about the
evil Holocaust' past that obfuscates the actual, earlier history of
judicial indifference and disregard. At the same time, this myth of
'particularly deserving'[102] Jews is often deployed as part of a

[2002] EWHC 1525, the Polish claimants' application was eventually successful after three appeals.
In the other, a South African man who claimed asylum based on his anti-apartheid beliefs and
eligibility for the South African draft, was told by four legal fora that, as a result of his 'close ties'
to Israel (where he had gone to university), and his 'Jewish race', he should move there instead (he
had also stated his opposition to Israeli military policy and his eligibility for the draft there), see *R v
Immigration Appeal Tribunal, ex parte Miller* [1988] Imm AR 1, QB; [1988] Imm AR 358, CA.

[99] *R v Immigration Appeal Tribunal, ex parte Shah* [1998] 4 All ER 30.
[100] *Horvath v Sec of State* [2001] 1 AC 489.
[101] *Fornah v Secretary of State* [2005] EWCA Civ 680, para. 38. A different approach can be found in
Al Almeri (FC) v RB Kensington & Chelsea [2003] EWCA Civ 235 where Lord Bingham implicitly
rebukes Buxton LJ's comment, in the court below, that 'Sophie's Choice' was a real choice: 'It would be
wholly unrealistic to suggest that a child selected by Sophie for the gas chamber had died of Sophie's
own choice.' However one might want to problematize the use of 'Holocaust' analogies, which in this
case was used to draw a parallel between 'Sophie's choice' and the lack of housing choice of a destitute
refugee, at least here the result was in the refugee's favour. See also *R v Sec of State for Education, ex
parte Talmud Torah Machzikei Hadass School Trust* (12 April 1985), where Woolf J found the Holocaust
background of the school's founders to be a relevant factor in understanding the school's ethos.
[102] *Adan v Secretary of State* [1997] 2 All ER 723.

discourse denying contemporary refugees safe haven. Finally, I have also argued that references to the Holocaust can act as a form of racialization, rendering contemporary Jewish litigants unappealing. Here, the Holocaust becomes a mark of foreignness, of strangerness to both the English and English law, and this echoes judicial discourse in a number of other, non-Holocaust-related, cases (see Chapters 2, 3, 4).

CONCLUDING REMARKS

I have focused here on the emergence and deployment of the Holocaust in English case law. While, prior to the end of the twentieth century, the judges had some language for describing the German-led systematic mass killing of Jewish Europeans, the phrase 'the Holocaust' did not become a standard refrain in the judicial repertoire in England until the 1990s. Prior to the 1970s, the Holocaust was not invoked, and references to the mass killings of Jewish Europeans were vague or non-existent. The case of *Nothman/Oppenheimer* in the early/mid 1970s represents a high-water mark of judicial engagement with German atrocities, while throughout this period generic uses of holocaust continued. The 1990s witnessed a proliferation of Holocaust rhetoric in English case law, and the virtual disappearance of the generic references to holocaust.

The next section examined some of these recent cases in more detail and my argument there had three elements. First, in the vast majority of cases containing the Holocaust or remarks about the events the phrase was intended to depict, the reference was mindless, made without awareness, an everyday, routine utterance in judgments that had nothing to do with mass killings of any kind. I include here the medical negligence, criminal law, family law, and human rights cases.[103] In one of the two most recent decisions, the Holocaust appears to facilitate reasoning that finds it justifiable to discriminate against former IRA members as if they were equivalent to Nazis, and the discriminating agency equivalent to Jewish

---

[103] It can be argued that animal rights cases are about state-sponsored mass killings, but I am not able to address that issue here. For a view defending Holocaust analogies in animal rights activism, see, for example, D. Sztybel, 'Can the Treatment of Animals be Compared to the Holocaust?' (2006) 11(1) *Ethics & the Environment* 97–132.

victims.[104] In the other, the Holocaust appears to show the judge's understanding of this mass murder, while she goes on to find that Jewish religious law violates English race relations law.[105] In these kinds of examples, the Holocaust works as a form of stock footage, engendering passivity and indifference to, and a misremembering of, not only the events the phrase is intended to recall, but also a lesser known wartime English history of indifference, internment, and collaboration.

Second, in the contemporary refugee decisions, the effect of the Holocaust's appearance in judicial discourse often facilitates the denial of the claim. References to the Holocaust and the myth of past, abstracted 'deserving Jews', often distance the judges from their moral responsibility in the here and now. In this sense, these decisions are in keeping with what Zygmunt Bauman has called the 'civilising tendency' of the Holocaust itself.[106] In other words, the Holocaust was itself partly the outcome of imposing a rationality divorced from moral concerns.

Third, I argue that in some cases, *Re P* being my primary example, references to the Holocaust, or to the events the phrase denotes even if the phrase is not used, work to construct Jewish litigants as strange, stubborn, and selfish. While there are not many such cases in my 'holocaust' sample, there are many more instances of such representations of 'the Jew' where the Holocaust does not make an appearance, as other chapters in this book make clear. Butler-Sloss J's narrative in *Re P* splices the Holocaust into this familiar English rendition on Jews and Jewishness; its performance there makes 'the Jew' of her judgment unappealing. Rather than offering any understanding of the Holocaust and its effects on the applicant father, Butler-Sloss J deploys the Holocaust as a mnemonic device to remember what is alien about 'the Jew'.[107]

Thus, contemporary appearances of the Holocaust can be seen as continuous with and also different from the older, wartime cases. Following the shift in racialization discourse I documented in Chapter 2, in a 'post-Holocaust' era an explicit linking of race

[104] *McConkey* v *Simon Community* [2009] UKHL 24.
[105] *R(E)* v *Governing Body of JFS* [2010] IRLR 136, SC.
[106] Z. Bauman, *Modernity and the Holocaust* (Ithaca: Cornell University Press 1989) 28.
[107] I am not suggesting Butler-Sloss J does this intentionally; I am arguing this is the 'work' the reference does in her judgment.

with bad character is less possible; judicial racialization processes became focused on identifying and condemning un-English behaviours. In 2000, the Jewish father in *Re P* remains as alien to the court as Sabine Greenberg, the 'illegal immigrant' of the *Exodus* case in 1947. Ironically, the father's status as a 'Holocaust survivor' facilitates this process of alienization.

Chapter 6

'THE WANDERING JEW HAS NO NATION':[1] JEWISHNESS AND RACE RELATIONS LAW

This chapter examines the interaction between Jews, Jewishness, and English law through a legal framework that explicitly seeks to protect minority groups from discrimination.[2] Unlike the other material I have explored in this book, in which Jews and Jewishness appeared in a range of substantive legal areas not directly concerned with 'race' or 'religion', UK race relations law aims to provide redress to minorities who have suffered from negative treatment based on their membership in a protected 'racial group'.

In England, the official history of minority groups is now usually told through this concept of 'race relations', a term in use since the 1960s. It refers to both the state of inter-racial relations, and successive governments' responses to the perception of such relations through legislation and policy initiatives. Until the late twentieth century, the dominant race relations narrative, as I shall discuss further below, was almost exclusively one of 'Black and White'; in other words, the perceived race relations 'problem' was represented as being one of the reception and assimilation of peoples of Afro-Caribbean and south Asian origin by the white English. More

---

[1] *Mandla v Dowell Lee* [1982] 3 All ER 1108, per Denning LJ.

[2] In April 2010, the Equality Act 2010 received Royal Assent. This Act replaces the Race Relations Act 1976 (as well as a number of other pieces of legislation). In this chapter, I continue to refer to the RRA 1976, as all the jurisprudence I discuss arose under this statute. RRA 1976 case law will continue to shape understandings of 'racial' and 'ethnic' groups under the Equality Act 2010, as the actual provisions remain unchanged.

recently, this gaze has alighted upon 'the Muslim', a figure in which concepts of race and religion cohere (as with 'the Jew'), while popular and governmental perceptions of the 'Afro-Caribbean problem' have honed in on the figure of the 'disaffected young Black man'.

In Chapter 2, I explored how issues to do with the reception and assimilation of newcomers arose vis-à-vis the migration of eastern European Jewish refugees around 100 years ago. And, in Chapter 1, I traced briefly some earlier histories of discrimination faced by Jewish people in previous centuries. While the phrase 'race relations' was never in use during these earlier periods, many of its perceived problems, particularly a notion of assimilation failure, are not at all new.

However, for the most part, academic accounts of race and racism in England fail to take account of these older histories, nor do scholars, whether mainstream or critical, usually attend to contemporary racialization processes that do not conform to dominant narratives of race (see discussion in Chapter 1). Popular and academic accounts of race relations in the UK largely dovetail. Both offer a similar story: the history of race relations begins with Black and Asian immigration in the middle parts of the twentieth century. Popular renditions start with the arrival of Afro-Caribbean immigrants aboard the *Empire Windrush* in 1948, which, for example, is described by the BBC as the first 'seminal moment' in 'UK race relations' (also ignoring the long history of south Asian, east Asian, and black presence in England).[3] Media and other similar accounts then tend to consist of a list of 'riots', racist incidents, and legislative initiatives from the middle and latter parts of the twentieth century, culminating in the Macpherson Report in 1999,[4] and reports of further 'racial conflict' in the early years of the new century. The 'race' of race relations means perceived skin colour, and/or, more recently, Muslimness, and the 'relations' white vs black/Asian.[5] Official statistics collection operates, more or less, on the same basis: 'The ethnic minority population includes many distinct

---

[3] News.bbc.co.uk/1/hi/uk/1517672.stm. Last accessed 5 July 2010.
[4] *The Stephen Lawrence Inquiry, A Report of an Inquiry by Sir William Macpherson of Cluny* (Cm. 4262-I, February 1999).
[5] See also the Commission for Racial Equality's 'race relations history': cre.gov.uk/40years/. No longer accessible, copy on file with author.

ethnic and religious groups. The original migrants came from different regions including the West Indies, Indian subcontinent and Africa.'[6] It is significant that neither Jews nor Sikhs, the paradigmatic ethnic groups for the purposes of the Race Relations Act 1976, are allowed to identify themselves as belonging to an 'ethnic group' in the UK census, only as a religious one.[7]

Most academic accounts in the social sciences do little to trouble this dominant race relations narrative, although some inject much-needed postcolonial perspectives into the frame. However, there is a resounding silence when it comes to racialization processes involving persons now deemed 'white'. Nor is there any acknowledgment that notions of 'white' and 'black' are not fixed but change over time in response to historical and social conditions. The racialization of Irish, Jewish, and Roma peoples in England, for example, is almost entirely ignored, including, how, historically, they were perceived as 'not white'. Unfortunately, this is largely the case in both socio-legal and critical legal work on 'race' and 'religion', as I explained in Chapter 1.

In the following pages, I first provide a brief parliamentary history of British race relations legislation. I then examine a number of legal cases in detail, both those involving Jewish claimants, and others ostensibly having nothing to do with Jews but which nonetheless draw on Jewishness in some way. In tracing this discourse, I make four key arguments. First, I show how the abstracted figure of 'the Jew' was deployed by all sides in parliamentary debates about race relations legislation. For supporters of legal intervention, references to Jews and the Holocaust enabled positive analogies with other groups coming under racist fire at various periods. For opponents of intervention, 'the Jew' provided a paradigmatic victim from which other immigrant groups and their experiences could be differentiated, a process similar to some uses of 'the Holocaust', as I explained in the previous chapter.

---

[6] J. Dobbs, H. Green, and L. Zealey, *Focus on Ethnicity and Religion*, *National Statistics* (Basingstoke: Palgrave Macmillan, 2006).

[7] I come back to the census issue in the next chapter. The Office for National Statistics has decided to continue with the omission of Jews and Sikhs from the 'ethnic group' category in the 2011 census; however the category of 'Arab' has been added: see 'Deciding which Tick-Boxes to Add to the Ethnic Group Question in the 2001 England and Wales Census' (Office for National Statistics, 2009); 'Final Recommended Questions for the 2011 Census in England and Wales: Ethnic Group' (Office For National Statistics, 2009).

My second argument is that despite all the talk about Jews in race relations cases after the Race Relations Act 1976 (RRA), their actual status as a 'racial group' under this legislation has never been adjudicated, only presumed. In other words, no English legal decision has ever elucidated how and why Jews fit into the Act's categories. Third, I demonstrate how, until late 2009, not a single Jewish claimant ever won a reported case under the RRA 1976, and that no Christian has ever been found to have engaged in discriminatory acts against Jewish persons (in reported cases under the RRA 1976). My intention is not to argue that Jews lose more cases than others, but that the contrast between this lack of success and the generic rhetoric about Jews in the cases (as I discuss below) is remarkable.[8] Finally, I reflect on how the book's themes of orientalization, secularism, Christianity and conversion play out in this legal context.

'THE JEW' IN PARLIAMENTARY DEBATE ON RACE RELATIONS LAW

Race Relations Act 1965

The first piece of race relations legislation in the UK was the Race Relations Act 1965. While subsequent legislation extended the scope, application, and administrative mechanisms of this Act in various ways,[9] the basic principles of non-discrimination and non-incitement of racial hatred, as well as the grounds upon which discrimination would be prohibited—'colour, race, or ethnic or national origins'—have remained virtually unchanged ('nationality'

---

[8] Unfortunately, as I explained in Chapter 1, a comparison between how Jews have fared under the RRA 1976 with other protected groups is beyond the scope of this project. Certainly, ample evidence suggests that a large proportion of complaints to employment tribunals citing 'racial grounds' are unsuccessful, and more unsuccessful than other types of discrimination cases: see, e.g., A. P. Brown and A. Erskine, 'A Qualitative Study of Judgments in Race Discrimination Employment Cases' (2009) 31(1) *Law & Policy* 42–159; M. Peters, K. Seeds and C. Harding, 'Findings From the Survey of Claimants in Race Discrimination Employment Tribunal Cases (SETA RRA)', Employment Relations Research Series No. 54, Department of Transport and Industry, 2006.

[9] This Act, for example, applied only to places of 'public resort' (i.e., hotels and restaurants) and not housing or employment, and, unlike subsequent Acts, was largely criminal not civil in terms of enforcement and was in this sense exemplary of the UK's gradual shift from understanding racial discrimination as a public order matter to one of 'race relations'. A general analysis of changes to the specific provisions in various incarnations of race relations law over the last fifty years is beyond the scope of my concerns here; however, where particular developments are relevant to my themes and arguments I will discuss them.

was added in 1976: see below). References to 'coloured' people and persons abound in the Home Secretary's speeches and clearly indicate that the driving force behind the government's introduction of race relations legislation was the perceived problems occasioned by growing Afro-Caribbean and Asian 'new arrivals' (and not, as Lady Hale claimed in 2009, 'the Holocaust'),[10] and, indeed, the 1965 Act had been preceded three years earlier by new, restrictive immigration law.[11]

Nevertheless, and perhaps unsurprisingly, the legislative debates from the mid 1960s are peppered with references to Nazi Germany and the mass killings of Jewish Europeans, demonstrating that these spectres were never far from at least some politicians' minds. While the fullest exposition on German anti-Jewish policies, and their relevance to the need for race relations law, was provided by Barnett Janner, a Jewish MP,[12] others, on both sides of the debate, made similar references. John Binns, while paying lip service to the 'gas chambers of Auschwitz', spent most of his speech outraged about 'Asiatics and Pakistanis who cannot speak a word of English . . . and come straight from the tribal villages of Pakistan and their ideas of personal hygiene are absolutely different from ours',[13] suggesting that had he been able to contribute to the Alien Act debate in 1904 he would have said something very similar about the Jewish eastern Europeans arriving on British shores (see Chapter 2). Henry Brooke MP noted that 'this House must never forget that about six million Jews were put to death as a result of Hitler', while, at the same time, arguing that antisemitism was virtually unheard of in England these days and was therefore no excuse for introducing freedom-infringing legislation of this sort.[14] Other MPs, contrarily, argued that antisemitic incidents in England

---

[10] Frank Soskice, MP, Hansard, cols 926, 942, 104 (3 May 1965). See Chapters 5 and 7 for discussion of Lady Hale's comments in the context of the *JFS* case.

[11] Commonwealth Immigrants Act 1962. That is *not* to say that this was the primary motivation for those non-Cabinet politicians championing the legislation, in particular the Act's original architects Barnett Janner and Anthony Lester. Indeed, Janner explicitly condemned the link with immigration control in his Commons speech, 3 May 1965, col. 960. See also, A. Lester, 'The Politics of the Race Relations Act 1976' in M. Anwar, P. Roach, and R. Sondhi (eds), *From Legislation to Integration: Race Relations in Britain* (Basingstoke: Macmillan, 2000) 24–39.

[12] *Hansard*, HC, cols 956–8, ibid.   [13] *Hansard*, HC, col. 1005 (16 July 1965).

[14] *Hansard*, HC, cols 962–3 (16 July 1965).

occurred both in the recent past and were currently on the rise, justifying the legislation partly on that basis.[15]

Several MPs, with varying motivations, were concerned as to whether the Act would even apply to Jews, and, in response to a direct question on this matter, the Home Secretary stated an unequivocal 'yes'.

It is certainly the intention of the Government that people of Jewish faith should be covered ... a person of Jewish faith, if not regarded as caught by the word 'racial' would undoubtedly be caught by the word 'ethnic', but if not caught by the word 'ethnic' would certainly be caught by the word 'national' ... he would certainly have an origin which many people would describe as an ethnic if not a racial one.[16]

The issue of whether the Act would apply to Jews was generally raised in connection with the meaning of the word 'ethnic'.[17] The Government's response to questions concerning the meaning of this word was simply to state that it was intended to avoid any ambiguity over the meaning of 'race'; in other words, 'ethnic' was meant to catch anyone it might be argued was not a 'race', but was still 'distinguished by skin colour'.[18] While there were a couple of references to Cypriots and Maltese falling into this category (and an implicit assumption that they would not be caught by 'national origins'), it seems clear that the term was not being used as one of art, but merely as a means of avoiding contentious debates about biological race.[19]

At the same time, the Home Secretary tied the word 'ethnic' to the phrase 'blood origin',[20] demonstrating that the two concepts— race and ethnicity—were by no means theorized or even disentangled at a basic level (witness the reference above to 'skin colour'). As I discuss later in the chapter, it was left to the judiciary, perhaps unfortunately, to try and work it out. Indeed, when a question about the application of the Act to 'gypsies' was raised, the Home

---

[15] See, e.g., *Hansard*, HC, Freeson MP, col. 965 (16 July 1965); Foot MP, ibid., cols 1039, 1043; Hogg MP, ibid., cols 1062–3.

[16] *Hansard*, HC, col. 933 (16 July 1965).

[17] See, for example, *Hansard*, HC, Buck MP, cols 1029–30 (16 July 1965); Renton MP, cols 969–70 (16 July 1965).

[18] *Hansard*, HC, Soskice MP, col. 932 (16 July 1965).   [19] Ibid., cols 971–2.

[20] Ibid., col. 933 (16 July 1965).

Secretary replied that this 'is one of the fringe questions which it is difficult to answer...possibly that is one of the puzzles which ultimately will come before the court'.[21] The Race Relations Act 1965 received Royal Assent in November, 1965; however, within a year, there was a concerted attempt to expand its provisions.

The Racial and Religious Discrimination Bill 1966, introduced by Lord Brockway, a campaigner for race relations legislation for some years previous, sought to expand both the Act's coverage (to housing and employment) and, additionally, include 'religion' in the list of grounds upon which discrimination was prohibited. A series of antisemitic incidents in the summer of 1966 was clearly a large part of the motivation,[22] as was a continued anxiety as to whether Jews were covered by the existing Act.[23] Nothing, however, came of this Bill and it was not until the spring of 1968 that legislation was introduced by the government to expand the Act's coverage to housing and employment. Religion, however, continued to remain off the agenda.

Race Relations Act 1968

The new Act extended the remit of the provisions to a wider array of public places, as well as housing and employment. It also made significant changes to the administrative and enforcement mechanisms. 'The Jew' figured once again in debates on the proposed Bill and, as on earlier occasions, was deployed by speakers on both sides of the issue. While by this point virtually no speaker paid attention to antisemitic incidents, several continued to make use of the abstracted figure of Jewish victimhood in other ways.

Opponents of the Bill, for example Rees-Davies, an MP not known for his empathy towards racial minorities, argued that the Bill might force Jews to employ Germans in their homes (Jews and Germans being clearly distinct persons in his mind),[24] while Lord Conesford used the example of Jews setting up their own insurance companies in order to avoid discrimination in insurance provision

[21] Ibid., col. 983 (16 July 1965).
[22] *Hansard*, HL, cols 2–4 (14 June 1966); also Lord Russell (7 July 1966); Lord Brockway, cols 1857–9 (19 December 1966).
[23] *Hansard*, HL, Lord Soper, col. 1862 (19 December 1966).
[24] *Hansard*, HC, col. 338 (9 July 1968).

as a reason why legislation was not necessary.[25] On the other hand, Lord Hirshfield, a Jewish peer, spoke of the need for 'the Jew to stand up fearlessly and give an example of humanity towards another minority group',[26] while Lord Walton referred to past anti-Jewish prejudice as a rationale for strengthening the legislation.[27]

By 1968, then, it seemed there was no question (within Parliament) that Jews were covered by the Act, and, at the same time, there was a clear perception that antisemitic incidents were largely a thing of the past (despite the outcry over them just two years previously). The new Act received Royal Assent in October, 1968, and, once again, was accompanied by legislation further restricting immigration.[28]

Race Relations Act 1976

The Bill that passed through parliament in 1976 contained, with some amendment, the provisions that currently govern the field, in so far as my subsequent discussion of race and ethnicity is concerned. Although the Equality Act 2010 repealed the RRA 1976, the definition of 'racial group' remains exactly the same. As explained by government ministers at the time, the impetus for legislating anew in the mid 1970s came partly from assessing the shortcomings of the previous legislation, and partly from the experience of passing the Sex Discrimination Act 1975. The new Act was to be modelled on that one.[29] The Bill included the new ground of 'nationality' and contained provisions for indirect discrimination, large private clubs, and a new Race Relations Commission empowered to take positive action. Once again, the stated motivation for the Act was to further the advancement of 'coloured' people; once again, government ministers tied race relations protections into an agenda of immigration control.[30]

Throughout the debates, the figure of 'the Jew' made several appearances. Enoch Powell, in railing against the Bill, suggested

---

[25] *Hansard*, HL, col. 86 (15 July 1968).   [26] Ibid., col. 80.
[27] *Hansard*, HL, col. 1304 (25 July 1968).   [28] Commonwealth Immigration Act 1968.
[29] See *Hansard*, HC, cols 1547–57 (4 March 1976).
[30] Ibid., col. 1547 (4 March 1976); see also N. Bamforth, M. Malik and C. O'Cinneide, *Discrimination Law* (London: Sweet & Maxwell, 2007) 778–9.

that the low birth rate amongst Jewish immigrants could not be compared to the explosion of the black population,[31] while Thomas Torney MP referred to Jews, pogroms, and concentration camps to underpin his support of the Bill.[32] Jill Knight MP, in opposing the entirety of the Bill but particularly a provision requiring employers to keep 'racial records', objected 'to the idea that anyone who is Jewish, for example, shall have this fact put down on his records. That brings back echoes of the 1930s.'[33] More than one member, in a question that appears never to have been answered, again raised the issue of whether Jews were covered by the Act,[34] while others referred to the gradual elimination of antisemitism through informal means as reason to avoid legislation,[35] or, in language reminiscent of debates ten years previously, argued that Jewish people should not be forced to employ Germans.[36]

During a Lords debate over an amendment to add 'religion' to the grounds, Lord Hailsham, an outspoken opponent of nearly all aspects of the Bill, had this to say on the subject:

Now Jews, if the noble Lord, Lord Janner, will forgive me, come all [sic] shapes, sizes and colours. There are black Jews called Falashas in Ethiopia; there are yellow Jews called something else in China; and there are white Jews with fair hair and blue eyes, with the best Aryan characteristics, in Europe. They come all shapes and sizes. They are not a race, and it is folly to believe they are. But some of them—not all of them, I am sorry to say, but some of them—have a religion. If you want to discriminate against Jews, it is no use discriminating against people with long noses; you must discriminate against people who will not eat bacon—and that is a religious discrimination.[37]

Although Lord Hailsham seems clear in this charming passage that if Jews suffer discrimination it is because of their religion, somewhat later in the same debate he remarked: 'Are the Jews a nation? In my opinion, they are not a race but they may be a nation.'[38] Lord Hailsham gave no indication as to how this suggestion might fit with his earlier remarks about race, or whether,

---

[31] *Hansard*, HC, col. 1583 (4 March 1976).   [32] Ibid., col. 1619.
[33] *Hansard*, HC, col. 1648 (8 July 1976).
[34] Ibid., cols 1847–8; HL, col. 55 (27 September 1976).
[35] *Hansard*, HC, col. 1866 (8 July 1976).   [36] *Hansard*, HL, col. 62 (27 September 1976).
[37] Ibid., cols 53–4 (27 September 1976).   [38] Ibid., col. 67.

if Jews were a nation, they would therefore be caught by the RRA 1976's ground of 'national origins'.

Also on this same day in the Lords, an amendment was introduced to remove the word 'ethnic' from the legislation, thus provoking one of the very few legislative debates on that term's meaning. However, Lord Harris, the Home Office Minster, simply repeated the justification from ten years previously, that its inclusion was intended as a catch-all. However, Lord Harris did slightly elaborate, arguing that 'ethnic' was intended to 'get away from the idea of physical characteristics' and 'introduce the idea of groups defined by reference to cultural characteristics, geographical location, social organisation, and so on'.[39]

Race Relations Amendment Act 2000, Equality Act 2006, and Equality Act 2010

The Race Relations Amendment Act 2000, the first substantive revision to the 1976 Act, imposed a positive duty on the public sector to promote race equality, as well as bringing public authorities within the ambit of the Act's jurisdiction (with some exceptions). Once again, 'the Jew' made several appearances in these debates. In defending the amendments in the Lords, Lord Lester, an architect of the RRA 1976 subsequently appointed to the House of Lords, made the following observation:

...discrimination based on ethnic or national origins is as much racial discrimination as the definition of racial discrimination in Article 1 of the United Nations Convention...Such discrimination involves treating one individual less favourably than another for what is not chosen by them but for what is innate in them at birth—their genetic inheritance— whether as ethnic Jews, Roma gypsies or Hong Kong Indians. It is as invidious and unfair as is discrimination based on the colour of a person's skin.[40]

While Lord Lester clearly differentiates 'ethnic' from 'skin colour', he nevertheless attaches a required 'genetic' component to it. Lord Peston, arguing the changes did not go far enough, offered a rather confusing narrative of ethnic, race, and religious discrimination:

---

[39] Ibid., col. 74.   [40] *Hansard*, HL, col. 144 (1999).

...I remembered that when I was a young man the Jewish boys at my school had to change their names in order even to secure an interview at medical school. You simply could not even get to the starting point of applying to medical school with a Jewish name. Boys who were called Cohen changed their names to Conn while those named Levi became Lefford. That was religious rather than race discrimination. But that is merely to argue a technicality.[41]

While Hilton Dawson MP made the following observation:

Recently in Lancaster... the leader of the city council—became the victim of a campaign of abuse and vilification. He is Jewish and he takes his religion seriously... that campaign was so concerted that the impact it had on that individual was probably disproportionate to the impact that it would have had on someone from a different racial background.[42]

Stephen Twigg MP, in his speech in support of the Bill, referred to historical antisemitism and Holocaust education.[43]

During the debates on this Bill, other parliamentarians, critical of how race relations case law had developed in the intervening years, deployed Jews and Sikhs to demonstrate the incoherence of Muslim exclusion and to argue for a religious discrimination provision:

The House of Lords made a decision, which I welcome, that Jews and Sikhs constitute a racial group and are entitled to protection under the Race Relations Act. They can be defined by their ethnic as well as their religious identity. So a black Jew from Ethiopia, a white Jew from Russia and a brown Jew from Lebanon are all treated as belonging to the same ethnic race for the purposes of English law, whereas black, white and brown Muslims from exactly the same countries are not.[44]

...the problem [is] how to give British Muslims the right to effective remedies for arbitrary discrimination and unequal treatment of the kind that people like myself have if we are discriminated against as Jews on racial grounds... When, as an officer in the Army, I experienced discrimination, I could never tell whether the anti-Semitism was on racial or religious grounds.[45]

---

[41] *Hansard*, HL, col. 565 (11 January 2000).   [42] *Hansard*, HC, col. 1251 (9 March 2000).
[43] Ibid., cols 1265–7.   [44] Lord Ahmed, *Hansard*, HL, col. 455 (28 October 1999).
[45] Lord Lester, *Hansard*, HL, col. 471, ibid. Religious discrimination is now prohibited (with exceptions) under the Equality Act 2010.

So, twenty-five years after the 1976 Act, over thirty-five years since the original articulation of 'racial groups' in 1965 upon which the 1976 Act relied, parliamentarians seemed no closer to arriving at a coherent understanding of Jewishness (leaving aside, for the time being, whether such an understanding is possible). Lord Lester believes Jewishness to be a genetic inheritance while at the same time acknowledging that the line between race and religion discrimination is thin and wobbly, Lord Peston claimed the discrimination resulting in the Anglicization of Jewish names was religious in nature, Hilton Dawson MP refers to a Jewish man taking his religion seriously but then calls the discrimination he faced 'racial', and so on. In a brief comment during the debate on what became the Equality Act 2006, Baroness Scotland remarked: 'The Government believes it is right than an ethnic group is not defined by its religion but that it can in part be so defined.'[46] As mentioned above, the Equality Act 2010 did nothing to change the definition of 'racial group' as originally set out in the RRA 1976.

Part of the story I have explored in this section of the chapter confirms a familiar narrative in both popular and academic accounts of race relations in Britain. Key points in the parliamentary debates include that the initial motivation for race relations legislation in the 1960s was clearly to do with increased black and Asian immigration and the perceived 'racial tensions' arising from this, and that legislation restricting immigration accompanied race relations legislation on each occasion. So far, this is a familiar story, and, for the most part, popular and academic accounts of the development of race relations in Britain simply provide variations on this theme.

However, for the purposes of a study on Jews, Jewishness and the judiciary, there are several additional aspects of the debates to which I wish to draw attention that have been otherwise ignored. My second point, then, is that in all of the debates over the 45 years, a number of speakers, on both sides, made use of the abstracted 'Jew' and antisemitism. Jews and the German-led mass killings of Jewish Europeans in the 1940s figured both as examples of why new law was needed, and as examples of why it was not. For both

---

[46] *Hansard*, HL, col. 665 (9 November 2005).

supporters and opponents of race relations legislation, Jews were deployed as paradigmatic victims of racism. For supporters, this move enabled positive analogies with groups coming under racist fire at the time; for opponents, the Jew as paradigmatic victim enabled speakers to disassociate 'the Jew' from these other immigrant groups in order to render the latter undeserving.

Third, there was consistent confusion over the meaning of 'ethnic group', 'race', 'religion' and 'national(ity)'. In the 1960s, 'ethnic', at least within the official discourse of government ministers, was clearly tied to 'blood origin' and 'skin colour'. In 1976, there appeared to be a move away from biological characteristics to cultural ones, while, in 2000, 'ethnic' was once again described as something 'innate'. So far as Jews were concerned, the narratives of MPs contained a wide array of understandings that explicitly (as in Lord Hailsham's speech) or implicitly raised questions about the legal status of Jews and Jewishness. Was Jewishness a faith, a race, an ethnicity, a nationality or perhaps all of these? It remained, then, for the judges to attempt to address this question.

THE CASE LAW

Judicial representations of Jews and Jewishness in race relations law occur in two trajectories of cases. One involves Jewish claimants. Over the course of the 45 years or so that such legislation has been in place, the number of reported cases involving Jewish claimants consists of a small handful, almost entirely concerning claims of employment discrimination. Cases involving other claimants, but where Jews and Jewishness are discussed or alluded to by the judges in some way, comprise the second trajectory. I will explore each in turn.

Cases Involving Jewish Claimants

The first reported judgment, *Seide* v *Gilette Industries*, occurred in 1980, and thus under the 1976 Act.[47] I have related the details of this case previously, in Chapter 2, where I explored historical

---

[47] *Seide* v *Gillette Industries Ltd* [1980] IRLR 427.

patterns and shifts in judicial representations of strange and unpleasant 'Jewish behaviour'. Briefly, the case concerned Mr Seide, a Jewish man, who complained that he had received less favourable treatment at work due to his Jewishness. An Industrial Tribunal, and an Appeal Tribunal, disagreed. I do not wish to re-examine this decision in detail here. However, there are two points to which I would draw attention. First, Slynn J, the judge in the *Seide* case, in upholding the Tribunal's decision that the Jewish claimant was responsible for what had happened to him, set the tone for the cases that follow. Second, in two sentences buried in the judgment, Slynn J pronounced on the meaning of 'Jewish', and this was, eventually, to have some future impact.

... the Tribunal accepted that 'Jewish' could mean that one was a member of a race or a particular ethnic origin as well as being a member of a particular religious faith... It seems to us that their approach to this question was the right approach.[48]

As I explore further below, this unargued and undeveloped remark stands as the sole, explicit judicial articulation concerning whether Jewishness comes within the ambit of the RRA 1976 (and, in 2009, was relied on again by a Supreme Court judge in the *JFS* case: see Chapter 7).

Three years later, Browne-Wilkinson J, in the case of *Garnel*, another employment appeal decision I explored in Chapter 2, made no reference to *Seide* v *Gillette* in his judgment similarly dismissing the Jewish claimant's argument.[49] Here, there was no question that the Act applied: 'Mr Garnel is, by race, a Jew... As is well known, many of our most talented musicians are, indeed, Jews by race...'[50]

Although the judge clearly had firm ideas about racial classifications, and thus the application of the Act was not ever in question, like Slynn J in *Seide* v *Gillette*, Browne-Wilkinson J nevertheless found that the Jewish claimant had brought his troubles upon himself (see further discussion in Chapter 2).

---

[48] Ibid., paras 21–2.
[49] *Garnel* v *Brighton Branch of the Musicians' Union* (13 June 1983).
[50] Ibid.

Four years after this, in *Simon v Brimham*, the Court of Appeal upheld an Industrial Tribunal and Employment Appeal Tribunal's rejection of a claim by a Jewish man.[51] Although the judgment consistently refers to the claimant's 'Jewish faith', Lord Balcombe confidently stated:

It is not in issue before us that, if there had been discrimination against Mr Simon on the grounds of his Jewish faith, that would have been discrimination on racial grounds.[52]

Presumably, the employer had not attempted to argue that any discrimination suffered had been on religious not racial grounds (thus rendering the Act inapplicable); however, the court's repeated references to Mr Simon's 'Jewish faith' suggests judicial confusion. Unlike Browne-Wilkinson J in the *Garnel* case, these Court of Appeal judges appeared reluctant to make racial pronouncements and were, perhaps, relieved to simply repeat the phrase 'Jewish faith' from the tribunal below which had used it without any interrogation.

Simon v Brimham made an appearance two years later, in *Tower Hamlets v Rabin*, another claim of employment discrimination by a Jewish man.[53] Here, the Industrial Tribunal at first instance had upheld the complaint; however, on appeal, Wood J overturned this decision, ensuring that this case conformed to the pattern initially set by *Seide v Gillette*. In the *Rabin* case, Mr Rabin, the claimant librarian, argued that he had been passed over for certain posts and had, in effect, been discouraged from applying for them, due to his observance of the Jewish Sabbath and consequent inability to work on Saturdays. Wood J found that there was no evidence Mr Rabin had suffered any detriment within the meaning of the Act—that, effectively, there had been no discriminatory treatment and the tribunal had erred in law. In coming to his decision, Wood J made the following observations:

Before leaving *Simon's* case [i.e., the judge's consideration of *Simon v Brimham*] it is important to remember that although mention is made of 'the Jewish faith', that case had nothing to do with religious tenets, it was purely a question of 'the Jewish race' . . . [in the present case] one jury

---

[51] *Simon v Brimham Associates* [1987] IRLR 307.   [52] Ibid.
[53] *Tower Hamlets LBC v Rabin* [1989] ICR 693.

might decide that it was obviously on religious grounds, and that another, that although seemingly upon religious grounds it was in fact upon racial grounds. It is however unnecessary for us to decide this interesting issue.[54]

The unsettling question of unpacking the distinction between race and religion was thus, again, avoided.

In *Wetstein* v *Misprestige*, a 1993 decision, Peppitt J described the appellant, Mrs Wetstein, as 'a Sabbath Observant Jew'.[55] Although the case raised a number of concerns, the only issue before the Employment Appeal Tribunal was whether the employer's Saturday work policy discriminated against Jews on racial grounds. The tribunal at first instance decided that it did not, and the Appeal Tribunal found this decision was not factually 'perverse', despite the Tribunal's acknowledgement that fewer members of the group 'Jews' could comply with the policy than the group 'non-Jews'. The question of whether this was a case of racial or religious discrimination was, oddly, not addressed.

In *Highdorn* v *Saleh*, Reid J, on behalf of another Employment Appeal Tribunal, dismissed the allegations of discrimination on the basis that they were out of time.[56] Although the case turned on other issues, the judge had this to say about 'Jewishness':

Mr Saleh asserts that the non-dismissal discrimination claim was based on a series of acts of discrimination against him as a Jew during his seven years of employment with the company. It was suggested on his behalf that the discrimination in a company which is Jewish-owned arose primarily from this overt Jewishness, he being an orthodox Jew, and a desire in the company to present an [*sic*] 'white anglo-saxon' image to the outside world and that 'no religious Jew could ever be promoted to these front-line positions'. This suggests that his complaint may in reality be one of religious discrimination (which is not at present actionable) rather than racial discrimination (which is). Be that as it may ...[57]

In considering these few reported cases with Jewish complainants, it is clear that they share certain characteristics. First, all Jewish claimants lose their cases, usually at first instance as well as on appeal and, in so doing, they are often spoken of as disruptive

[54] Ibid., 703–4.
[55] *Wetstein* v *Misprestige Management Services Ltd* (19 March 1993).
[56] *Highdorn Co Ltd* v *Saleh* (16 August 2002).   [57] Ibid., para. 20.

and/or paranoid in some way (see Chapter 2). Second, with the exception of *Seide* v *Gillette*, where the reference is very brief, Slynn J suggesting that Jews can be a race, an ethnicity, and a religion, the decisions contain no discussion of how or why Jews constitute a racial group whatsoever. According to Browne-Wilkinson J, in his *Garnel* judgment, Jews are simply and obviously a race; in *Simon* v *Brimham* it is unclear although the language of 'race' is also used; in *Tower Hamlets* v *Rabin* Jewishness is both race and religion; in the *Wetstein* case the question is not addressed at all; and in *Highdorn* v *Saleh* it is unclear, although implicitly it would appear Jewishness is both race and religion. With the exception of the brief references in the case of *Seide*, not a single judgment discusses whether Jews are an 'ethnic group'. Even the *JFS* case, as I go on to explore later and in Chapter 7, simply asserts Jewish inclusion. Thus, the inclusion of Jews in the RRA 1976 appears as simply a matter of judicial 'common-sense'. I now turn to a series of decisions that deploy 'the Jew' paradigmatically to develop the category of 'ethnic group', despite the absence of actual Jewish persons.

Jews and Jewishness without Jews

In 1983, the House of Lords issued their unanimous decision in *Mandla* v *Dowell Lee*, a judgment that remains to this day the leading one on the meaning of 'ethnic origins' in the Act.[58] The claimant, Sewa Mandla, was the father of a Sikh boy, Gurinder, whose school had refused his request to wear his dastar (turban). The Court of Appeal, upholding Gosling J's decision at first inst-ance, dismissed the Mandlas' argument, under the RRA 1976, that Sikhs were an ethnic group, Denning J making liberal use of 'the Jew' in his judgment.[59] In overturning the Court of Appeal's decision, the House of Lords made few references to Jews and Jewishness, although they relied on a New Zealand case about Jews to ground their claim that Sikhs were, in fact, an ethnic group for the purposes of the RRA 1976. The language used by both courts in the course of their decision-making contains nearly the full panoply of judicial approaches to representing Jews and Jewishness, and so I will spend some time unpacking each in turn.

---

[58] *Mandla* v *Dowell Lee* [1983] 2 AC 548.
[59] *Mandla* v *Dowell Lee* [1982] 3 All ER 1108.

At the Court of Appeal, Denning LJ drew from a series of antiquated dictionaries, trust law cases (see Chapter 3), and other texts to determine that Jews were an ethnic group but Sikhs were not.

Why are the Jews given as the best-known example of 'ethnic grouping'? What is their special characteristic which distinguishes them from non-Jews? To my mind it is a racial characteristic...If a man desires that his daughter should only marry 'a Jew' and cuts her out of his will if she should marry a man who is not 'a Jew', he will find that the court will hold the condition void for uncertainty. The reason is because 'a Jew' may mean a dozen different things. It may mean a man of the Jewish faith. Even if he was a convert from Christianity, he would be of the Jewish faith. Or it may mean a man of Jewish parentage, even though he may be a convert to Christianity. It may suffice if his grandfather was a Jew and his grandmother was not. The Jewish blood may have become very thin by intermarriage with Christians, but still many would call him 'a Jew'. All this leads me to think that, when it is said of the Jews that they are an 'ethnic group', it means that the group as a whole share a common characteristic which is a racial characteristic. It is that they are descended, however remotely, from a Jewish ancestor...When Hitler and the Nazis so fiendishly exterminated 'the Jews', it was because of their racial characteristics and not because of their religion. There is nothing in their culture of language or literature to mark out Jews in England from others. The Jews in England share all of these characteristics equally with the rest of us. Apart from religion, the one characteristic which is different is a racial characteristic...Jews are not to be distinguished by their national origins. The wandering Jew has no nation. He is a wanderer over the face of the earth. The one definable characteristic of the Jews is a racial characteristic. I have no doubt that, in using the words 'ethnic origins', Parliament had in mind primarily the Jews. There must be no discrimination against the Jews in England. Anti-Semitism must not be allowed. It has produced great evils elsewhere. It must not be allowed here.[60]

Thus, in reasoning that Jews were clearly covered by the RRA 1976, Denning LJ relied on their connection to 'a Jewish ancestor', however 'remote'. This was, according to him, a 'racial

---

[60] Ibid., 1112–13. Lord Denning's reference to the trust law cases in the early part of this quote is odd given that by the time of *Mandla*, Denning himself had participated in a judgment more or less overturning these uncertainty cases: see Chapter 3.

characteristic' which, in turn, also made them members of an 'ethnic group'. Denning LJ then went on to claim, in distinguishing Sikhs from Jews, that there were no racial distinctions between Sikhs and 'other peoples of India' and that 'they are only to be distinguished by their religion and culture'.[61] Effectively, however, Denning LJ was arguing that there was no distinction between 'race' and 'ethnic group'.

While the other judges in the Court came to the same conclusion as Denning LJ, and dismissed the Mandlas' case, in insisting on a biological element to 'ethnic' they did not once discuss Jews or Jewishness. Kerr J, for example, stated that only orthodox Sikhs wore turbans and that, 'viewed as a group... the Sikhs are Indians, and in particular Punjabis; they are not a people or a group having any ethnic or national origin'.[62]

> It follows in my judgment that Sikhs and Sikhism do not as such fall within the Race Relations Act 1976 at all, any more than members of the Church of England, Catholics, Muslims, Quakers, or Jehovah Witnesses; or any other groups which are only distinctive because they adhere to distinct religious, political or social beliefs and customs.[63]

By omitting Jews from his list, Kerr J may have agreed with Denning LJ that the defining characteristic of 'the Jews' was a racial characteristic that these other groups lacked, or he may simply have not known what to do with them.

Before the House of Lords, the lawyers for the Mandlas rested their main argument that Sikhs were an 'ethnic group' upon the New Zealand case *King-Ansell* v *Police*, a decision that had, apparently, not been brought to the attention of the Court of Appeal.[64] In this case, under New Zealand's Race Relations Act 1971, that country's Court of Appeal was asked to determine whether Jews constituted an 'ethnic group' for the purposes of that Act. The New Zealand Act similarly excluded a 'religion' ground and gave no more guidance than the RRA 1976 as to the meaning of 'ethnic group'. In coming to their decision, the New Zealand Court of Appeal relied, in part, on the expert evidence of Dr Cluny Macpherson, an anthropologist whose research area was the

---

[61] Ibid., 1114.   [62] Ibid., 1122.   [63] Ibid.
[64] *King-Ansell* v *Police* [1979] NZLR 531.

peoples and cultures of Pacific Islanders. His opinion, that Jews were an ethnic group and not a race, was reproduced fulsomely in the judgment. Although the New Zealand Court found Dr Macpherson's definition of 'ethnic group' too broad:

Nevertheless the evidence which he gave as to the customs and beliefs founded in an historical background, which in his opinion characterised the Jewish people, was of critical importance to the case... the concept of a group of persons in New Zealand having common ethnic origins would include a group marked off from the generality of our society by shared beliefs, customs and attitudes of the kind attributed by Dr MacPherson to the Jews.[65]

What these beliefs, customs and attitudes consisted of was not elucidated by the Court (so far as the reported judgment is concerned). In his concurring judgment, Woodhouse J stated that there was a:

...depth of Jewish history and the unbroken adherence of Jews to culture, traditions, and a mutually intelligible language, as well as religion, so that they have maintained a distinct and continuous identity as a people for longer perhaps than any other than the Egyptians ... undoubtedly Jews in New Zealand are a group of persons with ethnic origins of the clearest kind.[66]

Near the start of his lead judgment in *Mandla* v *Dowell Lee*, Lord Fraser, in what was, in effect, the only remark (other than paraphrasing from *King-Ansell* v *Police*) on Jewishness in the House of Lords decision, noted that 'it is inconceivable that Parliament would have legislated against racial discrimination intending that the protection should not apply either to Christians or (above all) to Jews'.[67] Lord Fraser elucidated the criteria for 'ethnic group' according to several characteristics, two of which he deemed 'essential':

(1) a long shared history, of which the group is conscious as distinguishing it from other groups, and the memory of which it keeps alive; (2) a cultural tradition of its own, including family and social customs and manners, often but not necessarily associated with religious observance.[68]

---

[65] Ibid., Richmond J, 535.   [66] Ibid., 535–6, 539.
[67] *Mandla* v *Dowell Lee* [1983] 2 AC 548, 561.   [68] Ibid., 562.

Other, less essential, features of ethnicity, according to Lord Fraser, included a common geographical origin, language, and religion, and being an oppressed minority or dominant majority within a larger community. An ethnic group could include both converts and exclude apostates. So long as someone was a part of or joined such a group, and felt themselves to be a member of it, 'then he is, for the purposes of the Act, a member'.[69] Lord Fraser noted that the following passage from the *King-Ansell* decision, in support of the finding that 'Jews in New Zealand' did form an ethnic group, 'summed up in a way upon which I could not hope to improve the views which I have been endeavouring to express':

> ...a group is identifiable in terms of its ethnic origins if it is a segment of the population distinguished from others by sufficient combination of shared customs, beliefs, traditions and characteristics derived from a common or presumed common past, even if not drawn from what in biological terms is a common racial stock. It is that combination which gives them an historically determined social identity in their own eyes and in the eyes of those outside the group. They have a distinct social identity based not simply on group cohesion and solidarity but also on their belief as to their historical antecedents.[70]

As Mr Dowell Lee had conceded that if a broad interpretation of 'ethnic group' was to be taken Sikhs would fit into it, Lord Fraser spent little time assessing whether Sikhs met these criteria. All the other justices concurred with Lord Fraser's approach.[71]

Over the years, *Mandla v Dowell Lee*, and, either explicitly or implicitly, *King-Ansell v Police*, were cited again and again as authority for the definition of 'ethnic group'. In *CRE v Dutton*, both the passage from *King-Ansell* reproduced above, as well as Lord Fraser's set of criteria in *Mandla*, allowed the Court of Appeal to find that 'gypsies' constituted an ethnic group for the purposes of the RRA 1976.[72]

---

[69] Ibid.   [70] *King-Ansell*, 543, quoted by Lord Fraser.

[71] Lord Templeman issued another, concurring, judgment. See H. Benyon and N. Love, '*Mandla* and the Meaning of "Racial Group"' (1984) 100 *LQR* 120–36 and Bamforth, Malik, and O'Cinneide, *Discrimination Law* for further discussion of distinctions between the two judgments. Note that Stocker LJ, who agreed with the decision but 'reluctantly', questions Lord Fraser's reasoning in a way that bears further scrutiny; however, his judgment has been all but ignored in subsequent ones.

[72] *Commission for Racial Equality v Dutton* [1989] IRLR 8.

In *Morgan* v *Civil Service Commission*, a non-Jewish man alleged that he was not appointed to a post with the British Library on the grounds that he was *not* Jewish.[73] In other words, he argued that the appointing panel was prepared to hire only Jewish persons to the post. Although he lost his case, the Industrial Tribunal at first instance, and as a preliminary issue, stated unequivocally but without any argument (citing the *Seide* case in a subsequent judgment):

We conclude that the question of Jewishness or non-Jewishness is a matter relating to 'race' and to 'ethnic and national origins', and that to discriminate against a person on the ground that he is non-Jewish is to discriminate on 'racial grounds' within the meaning of the Act.[74]

The Court of Appeal dismissed Mr Morgan's appeal in January 1993.[75]

In *Crown Suppliers* v *Dawkins*, the Employment Appeal Tribunal was asked to determine whether 'Rastafarians' qualified as an 'ethnic group'.[76] Tucker J, overturning the decision of the first Tribunal, said no; Rastafarians were not separate ethnically from native or diasporic Jamaicans and hence they did not meet the *Mandla* criteria; most importantly the 'essential' criteria of having a long, shared history (a sixty-year tradition was deemed to be not long enough).[77] This decision was confirmed by the Court of Appeal in 1993.[78]

In *BBC Scotland* v *Souster*, the Scottish Court of Session held that English (or Scottish) persons could be protected by the RRA 1976 on the grounds of 'national origins', but not on grounds of 'ethnic group'.[79] The Court found that there were clearly distinct, historical nations within Britain, from which a person could claim to derive their origin; however, neither 'the Scots' nor 'the English' qualified under the *Mandla* criteria as 'ethnic groups'. Quoting liberally from both *Mandla* and *King-Ansell*, Lord Cameron argued that:

---

[73] (12 December 1989), IT. The full decision was issued on 2–3 April 1990.   [74] Ibid.
[75] *Morgan* v *Civil Service Commission* (13 January 1993).
[76] *Crown Suppliers (PSA)* v *Dawkins* [1991] IRLR 327.   [77] Ibid., paras. 18–19.
[78] *Crown Suppliers* v *Dawkins* [1993] IRLR 284.
[79] *BBC Scotland* v *Souster* [2001] IRLR 150.

... while it may be that within Scotland there are groups, for instance, the Gaels, who might lay claim to being an ethnic group, it is within judicial knowledge that the racial group which can properly be described as the Scots has a much wider and broader based cultural tradition than that which would constitute one of the two essential conditions or characteristics for an ethnic group. By the same token, I consider that the same observation applies to the racial group which can properly be described as the English.[80]

Thus, both the Scottish and the English lacked the 'distinctiveness of community' to qualify as 'ethnic'.[81] I return to this below.

In *R v White*, a prosecution under the Crime and Disorder Act 1998, a provision containing the same definition of 'racial group' as the RRA 1976 was in question.[82] Again quoting extensively from *Mandla*, Pill J held that the word 'African' did not denote sufficient distinctiveness to qualify for the term 'ethnic group'; however, he did find that 'African' qualified as a 'race':

In ordinary speech, the word African denotes a limited group of people regarded as of common stock and regarded as one of the major divisions of humankind having in common distinct physical features. It denotes a person characteristic of the blacks of Africa...[83]

However, lest anyone suggest the judge believed all peoples from any single continent formed a race, he went on to suggest that 'South Americans' would not qualify as a 'race' as there was too great a 'range of physical characteristics in the population of that continent'.[84]

These cases suggest that English judges have as much difficulty coming to terms with processes of racialization in the 'race relations' field as in any other legal area. Far from the interpretation of the RRA 1976 providing a fruitful jumping-off point for the intelligent development of understandings of racial and ethnic categorization, these cases instead exhibit, for the most part, confusion at best, and appalling ignorance at worst. Lord Fraser's speech in *Mandla*, achieving biblical authoritative proportions in subsequent cases, even states that 'Christians' were protected by the RRA

---

[80] Ibid., 33–4.
[81] See also Bamforth, Malik and O'Cinneide, *Discrimination Law* 818–821.
[82] *R v White* [2001] All ER (D) 158.   [83] Ibid., para.17.   [84] Ibid., para.19.

1976. Did Lord Fraser think Christians were a race, or an ethnic group, or that they shared a national origin? Who knows.

However, my concern here is not with making a general critique of the judiciary's approach in this area, but, rather, to elucidate how the judges understand and represent Jews and Jewishness in these race relations cases 'without Jews'. In furtherance of this objective, I would draw attention to two key points: (1) the *Mandla* case implicitly established Jews (and explicitly Sikhs) as an ethnic group for the purposes of the RRA by adopting evidence about Jews adduced by a New Zealand anthropologist in the case of *King-Ansell*; (2) all other cases attempting to define 'ethnic group' applied these same criteria with varying results, 'Gypsies' faring best, English, Scottish, Rastafarians, and Africans were deemed to be unethnic for varying reasons.[85] However, the inclusion of Jews as an 'ethnic group' in the RRA 1976 has never been debated or reasoned in English case law—not in cases with Jewish parties, and not in cases without.

The JFS Case

In 2009, the Court of Appeal, and then the new Supreme Court (replacing the House of Lords), overturned a decision confirming a Jewish school's right to determine who was Jewish for the purposes of its admissions policy.[86] In *JFS*, the claimant/appellant was a Jewish man claiming discrimination on behalf of his son, and his ex-wife—who was a convert to Judaism. The Jewish school was the respondent being accused of discrimination. The school argued that it had relied on the authority of the Office of the Chief Rabbi (OCR) to determine who was Jewish for the purposes of admission.

---

[85] In *Heron Corp Ltd* v *Commis* (24 June 1980), a man describing his father as 'Arab' was rejected for a position as chauffeur to a Jewish business couple. His claim under the RRA 1976 was upheld by an EAT. The decision contained no discussion whatsoever of the meaning of 'Arab' or where and how that term might fit into 'race or national or ethnic origins'. The applicability of the Act to the group 'Arab' appears to have been assumed without question—whether 'Arab' is a race, an ethnicity, a national origin; whether the term 'Arab' was irrelevant; or whether the relevant category here was 'non-Jewish'—were all questions left unasked much less pursued. In *Advance Security UK Ltd.* v *Musa* (21 May 2008), the phrase 'Middle-Eastern Arab Jordanian' was considered to be a designation of an 'ethnic group' (although the complainant lost his case). There does not appear to have been any further case law on this question but note that 'Arab' is set to be a new tick-box in the 'ethnic group' question on the 2011 census: see sources in n. 7.

[86] *R (E)* v *Governing Body of JFS* [2010] IRLR 136, SC; *R (E)* v *Governing Body of JFS* [2009] 4 All ER 375, CA; *R (E)* v *Governing Body of JFS* [2008] ELR 445.

The OCR recognizes Jewishness matrilineally (as does almost every other branch of Judaism in the UK). The mother must be Jewish, and she can be Jewish in one of two ways: her mother was Jewish (by being born to a Jewish mother or having converted); or, she has converted to Judaism in an appropriate conversion process. This has been the method of determining Jewishness in Jewish religious law for centuries and was not peculiar to the English OCR's requirements. However, the OCR's strict approach to conversion, that they would not recognize conversions performed by any Jewish denomination other than their own, Orthodox one, had come under intense criticism within some English Jewish communities for some time.[87] In *JFS*, the OCR did not recognize the mother's conversion as it had been performed by a rival denomination and so did not recognize the son as Jewish under Jewish law; therefore neither did the school, as its admissions policy with respect to the definition of Jewishness was determined by the OCR.

The father argued that the determination of Jewishness through matrilineal descent constituted race discrimination. In other words, the mother and son were being discriminated against because they were not genetically Jewish (in the eyes of the school), Jews were a protected ethnic group under the RRA 1976, and thus any discrimination on the basis of being Jewish, or, as in this case, not being assessed as Jewish, was contrary to the Act. The school (and the Secretary of State for Education) argued that the reason for the non-admission was religious, and not racial (and, as a 'faith school', they had the legal right to engage in religious discrimination[88]). The JFS did not dispute that the mother and son could be Jewish ethnically; the school's position was that, as the mother's conversion was not recognized by the orthodox branch of Judaism to which the school belonged, the son could not be considered Jewish under Jewish law, and the school's admissions policy was explicitly determined by Jewish law as interpreted by the OCR. If the mother

---

[87] A conflictual relationship between Orthodox and other Jewish denominations goes back to the first synagogues that broke away from the United Synagogues and established themselves as separate to the Chief Rabbi's authority in the late nineteenth century. The *JFS* case and the resulting divisions within Jewish religious communities as a result should be read in this context, but this is not the place to delve more deeply into this matter.

[88] Schools officially designated as having a 'religious character' are permitted to discriminate on religious grounds: see Equality Act 2006, Part 2, s. 50.

had obtained a conversion through a recognized orthodox synagogue then that would have been fine. The Office of the School's
Adjudicator agreed with the school, and so the father launched an
action for judicial review.

The High Court Decision

Munby J's decision at first instance upheld the school's position.[89]
The judge first found that *Seide* v *Gillette* was authority for both
that (1) Jews were an ethnic group under the RRA 1976 and (2)
ethnicity and religion were two separate things. Munby J thus
reasoned that a person could be Jewish by religion and not by
ethnicity, and vice versa. While ethnicity involved some element
of biological descent the reverse was not necessarily the case—a
determination of descent did not necessarily involve a racial or
ethnic categorization. He found that this case was one of Jewish
'status'—descent was being used to determine a child's Jewish
status for the purposes of an admissions policy, not their race or
ethnicity. According to Munby J, determining this status was a
purely religious exercise—was this child Jewish according to
orthodox Jewish law? The discrimination was thus religious, and
therefore allowed under legal provisions for faith schools.[90] Munby
J's decision is far more comprehensive and nuanced than this short
summary suggests; however, I leave it here and return to it again in
the next chapter.

The Court of Appeal

Sedley LJ, writing for a unanimous Court of Appeal, wrote an
admittedly short decision overturning Munby J's.[91] With little
reasoning, commentary, or reference to the conversion question,
the Court found that: (1) citing *Mandla* as authority, Jews constituted a racial group under the RRA 1976 and any discriminatory
treatment based on a person's Jewish, or non-Jewish, status was
per se discriminatory, (2) the school clearly engaged in a racially
discriminatory act against a person it defined as 'not Jewish', and
(3) such an act could not be justified on any account.

---

[89] *R (E)* v *Governing Body of JFS* [2008] ELR 445.   [90] Ibid., para. 171.
[91] *R (E)* v *Governing Body of JFS* [2009] 4 All ER 375.

Applying this [the oft-quoted passage from Lord Fraser's judgment in *Mandla*: see above] to the present case, it appears to us clear (a) that Jews constitute a racial group defined principally by ethnic origin and additionally by conversion, and (b) that to discriminate against a person on the ground that he or someone else either is or is not Jewish is therefore to discriminate against him on racial grounds. The motive for the discrimination, whether benign or malign, theological or supremacist, makes it no less or more unlawful.[92]

The Court proclaimed that any test of Jewishness must be religious not racial.

While, in the High Court, Munby J had relied on the brief remarks of Slynn J in the *Seide* case to find that Jews were both an 'ethnic group' under the RRA and also a religious group and it was for the courts to make a factual determination as to whether the alleged discrimination was on racial or religious grounds,[93] in the Court of Appeal, on the other hand, Sedley LJ claimed *Seide* was of 'no assistance in a case where the religious belief in question is that of the alleged discriminator, not of the victim'.[94] Instead of relying on *Seide*, Sedley LJ found that *Mandla* was authority for the fact that 'Jews constitute a racial group',[95] despite *Mandla* not being any direct authority for this proposition at all (see my earlier discussion of this case). As I noted earlier in this chapter, with the exception of brief references in *Seide*, and also in *Morgan* (a case to which no court in *JFS* refers), no English case ever actually determined how or why Jews were covered by the RRA 1976. Only Denning LJ, in his *Mandla* judgment, attempted to do so (see the long extract reproduced earlier), a decision never cited or discussed by subsequent courts in any way (except, interestingly, by Lord Hope at the Supreme Court in *JFS*: see Chapter 7). There is also Lord Fraser's peculiar remark that 'it is inconceivable that Parliament would have legislated against racial discrimination intending that the protection should not apply either to Christians or (above all) to Jews' (see earlier discussion). That Lord Fraser appeared to consider Christians a racial group seems to have been conveniently forgotten by subsequent courts.

[92] Ibid., para. 32.
[93] *R (E) v Governing Body of JFS* [2008] ELR 445, para. 148.
[94] *R (E) v Governing Body of JFS* [2009] 4 All ER 375, para. 30.   [95] Ibid., para. 32.

Instead, all the courts in the *JFS* case rely on Lord Fraser's disquisition on ethnicity in *Mandla*, where he discussed the applicability of the RRA 1976 to Sikhs. In doing so, as I traced earlier, he relies on a New Zealand judgment about Jews, in which, as I noted previously, the judges there take their understanding of 'ethnic group' from the testimony of an anthropologist whose special expertise was the history and culture of Samoan peoples.[96]

What is also striking about this line of cases is how the judges deal with the question of conversion, and the relationship between conversion and ethnicity. In *King-Ansell*, the New Zealand case, the court did not address the question of conversion at all. Indeed, to do so would have greatly complicated the court's analysis as its holding about the meaning of ethnic group relegated religious belief to a minor consideration. In *Mandla*, Lord Fraser simply asserted, as if it was uncontroversial, that an ethnic group exhibiting sufficient of his elucidated characteristics 'would be capable of including converts, for example, persons who marry into the group, and of excluding apostates'.[97] In *JFS*, both Munby J and Sedley LJ reproduce these remarks without comment. But surely there is a debatable question as to whether one can 'convert' to an ethnicity? And, what does it mean to be an 'apostate' from ethnicity? These obviously religious terms, combined with Lord Fraser's comment that Christians were protected by the RRA 1976, surely demonstrate that *Mandla* provides questionable guidance on these matters.

In an even more problematic move, Sedley LJ went on to compare the school's policy to apartheid South Africa, arguing that it was no defence to such racism to argue that you might honestly believe black people were inferior to white.[98] The analogy to apartheid is misplaced (at the very least). Apartheid was based on a system of complex racial classification resulting in conditions of extreme social, political, and economic inequality throughout South African society. It also had the backing of the

---

[96] I am not suggesting that Dr Macpherson was unable to theorize more widely about ethnicity—only that so much significant English case law can be traced to this one intervention.

[97] *Mandla* v *Dowell Lee* [1983] 2 AC 548, 562.

[98] *R (E)* v *Governing Body of JFS* [2009] 4 All ER 375, para. 29.

South African courts of the time who found nothing wrong with it. Racial classification and ideology was 'the reason for' the system; for many, their form of Christianity also ordained white superiority. While religion might be a factor in supporting these racial laws, they were, at root, racially motivated and dependent on a system of racial classification and hierarchy. The idea that a black person in 'apartheid South Africa' could 'convert' to whiteness by undergoing a programme of indoctrination in white superiority, thereby also ensuring their children were classified as 'white', is obviously absurd. Thus, rather than seeing the inclusiveness of Judaism as a strength, that it is open to converts of any 'race' or 'ethnicity' or 'religion', the religious test of matrilineal descent instead here becomes equated with despicable racial classification.[99]

In the court below, it was this obvious judicial meddling in religious law that Munby J recognized would not be appropriate:

> The fact that ... religion is the true focus here is illustrated ... by the very fact that at the heart of all the three cases I am considering is a dispute—a quintessentially religious dispute—about the validity of the conversion of the applicant child's mother ... a dispute about what constitutes a valid conversion is simply not a matter which engages the 1976 Act at all; it is a question of religious doctrine on which the secular courts should be wary to treat.[100]

Munby J's long and detailed analysis leading him to this conclusion stands in stark contrast to the Court of Appeal's unreasoned assertions.

CONCLUDING REMARKS

This chapter has proceeded in three parts. In the first, I explored the history and context of UK race relations legislation. I argued there that the abstracted figure of 'the Jew' recurred in parliamentary debates over several decades, and that this figure was deployed by both supporters and opponents of legislative initiatives. Supporters drew on a history of antisemitism and the mass murder of Jewish

---

[99] I am grateful to Maleiha Malik for helping me to clarify these points. It is also worth noting the symbolic role played by 'apartheid South Africa' in English law, but I cannot pursue that any further here.

[100] *R (E)* v *Governing Body of JFS* [2008] ELR 445, para. 171.

Europeans during world war two as evidence of the need for legislative protections. Opponents referred to these same histories to ground their contention that racism was a thing of the past and/or to argue that contemporary groups were not akin to Jews and were thus undeserving of protections. I also argued that throughout these debates a consistent confusion was apparent over the meaning of various terms, including that of 'ethnic group', and also over whether Jews were or were not actually protected under race relations law.

In the second part of the chapter, I considered the case law where Jews and Jewishness were discussed as a matter of racial equality law. Here, I showed that, until 2009, no Jewish claimant had ever won a reported case under the RRA 1976. This outcome needs to be read in conjunction with my discussion in Chapter 2, where I showed how Jews complaining of race discrimination were usually found to have brought their misfortunes upon themselves. No judge in these cases ever referred to a wider English context of antisemitism as being in any way relevant to the Jewish individual's complaint. At the same time, no case ever actually got to grips with whether or not Jews were a protected group under the RRA 1976, and, if so, on what basis. Assumptions, not arguments, were made. I further argued that the leading case on the meaning of 'ethnic group', *Mandla* v *Dowell Lee*, was a poor precedent for anything, being, as it was, filled with confusions, contradictions, and patently bizarre remarks.

Finally, I considered the first two decisions in the *JFS* case. I argued that these judgments throw into relief the confusion between race and religion that characterizes so much of English law's approach to Jews and Jewishness. The High Court considered the case to be an internal religious dispute—the Court of Appeal considered it without doubt to be a case of racial discrimination. It remains notable that, in English law, a Jewish religious school can be found guilty of race discrimination against Jews (or non-Jews, depending on how you define it) while no Christian person or institution appears to have ever suffered a similar fate. At the start of this chapter, I noted that the ostensible purpose of race relations law was to provide redress to certain minority groups who suffered discrimination committed by those in other groups. In *JFS*, we have the irony of the only successful Jewish RRA 1976 litigant being one who took other Jews to court. In the final chapter, I use the Supreme Court's decision in the *JFS* case, affirming the Court of Appeal's, to review and illustrate the book's key arguments.

Chapter 7

'THE CHRISTIAN CHURCH WILL ADMIT CHILDREN REGARDLESS OF WHO THEIR PARENTS ARE':[1] THE *JFS* CASE AND OTHER FINAL THOUGHTS

I have taken the title quote of this chapter from the remarks of Lady Hale, one of seven judges in the UK's Supreme Court who found that a Jewish school had engaged in racial discrimination against Jews.[2] In my view, Lady Hale's comment exemplifies many of the themes of this book, and I will use it as a jumping-off point to analyse the *JFS* case and draw the arguments of the book together in this final chapter. But before turning to the Supreme Court's judgment in the *JFS* case in detail, I want to review the book's main arguments.

In Chapter 2, I explored a set of cases where ideas about nation, character, and alienness were to the fore. I argued that in the early and mid twentieth century, judges associated weak or bad character with Jewish immigrants from the east. Judges in these cases articulated an inextricable set of relations between the litigant's Jewishness, national origins and fundamentally 'unattractive' character. The depiction of Jewish litigants as 'unattractive' to the court persisted at least well into the 1950s. I then considered the cases from the latter half of the twentieth century, and into the twenty-first. I argued that a shift in discourse was noticeable. While the

---

[1] Lady Hale, *R (E)* v *Governing Body of JFS* [2010] IRLR 136, para. 69.
[2] As I elaborate below, five found direct discrimination, and seven found indirect discrimination (two others found none).

origins of Jewish persons ceased to be remarked upon, many judges continued to find them unattractive. Rather than explicitly linking this unattractiveness to racial make-up, these judges, in what they might prefer to call an 'unfortunate coincidence', instead found it present in the un-English behaviour of individual Jewish parties. I associated this discursive move with both the eventual recognition of the Holocaust, and with the emergence of 'race relations' law and culture. Over time, Jews were more infrequently explicitly represented as being problematic 'as a race', while their behaviour, manner(isms), and self-presentation continued to be read as alien and un-English. I argued that part of this process could even entail disavowing knowledge that a litigant was in fact Jewish—a form of 'racelessness' resulting in an expulsion of Jewishness that is, in itself, racial thinking.

Chapter 3 considered the very different approach to Jews and Jewishness contained in the law of trusts. In these cases, Jewish testators, by inserting restrictive clauses in their wills, attempted to prevent their progeny from marrying 'out'. I argued that, in finding Jewishness unknowable, the judiciary focused on Jewishness and Judaism itself, rather than individual Jews. Indeed, 'real' Jews appeared far from their minds. However, racializing and orientalizing processes were very present in how judges understood and represented 'the Hebraic' abstract Jew of ancient Israel. I argued that the relationship between class and orientalism was important to understanding this trust discourse. In other words, the Jewish testators at the heart of these cases were, largely, wealthy ones, many of whose families had lived in England for generations.

I also demonstrated that these trust cases contain significant discourses on Christianity; in marking out the 'uncertainty' of Jewishness and Judaism, the judges recuperate the solidity and universalism of the Church of England. Here too, there is a distinctive shift in rhetoric in the latter part of the twentieth century, as the judiciary, in seeking definitions of Jewishness, eventually defer to rabbinical authority. I also introduced the theme of conversion—and suggested that by finding Judaism unknowable and Christianity certain, we can discern a subtle process pointing to the de-Judification of England. This has become mirrored in trust law textbooks as the history of Jewishness in English trust law is almost entirely erased.

In Chapter 4, about child welfare cases, I took up this theme of conversion more explicitly. I argued that objections to minority persons and practices as harmful to children can involve not just racializing and orientalizing processes, but also conversionary ones. For example, finding circumcision cruel and harmful, in itself problematic for reasons I explore in the chapter, is not the end to the story. It is insufficient to consider minority practices in isolation, as many judges and academic commentators do, as if there was no anti-Jewish or anti-Islamic English history, including enormous pressures to convert, in which English Christians played the leading role.

I also argued that present in these cases was the same kind of Christian universalism we witnessed in the trust law judgments, although here more submerged, and defined as 'secularism'. And, in contrast to the trust cases, judges did not proclaim their ignorance of Jewishness (and other faiths/ethnicities) in these child welfare decisions; rather, they were keen to discuss it at length, in the context of an authoritative pronouncement on a child's welfare. At the same time, there was evidence in some judgments of a more nuanced, more sophisticated approach to considering ethnicity and religion. Some judges (and scholars) were able to move beyond the framework of blood and/or theology, to situate minority cultures in a wider, more sympathetic context.

The history and deployment of 'the Holocaust' was the subject of Chapter 5. I first traced the evolution of the term 'holocaust' in English case law, arguing that with two exceptions (one very minor), judges did not take note of the Holocaust regularly until the 1990s, although some euphemisms had been in place prior to then (for example, 'she failed to emerge from the ghetto of Krakow'[3]). Once the phrase did come into play, I argued that its deployment was significant in two major ways. First, the Holocaust came to be a routine utterance, its events usually having nothing to do with the case at hand. I argued that the Holocaust as 'stock footage' facilitated the rejection of contemporary claims for asylum, while focusing on an

---

[3] *Loudon v Ryder (No 2)* [1953] Ch 423.

abstract Jewish victim and fabricating a myth that these past victims had been deemed worthy of saving. Second, I argued that the Holocaust can also be seen to facilitate judicial presentations of the un-English behaviours I discussed in Chapter 2. Having 'survived the Holocaust' can stand in for alienness and psychological damage, and thus facilitate a similar process of orientalizing 'the Jew'.

In Chapter 6 I considered Jews and Jewishness in light of race relations law and culture. I first explored how parliamentarians made use of the abstracted Jewish victim on both sides of the debates on race relations legislation. I then considered the case law, both cases where individual Jewish people claimed to have been discriminated against on the basis of their Jewishness, and cases where there were no Jewish claimants, but nonetheless discussions of Jewishness were present.

I argued, first, that the question of whether Jewishness was even covered by the Race Relations Act 1976 had never been the subject of direct legal reasoning. Rather, an abstracted Jew had facilitated the development of the law in relation to other minority groups. And, second, that despite the abstracted Jew being at the centre of legal developments in relation to the 'ethnic group' category, no 'real' Jew, until 2009, had ever been successful in a reported Race Relations Act 1976 case, and this one success, paradoxically, came in a claim against fellow Jews. When combined with the ways in which Jewish persons are blamed for bringing negative treatment upon themselves (explored in Chapter 2), I argued that this area of law reveals a great deal of myth-making. I concluded that chapter with a discussion of the first two decisions in the *JFS* case, one of the most comprehensive judicial engagements with Jewishness in English case law in the last 100 or so years. It is to the final decision in that case that I now turn.

THE *JFS* CASE AT THE SUPREME COURT

Following the High Court and Court of Appeal decisions in 2008 (see discussion in Chapter 6), the *JFS* litigation came before the Supreme Court the following year. Five of nine judges at the Court found that the JFS had engaged in direct racial discrimination (two found there was indirect racial discrimination, and two found there was no discrimination), and, in coming to this conclusion, the majority undertook four major moves in reasoning. First, they asserted that there was no question that the group 'Jews' was protected by the RRA 1976. They either relied on *Mandla* for this assertion, or treated it as a matter of common sense. Second, they found that the matrilineal test was a racial test (as well as a religious test), as it was based fundamentally on examining the genetic descent of the mother. Third, several of the judges decided that the group 'Orthodox Jews' was a sub-ethnicity of the group 'Jews', and that another sub-ethnicity consisted of those Jews whose mother was not 'born Jewish'. Thus, through the imposition of the matrilineal test in a school admission policy, they reasoned that one sub-ethnicity was engaged in racial discrimination against another. Finally, they argued that the claim that the discrimination was religious and not racial was a red herring. Like Sedley LJ in the court below, they stated that religion was simply a *motive* for the test. What mattered were 'simply the factual criteria applied by the discriminator'.[4]

As part of this line of reasoning, the majority of the Court insisted that arguments about conversion were a diversion. It did not matter that anyone could convert—what mattered was that a racial test was in place: if the boy's mother had been 'born Jewish', he would have been admitted to the school. As Lady Hale declared:

M was rejected because of his mother's ethnic origins, which were Italian and Roman Catholic. The fact that the Office of the Chief Rabbi would have over-looked his mother's Italian origins, had she converted to Judaism in a procedure which they would recognise, makes no difference to this fundamental fact.[5]

All five judges also stated that even if there had been no direct discrimination, then the school had committed racial discrimination indirectly as there was no justification for the school's admissions policy. While Lords Hope and Walker disagreed with the reasoning of the majority on the question of direct discrimination,

---

[4] Lord Phillips, *R (E)* v *Governing Body of JFS* [2010] IRLR 136, para. 13.
[5] Ibid., paras 66–7.

they both concurred in finding the school responsible for indirect discrimination.

Lords Roger and Brown issued strong dissenting judgments. They found that religion was the *reason why* and not simply the motive for the difference in treatment. They insisted that the element of conversion in Judaism was crucial to the determination of the case, and not a red herring. In essence, they fully agreed with how Munby J had decided the case in the first instance (see Chapter 6)— this matter was fundamentally about a religious dispute within the Jewish community over the recognition of non-Orthodox conversions. Racial discrimination had nothing to do with it. As Lord Roger declared:

The majority's decision leads to such extraordinary results, and produces such manifest discrimination against Jewish schools in comparison with other faith schools, that one can't help feeling something has gone wrong ...Lady Hale says that M was rejected because of his mother's ethnic origins which were Italian and Roman Catholic. I respectfully disagree. His mother could have been as Italian in origin as Sophia Loren and as Roman Catholic as the Pope for all that the governors cared: the only thing that mattered was that she had not converted to Judaism under Orthodox auspices.[6]

As I noted above, while Lords Hope and Walker agreed with Lords Roger and Brown up to a point, they diverged on the question of indirect discrimination, the latter judges finding that the admissions policy was proportionate to achieving the school's legitimate aims, the former not.

As I have made clear throughout this book, my concerns in the cases are not, primarily, to do with outcome, nor, usually, with the doctrinal reasoning that leads judges to their results. I am interested, rather, in other kinds of way-findings. Jewish people and communities in England have had diverse and often conflicting responses to the final *JFS* decision. Personally, I find Munby J's decision at first instance persuasive, in terms of how the courts should approach an issue such as this. At the same time, I find the matrilineal test sexist (not racist) and therefore inappropriate to apply when allocating educational resources. I am thus in the

---

[6] Lord Roger, ibid., paras 226, 228.

curious position of disapproving of both the outcome of the case, and of the insistence of many Jewish denominations (not just the branch known as 'orthodox') on a non-Jewish woman's religious conversion in order to find her child Jewish. However, for the purposes of this book, the way-finding leading up to 'the result' in a case is of particular interest to me. So, I want to move now to consider how the majority judgments raise many of the concerns about knowledge production on which this book is focused.

ORIENTALIZING AND RACIALIZING PROCESSES

To return to the title quote of this chapter, in comparing Judaism with Christianity, and finding the latter intrinsically about equality, and the former not, Lady Hale offers a contribution to the judicial orientalizing of Jews and Jewishness, as well as to the furtherance of Christian universalism. But, when combined with the other remark of hers I reproduced above, suggesting that Jews cannot also be Italians, racialization also rears its head. Let me first make out the case for orientalism in the majority's decision, which, I would suggest, comes out most clearly in Lord Mance's judgment.

Lord Mance places the events which took place at the JFS in relation to the boy 'M' in a wide legal context. He references European Directives, the International Convention on the Elimination of Racial Discrimination, and the UN Convention on the Rights of the Child 1989.[7] In other words, the route he takes to reach his conclusion suggests that the Jewish matrilineal test contravenes European and international law, as well as the RRA 1976. This, in my view, is a 'civilizational' argument; on the one hand, there is the law of the Jews—archaic and discriminatory. On the other hand, there is the law of the Christians (Lord Mance might claim this world is 'secular', but for reasons extensively explored elsewhere in the book I disagree)—modern, just, and protective of individual rights.

To treat individual applicants to a school less favourably than others, because of the happenstance of their respective ancestries, is not to treat them as individuals but as members of a group defined in a manner

---

[7] Ibid., paras 80, 81, 90.

unrelated to their individual attributes…To treat as determinative the
view of others, which an applicant may not share, that a child is not
Jewish by reason of his ancestry, is to give effect not to the individuality
or interests of the applicant, but to the viewpoint, religiously and deeply
held though it be, of the school applying the less favourable treatment.
That does not seem to me either consistent with the scheme or appropriate in the context of legislation designed to protect individuals from
discrimination. I accept that parental responsibility and choice relating to
a child can determine the extent to which children are treated as having
certain attributes, e.g. memberships of a particular religion in the case of
Christian baptism. But neither parental birth nor the fact that a mother
has not converted to Orthodox Judaism at a time prior to a child's birth
can be regarded as within the concept of parental responsibility and
choice.[8]

Here, Lord Mance entirely divorces the 'individual' child from
her *Jewishness*—she is an unmarked 'individual' onto whom a
school is attempting to impose a religious edict. How an 'individual' Jewish person, whether they are religious or not, lives in
the world with their individuality separate to their Jewishness is
not clear. It seems more that the unmarked 'individual' is not
Jewish at all. When these remarks are combined with how Lord
Phillips chooses to begin his opening judgment, with the passage from Deuteronomy where God instructs the Jewish people
to destroy others and most certainly never marry them,[9] and
Lady Hale's remark about the fairness of Christian schools, the
overall orientalist tone of the majority's opinion is clear, including the implicit universalizing of Christianity—an 'individual' is
a Christian individual.

Lord Mance's comments are in keeping with rhetorical moves
I traced in earlier chapters, for example, in Chapter 2, where Jewish
litigants were described as unable to comprehend the rule of law,
while English courts and tribunals, and English law itself,
were lauded as the epitome of democracy, fairness, and propriety.

---

[8] Ibid., para. 90. As I explored in Chapter 2, the values of 'individuality' and 'liberty' are
particularly prized as essential aspects of 'English character', see also P. Mandler, *The English
National Character: The History of an Idea from Edmund Burke to Tony Blair* (New Haven: Yale
University Press, 2006) 52–7.

[9] Ibid., para. 1. I am aware that is the passage where religious Jews find the basis for the matrilineal
test and I am not suggesting Lord Phillips chooses it at random. However, I am noting that he did
choose to open his judgment with it, without any context provided beforehand whatsoever.

This comparison, between the Jewish world and the Christian (particularly the Protestant) world, between ostensibly Jewish insularity and Christian freedom, is also at the heart of current critiques of Islam—of the so-called 'clash of civilizations', and resonates with material I discussed in Chapter 4. There is a Christian triumphalism at play here.

RACIALIZATION

One of the ironies of the *JFS* decision is that as the Court calls the school a racial discriminator, the judges themselves indulge in some of the clumsiest racial description we have seen amongst the cases discussed in this book. For example, there is Lady Hale's view that a person cannot be both Jewish and Italian (see above), an understanding to which Lord Hope appears to subscribe when he describes the boy's parents: 'M's father is of Jewish ethnic origin. M's mother is Italian by birth and ethnic origin.'[10] In keeping with this line of thought is Lord Mance's remark suggesting that a 'Cohen' and an 'English woman' are two different species.[11] While the more appropriate phrase in this case would have been 'Christian woman' (although that, too, would have been problematic), Lord Mance's use of 'English woman' instead is more than yet another unfortunate coincidence. A 'Cohen' is clearly not 'English', and an 'English woman' is clearly not Jewish. These kinds of sentiments resonate with the 'blood' approach in the child welfare cases (see Chapter 4), where judges claim that the true essence of a person lies in their genetic descent. It is ironic that the Supreme Court criticizes the matrilineal test for just this approach. But there is also an odd contradiction in these remarks. The Court finds very explicitly that a convert joins the Jewish ethnic group—and, so, why is the mother's ethnicity described as Italian and Catholic? Is the Court not recognizing her conversion either? Or, is it that the judges just cannot conceive of Jewishness that is not, at its heart, in the blood?

More important, perhaps, are the implications of the Court's racializing discourse. Through its focus on genetics, the Court actually turns what Rabbi Tony Bayfield, in his intervention in

---

[10] Ibid., para. 166.   [11] Ibid., para. 87.

the case, called a 'mythical' kinship,[12] into a fixed racial category, which they then project as originating from within orthodox Judaism, in much the same way the judges in the trust cases projected their racial categories upon the dead Jewish testators (see Chapter 3). But the matrilineal test is usually just 'skin deep'—it normally stops at one generation. Jewish law presumes the older generations are Jewish unless a person cannot show evidence of the Jewishness of their own mother. And such evidence is not racial but religious and cultural, there is no genetic test for Jewishness. The evidence is found in such things as the *ketuba* (a Jewish marriage scroll), or in whether parents or grandparents are buried in Jewish cemeteries. These cultural/religious artefacts 'prove' the 'mythical kinship'. And, of course, through conversion, the process by which non-Jews become Jews—marginalized and deemed irrelevant by the court—none of this is necessary anyway. In contrast, it is the Supreme Court that insists that the matrilineal test has a 'blood' link to the ancient Jewish people—but, given some of the history of English courts with respect to Jews and Jewishness, as I explored in Chapter 3, this is perhaps not surprising.

Let me return for a moment to Jonathan Bradley's case (see Chapter 4). While it is true that, because his birth mother was not Jewish, the Bet Din did not accept Jonathan as Jewish until he underwent a conversion, once he did that there was no further issue. Jonathan—the young man described by the court as the son of a 'Kuwaiti Muslim Arab' (his mother effectively being erased from the equation)—could have been admitted to JFS without any difficulty whatsoever. However, the Supreme Court's focus on blood—there are eighteen references to either 'blood', 'birth' or 'genetic' in the judgments—returns us again to the trust line of cases—and is almost a reversal of the shift we saw there (see Chapter 3). Rather than deferring to Jewish religious authorities in relation to definitional questions about Jewishness, the Court is overruling them.

Jonathan Boyarin has argued that Jewishness is about an originary story, a genealogical narrative, something like the 'mythical kinship' that Rabbi Bayfield identified in his submission to the

---

[12] Ibid., para. 40. Rabbi Bayfield's comment in the case was provided in his capacity as Head of the Reform branch of Judaism in England.

court in *JFS*.[13] Pauline Christianity placed itself against a Jewish notion of 'inherited contract', replacing it with a different narrative—one about consent.[14] In *JFS*, we can see the same dynamics at play. The judges cut off the Jewish story, labelling it 'blood'-based and therefore 'racial', replacing it with a Christian myth of individuality and autonomy. This is the rejection of Jewishness at the heart of Christian, particularly Protestant, supersessionary, civilizational discourse. The fact that non-Jews have been welcomed into Jewishness through conversion for well over 2,000 years (ever since Jewishness acquired a more 'religious' rather than 'national' character[15]) does not fit the Christian triumphalist narrative, and so the judges simply ignore it.

Finally, when the Court strikes down the matrilineal test as 'racial', it paradoxically makes being an 'ethnic' Jew and not a 'religious' one even harder. In another irony, this plays into the hands of more hardline orthodox Jews who insist on the importance of theological belief and religious observance. Thus, the Supreme Court's decision in *JFS* actually marginalizes the ties that non-religious Jews have with Jewish culture and history, and also may make it more difficult for them to have their children admitted to the JFS as they will not be sufficiently observant. Indeed, the 'Certificate of Religious Practice' now adopted by the JFS in lieu of the matrilineal test may make it nigh impossible for children from non-religious families to be admitted to this over-subscribed school.[16] There is even a remark in the Supreme Court's decision claiming that Jewish 'atheists' are no longer part of the Jewish 'ethnic group'.[17] Lord Brown recognized the irony of imposing upon the school Christian ideas about worship:

---

[13] J. Boyarin, 'Another Abraham: Jewishness and the Law of the Father' (1997) 9 *Yale J. of Law & Humanities* 345–94.

[14] See also J. Weiler's review of the *JFS* decision, 'Discrimination and Identity in London: The Jewish Free School Case' *Jewish Review of Books* (2010).

[15] For a fascinating account of Jewish identities in antiquity, see S. Cohen, *The Beginnings of Jewishness: Boundaries, Varieties, Uncertainties* (Berkeley: University of California Press, 1999).

[16] See www.jfs.brent.sch.uk/admissions.aspx. The criteria now make synagogue attendance mandatory, and also include a past history of Jewish education and/or Jewish charity work.

[17] *R (E)* v *Governing Body of JFS* [2010] IRLR 136, para. 79. The remark appears in Lord Mance's judgment, however its placement suggests the claim may have been made by the lawyers for the school. In either case, it shows the confusion surrounding notions of ethnicity, as I discuss further below.

...to impose a religious practice test, besides being felt by many to be invasive, difficult to measure and open to abuse, would be contrary to the positive desire of schools like JFS to admit non-observant as well as observant children. Ironically, moreover, to impose such a test would narrow, rather than widen, the character of the school's intake so as to make it appear more, rather than less, discriminatory.[18]

It would seem that an effect of the Supreme Court's judgment is to turn the JFS into an exclusively religious school, making a child's 'ethnic ties' with Jewishness irrelevant—another irony, given race equality provisions purportedly protect Jewish persons on the basis of ethnicity.

SECULARISM, CHRISTIANITY, AND CONVERSION

To return, again, to the title quote of this chapter: 'The Christian Church will admit children regardless of who their parents are'. While Lady Hale is the only judge to explicitly compare Christianity with Judaism, finding the latter wanting, all the majority judgments result in a 'Christianization' of the JFS. As I noted above, by insisting on a test of religious observance rather than matrilineal descent, the Court is imposing a model of Christian worship on Jewish people (and this also returns us to the observance/ritual approach in the child welfare cases: see Chapter 4). This is a point made, in strong language, by Lord Brown:

Jewish schools in future, if oversubscribed, must decide on preference by reference only to outward manifestations of religious practice. The Court of Appeal's judgment insists on a non-Jewish definition of who is Jewish...ignoring whether the child is or is not Jewish defined by Orthodox Jewish law. That outcome I could not contemplate with equanimity.[19]

I would add that the Christian impositions in the majority decision are also very patriarchal. To the extent that, in Orthodox Judaism, outward, public observances are performed, they are largely performed by men. Many religious Jewish women, particularly more orthodox ones, do not engage in such public displays, but perform

---

[18] Ibid., para. 253.
[19] Ibid., paras 248, 258. See also Rabbi Bayfield's condemnation of such an approach in his submission, quoted by Munby J, *R (E)* v *Governing Body of JFS* [2008] ELR 445, para.101.

their religious rituals in the home.[20] While a test of 'observance' need
not ignore religious practice in the home, a test of 'worship'—a
Christian concept used by Lord Phillips, for example, several times
in relation to Jewish practice—might. Thus, in another irony, the
Supreme Court overturns a Jewish matriarchal test, substituting a
Christian, patriarchal one instead.[21]

Aside from these points, perhaps more subtly, the majority
judgments represent Christianity, implicitly and explicitly, as a
place of freedom and equality. As I discussed above, this has a
'civilizational' aspect in keeping with Said's development of the
concept of orientalism. But this discourse also obfuscates the legacy
of Christian racisms, as well as its history as an imperialistic,
violent, and colonial project (see discussion in Chapter 1). When
the majority's decision in *JFS*, that Jews are the racists,[22] is
combined with their total lack of acknowledgement of Christian
anti-Jewish persecution and discrimination in England (I have
discussed my view of Lady Hale's reference to the Holocaust in
Chapter 5), and the near total failure of Jewish claimants to win
their race relations cases and, instead, be blamed themselves for
their own suffering (see Chapters 2 and 6), Lady Hale's perhaps
offhand remark about the fairness of *Christian* schools takes on
more meaning.

Upon release of the Supreme Court's decision in the *JFS* case,
Trevor Phillips, the Chair of the UK's Equality and Human Rights
Commission, a body that intervened in the case on the side of the
family, issued the following statement:

This is an important verdict. Whilst not seeking to interfere with the
Jewish community's right to promote its religious ethos, the Commission
believed that it had to intervene in order to preserve the same protection
against racial discrimination for Jews as for anyone else—not least at a

---

[20] See also *R* v *Sec St Ed, ex parte E* [1996] ELR 312, where the judge does take notice of this.

[21] The test subsequently adopted by the JFS does not consider religious practice in the home
at all; however, it does count as valid 'charity work', which, arguably, is often women's work.
Perhaps this is also the place to note that the boy M's mother, so abstracted by the Court, did
not support the litigation against the school, remarking early on: 'The High Court is not the
place to discuss Jewish law': quoted by Munby J, *R(E)* v *Governing Body of JFS* [2008] ELR 445,
para. 89.

[22] One judge, Lord Clarke, explicitly approves of Sedley LJ's comparison of the matrilineal test
with 'apartheid South Africa', ibid., para. 150. Other judges explicitly claim they are *not* accusing the
school of being racist, but this is clearly semantic disingenuousness.

time when anti-Semitic groups are active across Europe. The decision of the Court achieves that end ... [23]

I would argue, in contrast to Phillips, that the *JFS* decision does quite the opposite.

'THE JEW', ABSTRACTIONS, AND MYTH-MAKING

Several myths permeate the Supreme Court's judgments. In Chapter 5, I discussed Lady Hale's reference to the Holocaust, and I will not pursue how such references function as problematic abstractions here. My first point, here, rather, is that there is an assumption throughout the entire decision that Jews have benefited from being protected by the RRA 1976. However, as I explained in Chapter 6, there is no evidence for this assertion as every Jewish claimant in a reported case had failed in their claim. Even references to the *Seide* decision in the *JFS* case suggest that Mr Seide won his case.[24] My comment here is about *how* Mr Seide's experience with English race relations legislation is narrated—as if English law had provided him with protection. Indeed, a reader of the Supreme Court's decision in *JFS* could be excused for thinking that Jews had benefited enormously from the Act, and were now seeking to avoid its jurisdiction.

Second, the myth that the *Mandla* case contained an authoritative discussion of Jewish ethnicity persists in *JFS*. Lord Fraser's words in *Mandla* v *Dowell Lee*, based on Dr Macpherson's testimony in the New Zealand case of *King-Ansell* (see Chapter 6), are repeated again and again in almost every judgment in *JFS*. Although Jews were not the subject of the *Mandla* case—Sikhs were—it is used nonetheless as authoritative precedent for finding it 'unquestionably true' that Jews are an 'ethnic group' for the purposes of the RRA 1976.[25] With one exception, the reference

---

[23] Quoted in EHRC, Press Release, 16 December 2009.

[24] Eg, *R (E)* v *Governing Body of JFS* [2010] IRLR 136, paras 186, 200. As I explained in Chapters 2 and 6, Mr Seide complained of antisemitism at work, but in fact lost his case as his own annoying behaviour was held to be responsible for the fact that he had been transferred to a different job. In cases involving Jewish claimants under the Race Relations Act 1976, the *Seide* case has stood as virtually the only precedent that Jews do constitute a 'racial group' for the purposes of the Act (see further in Chapter 6). However, only one judge on the Supreme Court refers to *Seide*, the rest use *Mandla* as authority, or none at all.

[25] Ibid., para. 121.

to *Seide* v *Gillette*, the judges do not draw on the previous case law concerning Jewish claimants at all.

But the failure of *Mandla* to resolve any of the complex issues to do with Jewish identity is readily apparent in the judges' confusing narratives of Jewishness. Lord Phillips, for example, states that religion is the 'dominant' criterion of Jewishness;[26] however, this is not the case for many self-identified Jewish people and, as I discussed in Chapter 6, in any event, the place of religion in Lord Fraser's formulation in *Mandla* is far from clear, and the British Government in 2006 clearly stated that religion was *not* the dominant criterion of 'ethnic group'.[27] A number of judges refer to someone being an 'Orthodox' or a 'Masorti' Jew 'by birth',[28] but would they similarly suggest that someone could be 'born' an Anglican or a Methodist? If so, isn't this a 'blood' test? And, how can this be reconciled with how judges in the family courts understand the cognitive abilities of children with respect to theology (see Chapter 4)?

As I noted above, several of the judges suggest that Catholicism and being Italian are also ethnicities. Certainly, in terms of the 'ethnic group' category and its case law, these claims are controversial to say the least. But for the purposes of this book, I am more interested in the silence around Protestantism. Would they find that Protestants were members of a Protestant ethnic group? Are Anglicans a 'sub-ethnicity' of that? Would they find that 'the English', like the Italians, also constituted such a group? There is an actual case on point here—*BBC Scotland* v *Souster*—which answers the 'English' question negatively.[29] It is not a 'coincidence' that these questions are avoided; instead, we have largely English Christian judges pronouncing on the qualities of various 'ethnics', leaving, once again, questions about who has the power to pronounce submerged. And, how is it that the Court 'knows' the boy in *JFS* is Jewish? They never explain this. As Hannah Arendt suggested,

---

[26] Ibid., para. 39.

[27] *Hansard*, HL, col. 665 (9 November 2005), Baroness Scotland on introducing the Equality Act 2006.

[28] Eg, *R (E)* v *Governing Body of JFS* [2010] IRLR 136, paras 74, 107, 109–110, 131.

[29] [2001] IRLR 150.

Whether the Jews are a religion or a nation, a people or a race, a state or a tribe, depends on the specific opinion non-Jews—in whose midst Jews live—have about themselves, but it certainly has no connection whatever with any germinal knowledge about the Jews.[30]

FURTHER EXPLORATIONS

In Chapter 1, I suggested two avenues for further research in relation to Jews and Jewishness—taking a longer historical lens than I have been able to do here, as well as tracing how English law has engaged with other minority peoples, including, for example, Muslims, Roma, and Catholics. There are obviously many more; however, here, I would like to suggest a further two in particular.

Character and Citizenship

As I complete this book, I notice the following headline: 'Immigrants To Be Taught How to Queue'.[31]

Foreigners applying to settle in the UK will have to learn about the revered British practice of forming an orderly queue... [Ministers] claim a lot of tension in communities is caused by immigrants not understanding that they must wait in line for services rather than barging to the front. This is not their fault, ministers say, but happens because in less-wealthy countries the only way to get access to necessities is to push yourself forward. But to elderly people waiting in bus queues, for example, such behaviour can be off-putting and frightening. Phil Woolas, the immigration minister, confirmed he was pushing the idea as part of moves to ensure immigrants integrate properly. He said: The simple act of taking one's turn is one of the things that holds our country together. It is central to the British sense of fair play and it is also better for everyone. Huge resentment is caused when people push in. Most immigrants in my experience want to play fair.[32]

While the papers understandably treated this story with humour, it shows that the link between character, nationality, and un-English behaviour remains alive and well. The 'immigrants' at the centre of the Government's gaze are not from the

---

[30] H. Arendt, *The Jewish Writings* (New York: Shocken, 2007) 68–9.
[31] Melissa Kite, *The Telegraph* (13 February 2010). This is just one example—the story appeared in every major British newspaper.
[32] Ibid.

white west/north, but from the brown east/south. They are from 'less wealthy' countries where people 'barge in'. And the 'elderly people' patiently waiting in bus queues are here completely white-washed.

In the next two months, March and April 2010: the Canadian province of Quebec introduces a Bill requiring women who wear the niqab to uncover their faces or be denied government services (including education and health care), a way of thinking that resonates with a recent British Home Secretary's complaints about 'the veil'; the lower house of the Belgian parliament passes a ban on wearing the burqa in public; while France, a country obsessed with the issue, also debates a total ban on the burqa.[33]

Scholarship on the 'civilizational' aspects of these kinds of policies, including work on 'the veil' and 'forced marriage' for example, has tended to focus on processes of racialization or neo-colonialism, and, to a lesser extent, the gendered politics of the obsession with how some Muslim women dress.[34] Usually, this is put into a 'post 9/11' theoretical framework of understanding. While this work is very welcome, it does leave underexplored the continuing relevance of much older civilizational discourses, including the sorts of 'conversionary' processes I have tried to elucidate in this book. In other words, *Christianity* remains relatively uninterrogated. How is 'Britishness' produced in relation to non-Christian faiths? How is the notion of 'playing fair' a Christian one, and what are the implications of this? How is the maintenance of religious dress and practice an attempt to assert communal and historical ties in the face of *conversionary* pressures?

Getting Ethnicity's Act Together

Under UK equality law, 'Jews' and 'Sikhs' are treated as ethnic groups. Yet, on the UK census form, it is impossible for Jewish or Sikh people to define themselves this way. Both appear only in the categories of 'religion', and the Office of National Statistics has taken

---

[33] On Quebec, see, for example, J. McNish and S. Boesveld, 'Quebec's niqab ban sets up a legal showdown', *The Globe and Mail* (25 March 2010); on the British example, see Maleiha Malik's critique, 'This Veil Fixation is Doing Muslim Women No Favours', *The Guardian* (19 October 2006); on Belgium, see 'Belgian Lawmakers Pass Burka Ban', *BBC News* (30 April 2010); on France, see 'France Plans Bill Banning Burqa For Spring', *France24* (12 March 2010).

[34] See references in Chapters 1 and 4.

a decision to maintain this state of affairs for the 2011 census.[35] In light of my critique of the *Mandla* case above and in Chapter 6, there is an urgent need—a legal and theoretical challenge—to develop conceptually what it means to be a member of an 'ethnic group' in law.

How significant should religious belief be to an understanding of 'ethnic group'? Is it 'dominant' as Lord Phillips suggested was the case for Jews in the *JFS* case, or is religion just one 'part' of the definition, as a Government minister claimed in 2006? Is it right that an ethnic group can contain 'converts or apostates' or consist of 'Christians' as Lord Fraser suggested in *Mandla*? If a convert to Judaism is immediately ethnicized into the Jewish ethnic group, why is an atheist not immediately thrown out of it? Is there any purchase in the notion of 'peoplehood', and how might this interact with 'ethnic group'? In *King-Ansell*, the New Zealand case highly persuasive on the House of Lords in *Mandla*, the court said that Jews were a 'people' analogous to 'the Egyptians'.[36] Is recognizing Jews as a 'people' too politically sensitive given current Middle East politics and rhetoric? In 1940, Hannah Arendt wrote:

I do not think it is utopian to hope for the possibility of a commonwealth of European nations with a parliament of its own. As for us [Jews] at least, this would be our sole salvation... Within such a commonwealth we could be recognised as a nation and be represented in a European parliament. For this 'solution' of the Jewish question, the conundrum of a people without land in search of a land without people—practically speaking, the moon, or a folktale free from politics—would finally have become meaningless.[37]

Arendt's proposal clearly has flaws. But that such an idea might appear utterly outlandish today only speaks to a lack of understanding of the complexity and multiple meanings of Jewishness.

The question of the relationship between race, ethnicity, nationhood, peoplehood, and religion in English law (and many other

---

[35] Office for National Statistics, 'Deciding which Tick-Boxes to Add to the Ethnic Group Question in the 2001 England and Wales Census' (Office for National Statistics, 2009); Office for National Statistics, 'Final Recommended Questions for the 2011 Census in England and Wales: Ethnic Group', (Office for National Statistics, 2009).

[36] *King-Ansell* v *Police* [1979] NZLR 531, 536, per Woodhouse J.

[37] J. Kohn and R.H. Feldman (eds), *The Jewish Writings* (New York: Shocken Books, 2007) 130 (orig. pub. 1940).

questions) cannot be resolved, or even properly addressed, without recognizing not just the history of Jewish people and Jewishness in English law, but also the contemporary dominance of Christianity in thinking about English values and national character. In the meantime, Jewish and other people in England will continue to live in the shadow of Christianity's enduring force—yet another 'unfortunate coincidence'.

BIBLIOGRAPHY

Agamben, G., *Remnants of Auschwitz: The Witness and the Archive* (New York: Zone Books, 1999)

Ahdar, R., 'Religion as a Factor in Custody and Access Disputes' (1996) 10 *International J. L. Policy & the Family* 177–99

Ahdar, R. and I. Leigh (eds), *Religious Freedom in the Liberal State* (Oxford: Oxford University Press, 2005)

Ahmed, S., *Strange Encounters: Embodied Others in Post-coloniality* (London: Routledge/Glasshouse, 2000)

Alderman, G., *Modern British Jewry* (Oxford: Oxford University Press, 1992)

Almog, O., *Britain, Israel and the United States, 1955–1958: Beyond Suez* (London: Frank Cass, 2003)

Anidjar, G., *The Jew, The Arab: A History of the Enemy* (Stanford: Stanford University Press, 2003)

Anidjar, G., *Semites: Race, Religion, Literature* (Stanford: Stanford University Press, 2008)

Ansari, A., *'The Infidel Within': Muslims in Britain Since 1800* (London: C. Hurst & Co., 2004)

Anthias, F., 'Evaluating "Diaspora": Beyond Ethnicity' (1998) 32(3) *Sociology* 557–80

Anwar, M., P. Roach, and R. Sondhi (eds), *From Legislation to Integration: Race Relations in Britain* (London: Palgrave Macmillan, 2000)

Arendt, H., *Eichmann in Jerusalem: A Report on the Banality of Evil* (New York: Penguin, 1963)

Arendt, H., *The Jewish Writings* (J. Kohn and R.H. Feldman (eds), New York: Shocken Books, 2007)

Asad, T., *Formations of the Secular: Christianity, Islam, Modernity* (Palo Alto: Stanford University Press, 2003)

Ashton, N. J., ' "A Special Relationship Sometimes in Spite of Ourselves": Britain and Jordan, 1957–73' (2005) 33(2) *J. of Imperial and Commonwealth History* 221–44

Auerbach, S., *Race, Law, and 'The Chinese Puzzle' in Imperial Britain* (New York: Palgrave Macmillan, 2009)

Avini, A., 'The Origins of the Modern English Trust Revisited' (1995–1996) 70 *Tulane L. Rev* 1139–63

Bale, A., *The Jew in the Medieval Book: English Antisemitism, 1350–1500* (Cambridge: Cambridge University Press, 2006)

Bamforth, N., M. Malik and C. O'Cinneide, *Discrimination Law, Theory and Context* (London: Sweet & Maxwell, 2008)

Banton, M., *Racial Theories* (Cambridge: Cambridge University Press, 1998)

Barkan, E., *The Retreat of Scientific Racism: Changing Concepts of Race in Britain and the United States Between the World Wars* (Cambridge: Cambridge University Press, 1992)

Bauman, Z., *Modernity and the Holocaust* (Cambridge: Polity, 1989)

Bauman, Z., *Modernity and Ambivalence* (Cambridge: Polity, 1991)

Benyon, H. and N. Love, '*Mandla* and the Meaning of 'Racial Group'' (1984) 100 *LQR* 120–36

Berkowitz, M., *The Crime of My Very Existence: Nazism and the Myth of Jewish Criminality* (Berkeley: University of California Press, 2007)

Bermant, C., *The Cousinhood: The Anglo-Jewish Gentry* (London: Eyre & Spotiswoode, 1971)

Bhandar, B., 'The Ties That Bind: Multiculturalism and Secularism Reconsidered' (2009) 36(3) *J. of Law & Society* 301–26

Blackstone, T., B. Parekh, and P. Sanders (eds), *Race Relations in Britain: A Developing Agenda* (London: Routledge, 1998)

Bloxham, D., *Genocide on Trial: War Crimes Trials and the Formation of Holocaust History and Memory* (New York: Oxford University Press, 2003)

Bloxham, D., 'Britain's Holocaust Memorial Day: Using the Past in the Service of the Present' (2003) 21(1) *Immigrants and Minorities* 41–62

Bolchover, R., *British Jewry and the Holocaust* (Cambridge: Cambridge University Press, 1993)

Bonnett, A., *The Idea of the West: Culture, Politics and History* (London: Palgrave, 2004)

Boyarin, D., *Unheroic Conduct: The Rise of Heterosexuality and the Invention of the Jewish Man* (Berkeley: University of California Press, 1997)

Boyarin, D., D. Itzkovits and A. Pellegrini (eds), *Queer Theory and the Jewish Question* (New York: Columbia University Press, 2003)

Boyarin, J., *Thinking in Jewish* (Chicago: University of Chicago Press, 1996)

Boyarin, J., 'Another Abraham: Jewishness and the Law of the Father' (1997) 9 *Yale J. of Law & Humanities* 345–94

Boyarin, J., *The UnConverted Self: Jews, Indians, and the Identity of Christian Europe* (Chicago: University of Chicago Press, 2009)

Boyarin, J. and D. Boyarin, *Jews and Other Differences: The New Jewish Cultural Studies* (Minneapolis: University of Minnesota Press, 1997)

Bradney, A., *Religion, Rights and Laws* (Leicester: Leicester University Press, 1993)

Bradney, A., *Law and Faith in a Sceptical Age* (London: Routledge, 2009)

Bradney, A., 'The Inspection of Ultra-Orthodox Jewish Schools: "The Audit Society" and "the Society of Scholars"' (2009) 21(2) *CFLQ* 133–54

Bridge, C., 'Religion, Culture, and Conviction—The Medical Treatment of Young Children' (1999) 11(1) *CFLQ* 1–16

Brown, A. P. and A. Erskine, 'A Qualitative Study of Judgments in Race Discrimination Employment Cases' (2009) 31(1) *Law & Policy* 142–59

Brown, W., *Regulating Aversion: Tolerance in the Age of Identity and Empire* (Princeton: Princeton University Press, 2006)

Burton, A., *At the Heart of the Empire: Indians and the Colonial Encounter in Late-Victorian Britain* (Berkeley: University of California Press, 1998)

Bush, J.A., '"Include Me Out": Some Lessons of Religious Toleration in Britain' (1991) 12 *Cardozo Law Review* 881–923

Bush, J.A., '"You're Gonna Miss Me When I'm Gone": Early Modern Common Law Discourse and the Case of the Jews' (1993) 5 *Wisconsin Law Journal* 1225–85

Butler, J., 'Sexual Politics, Torture, and Secular Time' (2008) 59 *The British J. of Sociology* 1–23

Butler-Sloss, E., 'Matters of Life and Death' in C. Chartres (ed.), *Why I Am Still an Anglican; Essays and Conversations* (London: Continuum, 2006)

Butler-Sloss, E., 'A Christian and a Judge in Family Matters: Squaring Belief with Judicial Duties' (2006) The Niblett Memorial Lecture, Sarum College, 1–8

Carter, P., 'Polite "Persons": Character, Biography and the Gentleman' (2002) 12 *Transactions of the Royal Historical Society* 333–54

Centre for Contemporary Cultural Studies, *The Empire Strikes Back: Race and Racism in 70s Britain* (London: Routledge, 1982)

Cesarani, D., 'The Anti-Jewish Career of Sir William Joynson-Hicks, Cabinet Minister' (1989) 24 *J. of Contemporary History* 461–82

Cesarani, D., *Justice Delayed: How Britain Became a Refuge for Nazi War Criminals* (London: Mandarin, 1992)

Cesarani, D. (ed.), *The Making of Modern Anglo-Jewry* (Oxford: Blackwell, 1990)

Cesarani, D. and T. Kushner, *The Internment of Aliens in Twentieth-Century Britain* (London: Frank Cass, 1993)

Cheyette, B., *Constructions of 'The Jew' in English Literature and Society* (Cambridge: Cambridge University Press, 1993)

Cheyette, B., 'English Anti-Semitism: A Counter-narrative' (forthcoming) *Textual Practice*

Cheyette, B. (ed.), *Between 'Race' and Culture: Images of 'The Jew' in English and American Literature* (Stanford: Stanford University Press, 1996)

Cheyette, B. and L. Marcus (eds), *Modernity, Culture and 'the Jew'* (Stanford: Stanford University Press, 1998)

Cohen, Deborah, 'Who Was Who?: Race and Jews in Turn-of–the-century Britain' (2002) 41(4) *The J. of British Studies* 460–83

Cohen, Derek and D. Heller, *Jewish Presences in English Literature* (Montreal: McGill-Queen's University Press, 1990)

Cohen, S., *The Beginnings of Jewishness: Boundaries, Varieties, Uncertainties* (Berkeley: University of California Press, 1999)

Cole, T., *Selling the Holocaust: From Auschwitz to Schindler: How History is Bought, Packaged, and Sold* (New York: Routledge, 2000)

Coles, R., *The Spiritual Life of Children* (Boston: Houghton Mifflin, 1990)

Colley, L., *Britons: Forging the Nation 1707–1837* (New Haven: Yale University Press, 1992)

Connolly, M., *Townshend-Smith on Discrimination Law: Text, Cases and Materials* (London: Cavendish, 2004)

Cooper, D., 'Defiance and Non-Compliance: Religious Education and the Implementation Problem' (1995) 48 *Current Legal Problems* 253–79

Cooper, D., *Governing Out of Order: Space, Law and the Politics of Belonging* (London: Rivers Oram, 1998)

Cooper, D. and D. Herman, 'Jews and Other Uncertainties: Race, Faith and English Law' (1999) 19 *Legal Studies* 339–66

Crenshaw, K., N. Gotanda, G. Peller and K. Thomas (eds), *Critical Race Theory: The Key Writings That Formed the Movement* (New York: New York University Press, 1996)

Darian-Smith, E. *Religion, Race, Rights: Landmarks in the History of Modern Anglo-American Law* (Oxford: Hart, 2010)

De Vries, H., *Religion, Beyond a Concept* (New York: Fordham University Press, 2008)

De Vries, H. and L. Sullivan (eds), *Political Theologies* (New York: Fordham University Press, 2006)

De Vries, H., *Introduction* in H. De Vries and L. Sullivan (eds), *Political Theologies* (New York: Fordham University Press, 2006)

Delgado, R., J. Stefanic, A. Harris (eds), *Critical Race Theory* (New York: New York University Press, 2001)

Dench, G., *Minorities in the Open Society* (New Brunswick: Transaction, 1986)

Dobbs, J., H. Green and L. Zealey, *Focus on Ethnicity and Religion, National Statistics* (Basingstoke: Palgrave Macmillan, 2006)

Dobson, R.B., *The Jews of Medieval York and the Massacre of March 1190* (York: University of York, Bothwick Paper No. 45, 1974)

Douglas, L., *The Memory of Judgment: Making Law and History in the Trials of the Holocaust* (New Haven: Yale University Press, 2001)

Duncan, J. S., 'The Struggle to be Temperate: Climate and "Moral Masculinity" in Mid-Nineteenth Century Ceylon' (2000) 21(1) *Singapore J. of Tropical Geography* 34–47

Edge, P., 'Male Circumcision After the Human Rights Act 1998' (2000) 5 *J. of Civil Liberties* 320–37

Eekelaar, J., 'Children between Cultures' (2004) 18 *International J. of Law, Policy and the Family* 178–94

Endelman, T., *The Jews of Britain, 1656 to 2000* (Berkeley: University of California Press, 2002)

Evans, R. J., *Telling Lies about Hitler: The Holocaust, History and the David Irving Trial* (London: Verso, 2002)

Feldman, D., *Englishmen and Jews: Social Relations and Political Culture 1840–1914* (New Haven: Yale University Press, 1994)

Feldman, D., 'Was Modernity Good for the Jews?' in B. Cheyette and L. Marcus (eds), *Modernity, Culture and 'the Jew'* (Stanford: Stanford University Press, 1998) 171–87

Finkelstein, N. G., *The Holocaust Industry: Reflections on the Exploitation of Jewish Suffering* (London: Verso, 2000)

Fitzgerald, T., *Discourses on Civility and Barbarity* (Oxford: Oxford University Press, 2007)

Fitzgerald, T. (ed.), *Religion and the Secular: Historical and Colonial Formations* (London: Equinox, 2007)

Fitzpatrick, P., 'Racism and the Innocence of Law' (1987) 14 *J. of Law and Society* 119–32

Fitzpatrick, P., *The Mythology of Modern Law* (London: Routledge, 1992)

Fox, M. and J. McHale, 'In Whose Best Interests?' (1997) 60 *Modern Law Review* 700–9

Fox, M. and M. Thomson, 'A Covenant with the Status Quo? Male Circumcision and the New BMA Guidance to Doctors' (2005) 31 *J. of Medical Ethics* 463–9

Fox, M. and M. Thomson, 'Short Changed? The Law and Ethics of Male Circumcision' (2005) 13 *International J. of Children's Rights* 161–81

Fox, M. and M. Thomson, 'Older Minors and Circumcision: Questioning the Limits of Religious Actions' (2008) 9 *Medical Law International* 283–311

Fraser, D., *The Jews of the Channel Islands and the Rule of Law, 1940–1945* (Brighton: Sussex Academic Press, 2000)

Fraser, D., *Law after Auschwitz* (Durham: Carolina Academic Press, 2005)

Fraser, D., 'To Belong or not to Belong: the Roma, State Violence and the New Europe in the House of Lords' (2001) 21(4) *Legal Studies* 569–93

Fraser, D., '"This is not like any other legal question": A Brief History of Nazi Law before U.K. and U.S. Courts' (2003–04) 19 *Connecticut J. of International Law* 59–125

Fredman, S., *Discrimination Law* (Oxford: Oxford University Press, 2002)

Freeman, M., 'Is the Get Any Business of the State?' in R. O'Dair and A. Lewis (eds), *Law and Religion* (Oxford: Oxford University Press, 2001)

Freeman, M., 'Whose Life is it Anyway?' (2001) 9 *Medical Law Review* 259–80

Friedlander, S. (ed.), *Probing the Limits of Representation: Nazism and the 'Final Solution'* (Cambridge: Harvard University Press, 1992)

Friedman, J., 'Jewish Conversion, the Spanish Pure Blood Laws and Reformation: A Revisionist View of Racial and Religious Antisemitism' (1987) 18(1) *Sixteenth Century Journal* 3–30

Gainer, B., *The Alien Invasion: The Origins of the Aliens Act of 1905* (London: Heinmann Education Publishers, 1972)

Garrard, J. A., *The English and Immigration 1880–1910* (Oxford: Oxford University Press, 1971)

Gilbert, H., 'Time to Reconsider the Lawfulness of Ritual Male Circumcision' (2007) *European Human Rights Law Review* 279–94

Gilman, S. L., *Difference and Pathology: Stereotypes of Sexuality, Race, and Madness* (Ithaca: Cornell University Press, 1985)

Gilman, S. L., *The Jew's Body* (New York: Routledge, 1991)

Gilman, S. L., *Freud, Race, and Gender* (Princeton: Princeton University Press, 1993)

Gilroy, P., *The Black Atlantic: Modernity and Double Consciousness* (London: Verso, 1993)

Gilroy, P., *After Empire: Melancholia or Convivial Culture?* (London: Routledge, 2004)

Glasser, C., 'Radicals and Refugees: The Foundation of the Modern Law Review and English Legal Scholarship' (1987) 50 *Modern Law Review* 688–708

Godfrey, G., 'The Judges and the Jews' (2003) *Ecclesiastical Law Journal* 50–61

Goldberg, D. T., *Racist Culture* (Malden, MA: Blackwell, 1993)

Goldberg, D. T., *The Racial State* (Malden, MA: Blackwell, 2001)

Goldhagen, D., *Hitler's Willing Executioners: Ordinary Germans and the Holocaust* (New York: Knopf, 1996)

Goldstein, E., *The Price of Whiteness: Jews, Race, and American Identity* (Princeton: Princeton University Press, 2006)

Goldstein, J., 'The Wandering Jew and the Problem of Psychiatric Anti-semitism in Fin-de-siecle France' (1985) 20 *J. of Contemporary History* 521–52

Goodrich, P. and L. Mills, 'The Law of White Spaces: Race, Culture, and Legal Education' (2001) 51(1) *J. of Legal Education* 15–38

Grabham, E., '"Flagging" the Skin: Corporeal Nationalism and the Properties of Belonging' (2009) 15 *Body & Society* 63–82

Graycar, R. and J. Morgan, *The Hidden Gender of Law* (Annandale: Federation Press, 2nd edn, 2002)

Green, K. and H. Lim, 'What is This Thing about Female Circumcision?: Legal Education and Human Rights' (1998) 7 *Social & Legal Studies* 365–88

Griffiths, R., 'The Reception of Bryant's *Unfinished Victory*: Insights into British Public Opinion in Early 1940' (2004) 38 *Patterns of Prejudice* 18–36

Grimley, M., 'The Religion of Englishness: Puritanism, Providentialism, and "National Character" 1918–1945' (2007) 46 (4) *J. of British Studies* 884–906

Gruber, R., *Exodus 1947: The Ship that Launched a Nation* (New York: Random House, 1999)

Halamish, A., *The Exodus Affair: Holocaust Survivors and the Struggle for Palestine* (Syracuse: Syracuse University Press, 1998)

Hale, B., D. Pearle, E. Cooke, and D. Monk, *The Family, Law & Society: Cases and Materials* (Oxford: Oxford University Press, 2009)

Hall, C., K. McCelland and J. Rendall, *Defining the Victorian Nation: Class, Race, Gender, and the Reform Act of 1867* (Cambridge: Cambridge University Press, 2000)

Hall, K. F., *Things of Darkness: Economies of Race and Gender in Early Modern England* (Ithaca: Cornell University Press, 1995)

Hamilton, C., *Family, Law, Religion* (London: Sweet & Maxwell, 1995)

Haron, M., 'Britain and Israel, 1948–1950' (1983) 3(2) *Modern Judaism* 217–23

Harrington, J. and A. Manji, '"Mind with Mind and Spirit with Spirit": Lord Denning and African Legal Education'(2003) 30(3) *J. of Law and Society* 376–99

Harris-Short, S., and J. Miles, *Family Law: Text, Cases and Materials* (Oxford: Oxford University Press, 2007)

Hayes, P., 'Giving Due Consideration to Ethnicity in Adoption Placements—A Principled Approach' (2003) 15(3) *CFLQ* 255–68

Hayton, D., *Commentary and Cases on the Law of Trusts and Equitable Remedies* (London: Sweet & Maxwell, 12th edn, 2005)

Henriques, H.S.Q., *The Jews and English Law* (Clifton: Augustus M. Kelley, 1974, orig. pub. 1908)

Herman, D., *The Antigay Agenda: Orthodox Vision and the Christian Right* (Chicago: University of Chicago Press, 1997)

Herman, D., '"An Unfortunate Coincidence": Jews and Jewishness in 20th Century English Judicial Discourse' (2006) 33 *J. of Law and Society* 277–301

Herman, D., ' "I Do Not Attach Great Significance To It": Taking Note of "the Holocaust" in English Law' (2008) 17 *Social & Legal Studies* 427–52

Herman, D. and D. Cooper, 'Anarchic Armadas, Brussels Bureaucrats, and the Valiant Maple Leaf: Sexuality, Governance, and the Construction of British Nationhood Through the Canada–Spain Fish War' (1997) 17(3) *Legal Studies* 415–33

Herman, L., *Engaging the Disturbing Images of Evil: How Do Those Born After Remember Auschwitz?* (Saarbrucken: VDM Verlag, 2009)

Herman, S., 'Legacy and Legend: The Continuity of Roman and English Regulation of the Jews' (1991–2) 66 *Tulane Law Review* 1781–1851

Herring, J., *Family Law* (Harlow: Pearson, 2009)

Hickman, M., 'Reconstructing Deconstructing 'Race': British Political Discourses about the Irish in Britain' (1998) 21(2) *Ethnic and Racial Studies* 288–307

Hill, M. M. and L. N. Williams, *Auschwitz in England: A Record of a Libel Action* (London: MacGibbon & Kee, 1965)

Hirsch, D., 'Dickens's Queer "Jew" and Anglo-Christian Identity Politics: The Contradictions of Victorian Family Values' in D. Boyarin, D. Itzkovitz, A. Pellegrini (eds), *Queer Theory and the Jewish Question* (New York: Columbia University Press, 2003) 311–33

Holly, D. C., *Exodus 1947* (Annapolis: Naval Institute Press, rev. edn, 1995, orig. pub. 1965)

Holmes, C., *Anti-Semitism in British Society 1876–1939* (New York: Holmes & Meir, 1979)

Hunter, R., C. McGlynn and E. Rackley (eds), *Feminist Judgments: From Theory to Practice* (Oxford: Hart Publishing, 2010)

Itzkovits, D., 'Secret Temples' in J. Boyarin and D. Boyarin, *Jews and Other Differences: The New Jewish Cultural Studies* (Minneapolis: University of Minnesota Press, 1997) 176–202

Jackson, B., 'Brother Daniel: The Construction of Jewish Identity in the Israel Supreme Court' (1993) 17 *Intl J. for the Semiotics of Law* 115–46

Jakobsen, J. R. and A. Pellegrini (eds), *Secularisms* (Durham: Duke University Press, 2007)

Jivraj. S., *Interrogating 'Religion' and 'Race' in Child Welfare and Education Law* (PhD Thesis, University of Kent, forthcoming)

Jivraj, S. and D. Herman, ' "It is Difficult for a White Judge to Understand": Orientalism, Racialisation, and Christianity in English Child Welfare Cases' (2009) 21(3) *CFLQ* 283–308

Johnson, P., *A History of the Jews* (London: Weidenfeld & Nicholson, 1987)

Jones, R. and W. Gnanapala, *Ethnic Minorities in English Law* (Stoke-on-Trent: Trentham Books, 2000)

Julius, A., *Trials of the Diaspora: A History of Anti-Semitism in England* (Oxford: Oxford University Press, 2010)

Kaniuk, Y., *Commander of the Exodus* (New York: Grove Press, 1999)

Karsov, N. and S. Szechter, *Monuments are not Loved* (London: Hodder and Stoughton, 1970)

Katz, D. S., *The Jews in the History of England 1485–1850* (Oxford: Clarendon Press, 1994)

Katz, J., *From Prejudice to Destruction: Antisemitism, 1700–1933* (Cambridge: Harvard University Press, 1980)

Kline, M., 'The "Colour" of Law: Ideological Representations of First Nations in Legal Discourse' (1994) 3 *Social & Legal Studies* 451–76

Knepper, P., 'British Jews and the Racialisation of Crime in the Age of Empire' (2007) 47(1) *British J. of Criminology* 61–79

Knights, S., *Freedom of Religion, Minorities and the Law* (Oxford: Oxford University Press, 2007)

Kumar, K., *The Making of English National Identity* (Cambridge: Cambridge University Press, 2003)

Kushner, T., *The Persistence of Prejudice: Antisemitism in British Society During the Second World War* (Manchester: Manchester University Press, 1989)

Kushner, T., *The Holocaust and the Liberal Imagination* (Oxford: Blackwell, 1994)

Kushner, T., 'Remembering to Forget: Racism and Anti-racism in Postwar Britain' in B. Cheyette and L. Marcus (eds), *Modernity, Culture and 'the Jew'* (Stanford: Stanford University Press, 1998) 226–41

Kushner, T. (ed.), *The Jewish Heritage in British History: Englishness and Jewishness* (London: Frank Cass, 1992)

La Capra, D., *History and Memory After Auschwitz* (Ithaca: Cornell University Press, 1998)

La Capra, D., *Writing History, Writing Trauma* (Baltimore: Johns Hopkins University Press, 2001)

La Capra, D., 'Representing the Holocaust: Reflections on the Historians' Debate' in S. Friedlander (ed.), *Probing the Limits of Representation: Nazism and the 'Final Solution'* (Cambridge: Harvard University Press, 1992) 108–42

Lacey, N., *A Life of H.L.A. Hart: The Nightmare and the Noble Dream* (Oxford: Oxford University Press, 2004)

Lawson, T., 'The Anglican Understanding of Nazism 1933–1945: Placing the Church of England's Response to the Holocaust in Context' (2003) 14(2) *Twentieth Century British History* 112–37

Lentin, A., 'Replacing "Race", Historicising "Culture" in Multiculturalism' (2005) 39(4) *Patterns of Prejudice* 379–96

Lentin, R., *Representing the Shoah for the Twenty-First Century* (Oxford: Berghan Books, 2004)

Lester, A., 'The Politics of the Race Relations Act 1976' in M. Anwar, P. Roach, and R. Sondhi (eds), *From Legislation to Integration: Race Relations in Britain* (Basingstoke: Macmillan, 2000) 24–39

Levy, A., *Reuben Sachs* (London: Persephone, 2001, orig. pub. 1888)

Lewis, R., *Gendering Orientalism: Race, Femininity and Representation* (London: Routledge, 1996)

London, L., *Whitehall and the Jews 1933–1948: British Immigration Policy and the Holocaust* (Cambridge: Cambridge University Press, 2003)

Mac An Ghaill, M., 'The Irish in Britain' (2000) 26(1) *J. of Ethnic & Migration Studies* 137–64

Mac An Ghaill, M., 'British Critical Theorists: The Production of the Conceptual Invisibility of the Irish Diaspora' (2001) 7(2) *Social Identities* 179–201

Macklin, G., '"A Quite Natural and Moderate Defensive Feeling"?: The 1945 Hampstead "Anti-alien" Petition' (2003) 37 *Patterns of Prejudice* 277–300

Maidment, S., 'The Legal Effect of Religious Divorces' (1974) 37 *Modern Law Review* 611–26

Makdisi, G., 'The Guilds of Law in Medieval Legal History: An Inquiry into the Origins of the Inns of Court' (1985–1986) 34 *Cleveland St. L. Rev* 3–18

Makdisi, J., 'Islamic Origins of the Common Law' (1999) 77(5) *North Carolina L. Rev* 1635–1739

Malik, M., *Feminism and Minority Women* (Cambridge: Cambridge University Press, 2010)

Mandler, P., *The English National Character: The History of an Idea from Edmund Burke to Tony Blair* (New Haven: Yale University Press, 2006)

Marrus, M. R., *The Holocaust in History* (London: Penguin, 1987)

Martin, J. E., *Modern Equity* (London: Sweet & Maxwell, 18th edn, 2009)

Masson, J., R. Bailey-Harris, R. Probert, *Cretney: Principles of Family Law* (London: Sweet & Maxwell, 2008)

Masuzawa, T., *The Invention of World Religions* (Chicago: University of Chicago Press, 2005)

Matar, N., *Islam in Britain 1558–1685* (Cambridge: Cambridge University Press, 1998)

McClintock, A., *Imperial Leather: Race, Gender and Sexuality in the Colonial Contest* (London: Routledge, 1995)

McColgan, A., *Discrimination Law* (Oxford: Hart, 2005)

McColgan, A., 'Class Wars? Religion and (In)Equality in the Workplace' (2009) 38(1) *ILJ* 1–29

Merrills, J. G., 'One Nationality or Two? The Strange Case of *Oppenheimer* v. *Cattermole*' (1974) 23 *International & Comparative Law Quarterly* 143–59

Merrills, J. G., '*Oppenheimer* v. *Cattermole*—The Curtain Falls' (1975) 24 *International & Comparative Law Quarterly* 617–34

Metzger, M. J., '"Now by my hood, a Gentle and no Jew": Jessica, The Merchant of Venice, and the Discourse of Early Modern Identity' (1998) 113(1) *PMLA* 52–63

Miles, R., *Racism After 'Race Relations'* (London: Routledge, 1993)

Miles, R. and M. Brown, *Racism* (London: Routledge, 2nd edn, 2003)

Mirza, Q., 'Critical Race Feminism: The Anglo-American Experience' Paper presented at the Annual Meeting of the Law & Society Association, Chicago, May 2004

Motha, S., 'Veiled Women and the *Affect* of Religion in Democracy' (2007) 34 *J. of Law and Society* 139–62

Motha, S., 'Liberal Cults, Suicide Bombers, and other Theological Dilemmas' (2008) 5 *J. of Law, Culture and the Humanities* 228–46

Mundill, R. R., *England's Jewish Solution: Experiment and Expulsion, 1262–1290* (Cambridge: Cambridge University Press, 1998)

Novick, P., *The Holocaust in American Life* (New York: Houghton Mifflin, 1999)

Oakley, A. J., *The Modern Law of Trusts* (London: Sweet & Maxwell, 9th edn, 2008)

Office for National Statistics, 'Deciding which Tick-Boxes to Add to the Ethnic Group Question in the 2001 England and Wales Census' (Office for National Statistics, 2009)

Office for National Statistics, 'Final Recommended Questions for the 2011 Census in England and Wales: Ethnic Group' (Office for National Statistics, 2009)

O'Dair, R. and A. Lewis (eds), *Law and Religion* (Oxford: Oxford University Press, 2001)

Oliver, P., S. Douglas-Scott and V. Tadros (eds), *Faith in Law: Essays in Legal Theory* (London: Hart, 2000)

Omni, M. and H. Winant, *Racial Formations in the United States: From the 1960s to the 1990s* (London: Routledge, 1994)

Panayi, P., *Immigration, Ethnicity and Racism in Britain, 1815–1945* (Manchester: Manchester University Press, 1994)

Persoff, M., *Faith Against Reason: Religious Reform and the British Chief Rabbinate, 1840–1990* (Edgware: Valentine Mitchell, 2008)

Peters, M., K. Seeds and C. Harding, 'Findings from the Survey of Claimants in Race Discrimination Employment Tribunal Cases (SETA RRA)' (Employment Relations Research Series No. 54, Department of Transport and Industry, 2006)

Petrie, J., 'The Secular Word HOLOCAUST: Scholarly Myths, History, and 20th Century Meanings' (2000) 2(1) *J. of Genocide Research* 31–63

Pfeffer, J.I., *'From One End of Earth to the Other': The London* Bet Din, *1805–1855, and the Jewish Convicts Transported to Australia* (Brighton: Sussex Academic Press, 2010)

Poulter, S., *English Law and Minority Ethnic Customs* (London: Butterworths, 1986)

Poulter, S., *Ethnicity, Law and Human Rights* (Oxford: Oxford University Press, 1999)

Ragussis, M., *Figures of Conversion: 'The Jewish Question' & English National Identity* (Durham: Duke University Press, 1995)

Randall, D., 'Rearwindow: Exodus 1947: Another Ship, Another Time' *Independent on Sunday* (2 September 2001)

Razack, S., 'Imperilled Muslim Women, Dangerous Muslim Men and Civilised Europeans: Legal and Social Responses to Forced Marriages' (2004) 12 *Feminist Legal Studies* 129–74

Reece, H., 'Subverting the Stigmatization Argument' (1996) 23 *J. of Law and Society* 484–505

Reisenover, E.M., 'Anti-Jewish Philosemitism: British and Hebrew Affinity and Nineteenth Century British Antisemitism' (2008) I(1) *British Scholar* 79–104

Richmond, C., 'Englishness and Medieval Anglo-Jewry' in T. Kushner (ed.), *The Jewish Heritage in British History: Englishmen and Jewishness* (London: Frank Cass, 1992)

Robillard, St. J. A., *Religion and the Law* (Manchester: University of Manchester Press, 1984)

Roediger, D., *The Wages of Whiteness: Race and the Making of the American Working Class* (London: Verso, 1999, orig. pub. 1991)

Romain, J. A., *The Jews of England: A Portrait of Anglo-Jewry Through Original Sources and Illustrations* (London: Michael Goulston Educational Foundation and Jewish Chronicle Press, 1988)

Ronen, Y., 'Redefining the Child's Right to Identity' (2004) *International J. of Law, Policy and the Family* 147–77

Rose, G., *Mourning Becomes the Law* (Cambridge: Cambridge University Press, 1996)

Rosenblatt, J. P., *Renaissance England's Chief Rabbi: John Seldon* (Oxford: Oxford University Press, 2006)

Roth, C., *A History of the Jews in England* (Oxford: Oxford University Press, 1941)

Said, E., *Orientalism* (New York: Vintage, 1979)

Sandland, R., 'The Real, the Simulacrum, and the Construction of "Gypsy" in Law' (1996) 23(3) *J. of Law and Society* 383–405

Santner, E. L., 'History Beyond the Pleasure Principle: Some Thoughts on the Representation of Trauma' in S. Friedlander (ed.), *Probing the Limits of Representation: Nazism and the 'Final Solution'* (Cambridge: Harvard University Press, 1992) 143–54

Schiek, D., L. Waddington, M. Bell, *Non-Discrimination Law* (Oxford: Hart, 2007)

Seymour, D., *Law, Antisemitism and the Holocaust* (London: Routledge/Cavendish, 2007)

Shapiro, J., *Shakespeare and the Jews* (New York: Columbia University Press, 1996)

Shapiro, J. A., 'The Shetar's Effect on English law—A Law of the Jews Becomes the Law of the Land' (1983) 71 *The Georgetown Law Journal* 1179–200

Silverman, M., 'Refiguring "the Jew" in France' in B. Cheyette and L. Marcus (eds), *Modernity, Culture and 'the Jew'* (Stanford: Stanford University Press, 1998)

Sinha, M., *Colonial Masculinity: The 'Manly Englishman' and the 'Effeminate Bengali' in the Late Nineteenth Century* (Manchester: Manchester University Press, 1995)

Solomos, J., *Race and Racism in Britain* (Basingstoke: Palgrave Macmillan, 3rd edn, 2003)

Solomos, J. and L. Back, *Race, Politics and Social Change* (London: Routledge, 1995)

Stepan, N., *The Idea of Race in Science: Great Britain 1800–1960* (Basingstoke: Macmillan, 1982)

Steyn, J., *The Jew: Assumptions of Identity* (London: Cassell, 1999)

Stolleis, M., *The Law Under the Swastika* (Chicago: University of Chicago Press, 1998)

Sztybel, D., 'Can the Treatment of Animals be Compared to the Holocaust?' (2006) 11(1) *Ethics & the Environment* 97–132

Thomson, M., *Endowed: Regulating the Male Sexed Body* (London: Routledge, 2008)

Tuitt, P., *Race, Law and Resistance* (London: Glasshouse, 2004)

Vakulenko, A., 'Islamic Dress in Human Rights Jurisprudence: A Critique of Current Trends' (2007) 7(4) *Human Rights Law Review* 717–39

Valman, N., *The Jewess in Nineteenth-Century British Literary Culture* (Cambridge: Cambridge University Press, 2007)

Van Praagh, S., 'Faith, Belonging, and the Protection of Our Children' (1999) XVII *Windsor Yearbook of Access to Justice* 154–203

Voeltz, R., '"… A good Jew and a good Englishman": The Jewish Lads' Brigade, 1894–1922' (1988) 23 *J. of Contemporary History* 119–27

Walker, J. W. St. G., *'Race,' Rights and the Law in the Supreme Court of Canada* (Waterloo: Wilfrid Laurier University Press, 1997)

Walkowitz, J., 'The Indian Woman, the Flower Girl, and the Jew: Photojournalism in Edwardian London' (1998–1999) 42 *Victorian Studies* 3–46

Weiler, J. H. H., 'Discrimination and Identity in London: The Jewish Free School Case' (2010) 1 *Jewish Review of Books* (Spring)

Wheeler, R., *The Complexion of Race: Categories of Difference in Eighteenth-Century British Culture* (Philadelphia: University of Pennsylvania Press, 2000)

Wiesberg, R. H., *Vichy Law and the Holocaust in France* (New York: New York University Press, 1996)

Williams, B., '"East and West": Class and Community in Manchester Jewry, 1850–1914' in D. Cesarani (ed.), *The Making of Modern Anglo-Jewry* (Oxford: Blackwell, 1990)

Wilson, K., *The Island Race: Englishness, Empire and Gender in the Eighteenth Century* (London: Routledge, 2003)

Wing, A., R. Delgado, D. Bell (eds), *Critical Race Feminism: A Reader* (New York: New York University Press, 2003)

Wray, H., 'The Aliens Act 1905 and the Immigration Dilemma' (2006) 33(2) *J. of Law & Society* 302–23

Young, J. E., *The Texture of Memory: Holocaust Memorials and Meaning* (New Haven: Yale University Press, 1993)

Young, R., *Colonial Desire: Hybridity in Theory, Culture and Race* (New York: Routledge, 1995)

Zelizer, B., *Remembering to Forget: Holocaust Memory Through the Camera's Eye* (Chicago: University of Chicago Press, 1998)

INDEX